Praise for *Questioning God?*

Questioning God? makes a compelling case for the Christian worldview, showing how philosophy, history, psychology, and science point toward the truth of the gospel. It doesn't dodge the hard questions, wrestling with many of the most nettlesome objections raised by skeptics. This book is practical and to the point, filled with common-sense illustrations, and it's sure to help any open-minded thinker take steps closer to God.

— **Lee Strobel**, best-selling author of *The Case for Christ* and Founding Director of the Strobel Center for Evangelism and Applied Apologetics at Colorado Christian University

I was an aggressive spiritual seeker for most of my life and eventually stopped my search when I found Christ at the age of 33. I had many questions and doubts about God and endured an arduous journey to get the answers that made sense to my analytical mind. This book contains the answers I wish I had heard as a younger man on my path to truth. It has been said that Christianity is often tried but rarely tested. *Questioning God?* applies evidence-based research and deductive reasoning (the only kind that makes sense to me) to test the Christian worldview, and the results are compelling and transformational.

— **Barry Zito**, Cy Young Award winner, World Series Champion, Recording Artist & Producer

If you are a "Why" person regarding the Christian faith—this is a must read. John Hopper's *Questioning God?* is a 5-Star resource for both doers and doubters; seekers and skeptics. It will help you reason critically, react transparently, and respond purposefully. Hopper is right: there are answers to questions worth asking.

— **Mark M. Yarbrough**, PhD President, Dallas Theological Seminary

John Hopper's *Questioning God?* is a delightful book that fills an important need in today's apologetical literature. In a unique way, Hopper's book is . . . important and useful for these reasons: (1) It is written in a very laid-back, inviting conversational style. (2) It is specifically written as a provision of answers to fifteen specific and important questions frequently raised in discussions of Christianity. (3) While useful to believers, its particular audience is unbelieving seekers and Hopper clearly understands this audience. Thus, his book helps a believer to share his or her faith by using the book as a resource or handout. I am optimistic about the impact of *Questioning God?* and am glad to have it in my own toolbox.

> — **J. P. Moreland**, Distinguished Professor of Philosophy, Talbot School of Theology, Biola University and author of *A Simple Guide to Experience Miracles*

In his book, *Questioning God?*, John Hopper has looked at the big questions about God with a fresh set of eyes and in a manner that is very informative but very conversational. I couldn't put it down. I can't wait to share it with friends and look forward to hearing stories of great conversations!

> — **Bruce Matthews**, Pro Football Hall of Fame Class of 2007

Questioning God? provides a real opportunity for the reader to think through big questions regarding their spiritual beliefs. John's ability to use plain language and common sense in a thoughtful way is reflected throughout this book. If you are a skeptic, seeker, or candidly a believer who has some real questions regarding God, this book hits the target!

> — **Jack Plating**, retired Executive Vice President & Chief Operating Officer, Verizon Wireless

Questioning God?

Answers to Questions
Worth Asking

John Hopper

First printing 2021
Printed in the United States

Published by:
Search Ministries, inc.
4330 W. Vickery Blvd., Suite 150
Fort Worth, TX 76107
searchnational.org
800.617.3272

Hardcover ISBN: 978-0-9899096-2-4

To Ann,
the one I adore
until death do us part

To Eric, Ian, Hudson, and Corrie,
who make a father proud

Contents

Introduction

I like to make sense of things. I always have. I suppose that has its advantages, but it also means I'm prone to staying up late at night with a pile of books or fiddling with something for way too long trying to see how it works. Some people are good with believing what they're told. But that's never really worked for me; it's got to make sense before I jump on board.

Too often when people are exposed to Christianity, they are told this or that to believe about God, or Jesus, or the Bible, but they are never told *why* they should believe any of it. It's as if you just have to "take it all by faith," even if none of it seems plausible. If that's what you've experienced, I feel your pain. If Christianity involves anything worth believing, it ought to make sense first.

You'd understand if you couldn't get your questions answered about Christianity by an atheist or a Buddhist, but it seems more than reasonable to expect something more from Christians. I'm sorry to say, however, that Christians often can be of little help when it comes to the "whys" of Christianity. Not only can they find themselves short on good answers to good questions, but sometimes they also make it clear they aren't comfortable with you even asking your questions in the first place!

If I had my way, I'd change all that. I'd make sure the world included spaces where people could ask any question they want—friendly places where people didn't try to prove the other person wrong but instead where everyone could put facts and perspectives and logic on the table to be considered by all. If you're picking up this book, I'm thinking you might want to be in a room like that too, even if only to satisfy your curiosity.

I suppose the big reason I'd like to create spaces where people can ask their questions is because I believe that reasonable questions are worthy of reasonable answers. I've heard many friends tell me that when they brought up questions about God or the Bible to a parent or a priest or the guy working in the adjacent cubicle, the best they received in reply was "You just need to have faith." That kind of answer didn't cut it for my friends, and it didn't cut it for Jesus either.

Jesus had a cousin named John, at least that's what the Bible tells us. John was famous before Jesus ever was, and he kept telling people to get ready because the Messiah was coming soon. Then Jesus showed up where John was preaching, and John didn't hesitate for a moment. He tells his crowd that the awaited Messiah is Jesus, and within minutes a voice from heaven confirms just what he said.[1]

A few years later, John's preaching gets him in trouble. He calls out the king for marrying his brother's wife, and he's placed on death row.[2] Now, I don't know about you, but when the hammer is about to fall, I find it easy to doubt whether the efforts that landed me in my predicament were worth it. And that was certainly the case for John. He was about to lose his head, and he could not help but wonder if all his years of teaching were for naught. So he sent a message from his jail cell to Jesus. He asks Jesus if he really is the one—if he really is the Messiah.[3] If you read the Bible just a bit, you will find out that John was about as big a God-follower as there gets, and yet after years of telling others to believe he begins to doubt. He starts to ask questions. That right there is telling. It gives us, shall we say, permission to ask the questions we have too.

But that's not the end of the story. John doesn't just ask his question. Jesus answers him. And Jesus' response is rather instructive. Jesus does not say, "Come on, John! I can't believe you're full of doubts now. Why don't you just have faith?" Instead, Jesus says something wholly different. He sends back a message about the evidence. He tells John of the blind who see, the lame who walk, and the dead who are raised.[4] In other words, he says, "John, here are the facts. You decide for yourself who I am."

Of course, at this point, you might not believe any of the "evidence" of which Jesus spoke, but that's a discussion for later. My point in mentioning Jesus' approach is that I hope it is mine as well. In this book I aim simply to put the facts on the table and let you decide for yourself whether there is any credence to the idea of God, the Bible, or Christianity.

In many cases, as I said, things don't make sense to me unless I can see them for myself. And I don't expect anything different from you. You have questions. Good questions. They deserve well-reasoned answers. I hope you find them here.

Visit **questioninggod.com** for more about *Questioning God?*

PART ONE:
GOD

Life Is Good, So Why Be Concerned with God?

"I'm free!" the young woman excitedly declared. As far as my new friend was concerned, she was happy to be an atheist. I mean really happy. At one time she had believed in God, but when she threw God aside, she finally felt free to be herself. God had done nothing for her, and even if by some remote possibility God did exist, why even bother? She felt better off without him.

This woman is not alone. While it was once true that the bulk of Americans frequented a house of worship, many today give God little more than an occasional nod. In some cases, people proudly denounce the idea of God, but based on my conversations, a significant number simply find God boring, restrictive, or irrelevant. That's why they say things like, "Life is good, so why should I be concerned with God?" or more strongly, "Believe in God if you must, but don't think you're better than one who doesn't." Perhaps these are words you have spoken yourself, and understandably so. If God is just an imaginary friend meant to make us feel better or motivate good behavior, then spending time worrying about God is at best an optional proposition. But maybe there is more to be considered. Maybe being free of God has greater implications than you've ever considered.

I am not much of a car person. Not only do I fail to understand how everything under the hood works, but I don't even know what everything is supposed to do. In one sense, I don't seem to use any of the stuff tucked beneath the hood. I use the steering wheel, some of the dashboard gauges are valuable to me, and I appreciate the headlights and the brake pedal nearly every day. Those things have obvious value to me, but do I really need all the stuff under the hood? The answer, of course, is yes. All I must do is to remove a gasket from the carburetor or the wiring from the starter to see that there is great value to what's under the hood.

I wonder if that is the same with God. At times people say, "I see how this or that works to make life good, but this God thing seems rather useless." But maybe they'd have a different appreciation of God if they considered what would be true if God were removed from under the hood of life.

A Bit about God

Before we go any further, it might be helpful if I provide a basic definition of God. People all across the planet have different ideas of God, ranging from something of a fairy godmother to an opaque cosmic Star Wars kind of Force. The definition I provide might not be the same as yours, but at least you will know where I am coming from. I won't get extra detailed at this point, but I will state a few basics—a few basics largely held by the world's major monotheistic religions:

- God is self-existent and eternal. In other words, God has always been here and always will be.
- God is a powerful creator who made the universe in which we live.
- God is interested in his creation and is particularly concerned about what you and I do and say and think.
- God is willing to grant us blissful immortality provided we meet certain conditions.

Again, that's not a lot of detail, but I think it is enough to go on for now. Let's consider what we'd have if this kind of God, or anything remotely like this God, didn't exist.

A World of Chance

I am not sure who came up with the idea of dice. Information on the internet says it probably had to do with the ancients of Egypt or China. It seems they once were used for divining the future. If you wondered whether to plant this crop or that, or fight a particular enemy, to the craps table you went. I don't think anyone really uses dice in that way anymore. When we think of dice today, we think of chance, pure random chance. There's nothing magical or divine about rolling a double six. Roll two dice long enough and the pair is bound to show up. Chance has a way of making that happen.

I know it's a bit more complicated than that, but I think that's the way many people look at the world today. From the earliest age, we are told in classrooms far and wide that the universe and all that is within it is explained by a long, long series of dice rolls. Take biological life, for example. It is said that the universe through its own set of chance happenings ended up producing the elements on that periodic chart posted in every science class. Those elements bumped into each other by chance and produced a few molecular compounds. Throw the dice a few more times (or a few more zillion times) and you get the first protein and eventually the first simple cell. Fast-forward a couple billion years and humans come on the scene, joining cockroaches and elephants.

At first blush, a world of chance might not be all that bad. I mean, if chance is responsible for it all, it has certainly made for some spectacular life forms, on a beautiful planet, in an awe-inspiring universe. But even if chance has had a big role in making the universe in which we live, I still think we do well not to remove God from under the hood. If we do, there is just too much we lose. Let me show you what I mean.

The Loss of Meaning

Sometimes I wonder what my dog is thinking. It seems like finding food and taking walks and chasing squirrels are high on the list. But is there anything more? Does my dog ever think about the meaning of life? Does my dog wonder whether what he has accomplished today amounts to anything? I doubt my dog has those kinds of thoughts, but I have a hunch people do. Such thoughts show up in questions like "Why are we here?" or in eulogies that tell us that a person's life really did matter. They also show up when we are assigned to do a task that seems to have no recognizable value. Meaning is so important to us that when it eludes us, it's hard to find the motivation to continue. But here's the tricky part, where the dice come in: If you and I are here by chance and chance alone—if there is no God in the picture who created us—can it be said that there is any real meaning to our existence? That might seem like a mind-bending question, but I am not sure it needs to be.

Suppose a Scrabble box with all the usual tiles sits on your table. Your cat, in an attempt to get away from your dog, jumps up on the table and knocks the box to the floor. In the process, all the lettered tiles are spread across the ground. After seeing the mess, I am guessing you'd say some choice words to your furry friends, sigh, and then get to work picking up the pieces. What I doubt you would do is look intently at the tiles on the floor to decipher the meaning of their configuration. You couldn't care less that a "P" ended up next to an "R" or that an "X" wound up far away from an "A." Even if a few letters landed to make a word like "YES," you might take a picture and post it to your friends on Facebook, but I seriously doubt you would take it as a sign you should marry the guy you met yesterday. And that's because "YES" came about by chance. There is no real meaning to it.

But if this is the case with Scrabble tiles, what does that say about our lives if we are nothing more than the product of chance? Can we really say there is any real meaning to our existence? According to some atheist thinkers, the answer is "No." For example, Nobel Prize-winning physicist Steven Weinberg writes:

> It is almost irresistible for humans to believe that we have some special relation to the universe, that human life is not just a more-or-less farcical outcome of a chain of accidents reaching back to the first three minutes, but . . . The more the universe seems comprehensible the more it also seems pointless.[1]

William Provine, a distinguished biology professor at Cornell University, shared a similar view during a debate at Stanford University: "Let me summarize my views . . . There are no gods . . . There is no ultimate foundation for ethics, *no ultimate meaning in life.*"[2]

Not only is it existence by chance that lends itself to meaninglessness, but so too does the ultimate winding down of the universe. At some point, the stars will all burn out and leave behind an uninhabitable world. That means that whether we try to "leave the world a better place" or make a mess of it, the result will be the same. I think this is what the great German philosopher Arthur Schopenhauer was getting at when he declared that all of humanity will be "given over at last to annihilation" and as a result all our striving "is essentially vain."[3] This point has not escaped American film director Woody Allen, who finds the thought of annihilation "stupefying in its terror," because it "renders anyone's accomplishments meaningless."[4] In particular, Allen is concerned about finding motivation in a meaningless world, and I think he is on to something. If our efforts in one direction or another don't amount to much in the end, it is like the prospect of moving a pile of rocks from one side of a prison camp to another until you die.

Now, it is important to note that the thinkers mentioned above are not God-believing people who have somehow pieced together a sneaky argument to suggest that without God there is no objective meaning to life. Rather, the people I have noted are those who hold firmly to the idea that life has come about by chance. And from this premise, they have concluded that life in turn has no real meaning. Of course, that doesn't mean they can't label something meaningful if they wish, but any such labeling should not be taken seriously if we are here by nothing more than a roll of the dice.

When I began this chapter, I suggested that the existence of God is more important than we think. Maybe God is like that thing under the hood that seems only to take up space but, once you take it out, you recognize that it contributes more than you knew. In this case, if God is taken out of our world, we are left without any ultimate meaning to life. I think that's a pretty big loss, but as you will see, we are only getting started.

The Loss of Purpose

It wasn't long ago that I sat in a beautiful backyard with tall pine trees and a bright blue pool along with about 30 other men. Some called themselves Christians, some not so much, and we talked about life and God. I don't remember much about that evening, apart from some words that were spoken near the end of the conversation. A man who would fit most people's definition of success, and who had said little up to that point, bravely expressed, "I'd just like to know the purpose of life." Boy, wouldn't we all?!

Talking about the weather, the stock market, or even each other's kids can get stale after a while. So, if I am feeling comfortable with people, I ask them deeper questions than what they think about the local sports teams or the latest movie. At first, they may be a little taken aback, but in the end most people are glad I got a more substantive conversation started. Sometimes I ask the purpose question as my backyard friend essentially did. I can't say I've catalogued the responses I've received, so I don't know what the most common answer is, but here are some thoughts people have shared with me over time.

The purpose of life is:

- To leave earth a better place than when you came
- To take care of your family and pass on your values
- To make something of yourself
- To be the best that you can be
- To be a good person
- Whatever you want it to be

My guess is that you too could add an idea to this list. Probably your most truthful answer to the purpose question would center on what it is that gets you up in the morning and drives you to do what you do. Whether you recognize it or not, that is your purpose. It is what you see as the worthwhile aim of your life, or at least of your day. You may think your purpose is better than that of others. Or maybe you think it is rather mundane. But, whatever the case, I am not sure your particular purpose has any real merit. That sounds rude, I admit, but I am not singling you out. I am not sure anyone's purpose has much merit to it, at least not if we go back to the whole idea that life on earth is just the result of random chance and dice rolls.

Purpose is the kind of thing that comes about because of personal intention. It's not the kind of thing that comes about by chance. You might say, "The reason I put the towels on the lower shelf is so my kids can reach them on their own." In that case, the purpose of the towels' location is the result of your intention. But if someone bumped you while you carried the laundry basket and you dropped it, spilling its contents, it is unlikely you would talk about the purpose of the towels' current crumpled state. If purpose requires intention, however, what does that say about our lives if we are only here by a long string of random chance events? Like it or not, it says our lives have no objective purpose. Richard Dawkins, a famed atheist, couldn't agree more:

> In a universe of blind physical forces and genetic replication, some people are going to get hurt, other people are going to get lucky, and you won't find any rhyme or reason in it, nor any justice. The universe we observe has precisely the properties we should expect if there is, at bottom, no design, no purpose, no evil and no good, nothing but blind, pitiless indifference.[5]

You see, if you and I are here not by intention but by "blind physical forces," there is no real purpose to our existence. We just bump along in life in one fashion or another, hoping we are one of the lucky few who don't get hurt along the way.

Now, at this point you might object, saying, "What do you mean no purpose? I most certainly have purpose to my life, and so do countless others. And none of this philosophical double-talk is going to convince me otherwise." I get it. I think most of us live our days as though there is real purpose to life. In fact, it seems to me we can't maintain much mental health if we don't act out one purpose or another. But the question is not whether we think or behave *as though* there is a purpose; the question is whether an *objective* purpose really exists. If objective purpose does exist, then there must be personal intention behind our existence.[6]

One of my favorite philosophers is Loyal Rue, not because I know him or because I have read much of what he has written but only because I think he has a great name! I also like him because I think he is honest. He readily admits that if there is no God, then there is no real purpose. He doesn't end there, though. Rue also admits it's just too hard to live thinking that way. In fact, he says we all do well to live by some "Noble Lie," one "that deceives us, tricks us, compels us beyond self-interest, beyond ego, beyond family, nation [and] race," because Rue tells us "without such lies, we cannot live."[7]

I get it when you protest and say that you do in fact have a purpose. Most everyone does have some reason for living. But in a world without God, it's hard to say those purposes amount to anything more than a game we play. Perhaps it is an important game, because if Loyal Rue is right, we cannot live without purpose. Nonetheless, it is still a game if God is not under the hood of our universe.

The Loss of Free Will

Last night before I went to bed, I set my alarm. When it went off, I got up out of bed, went through my normal routine, and got dressed for the day. Soon I headed off to a meeting with some others and returned to my office to enjoy a cup of coffee before writing these words. Most people would say that these were all choices I freely made. I did not have to set my alarm or get up when it went off. I did not have to go to the meeting or put myself back in front of a keyboard. But while I might have had a sense of free will, if we are creatures that exist solely because of a long string of random chemical interactions, it's hard to think that my free will is anything more than a feeling.

As a parent of four kids, I have been involved in plenty of science projects, but a crowd favorite was the making of a "volcano." You probably know the scene. We surrounded a cup or bottle with a little mound of dirt, and then added some vinegar, soap, and water, plus a little food coloring for flair. If we left things like that, it would all be rather boring, but then came the final step—adding a spoonful of baking soda. That's when the volcano erupted, as did the oohs and ahhs of the little onlookers. As the mess was made, I may have tried to tell my kids the science behind it all, but one thing was for sure: I never spoke as if the vinegar and baking soda *chose* to produce the reaction that they did. It simply would have been wrong to imply that the eruption took place as a result of some free will on the part of either substance. Vinegar and baking soda are going to do what they do based solely on their fixed properties, and that's that.

But if it would be wrong to talk of vinegar and baking soda having a free will, wouldn't it be equally wrong to talk about you and I having a free will if we are nothing more than biochemical machines reacting to our environment? Sam Harris, best-selling author and neuroscientist, thinks so. He writes: "Free will *is* an illusion. Our wills are simply not of our own making. Thoughts and intentions emerge from background causes of which we are unaware and over which we exert no conscious control. We do not have the freedom we think we have."[8]

For some, the loss of real free will is no big deal as long as we still feel like we have it. Cris Evatt, author of *The Myth of Free Will*, writes: "We *all* feel like we have free will. Deeply understanding that free will is a myth and illusion need not strip you of that comfy, inborn, blissful feeling of being a 'me,' . . . But it is possible to let go of fantasy and, at the same time, enjoy the feeling."[9] But I am not sure Evatt's take on free will is one that leaves me feeling very blissful or comfy. First of all, there is something strange about her call to let go of fantasy (i.e., the myth of free will), while at the same time encouraging us to embrace a blissful feeling that has no basis. I mean why not go all in and reject the myth and the feeling? My guess is Evatt does not want to let go of the feeling of free will because that would lead to the same kind of despair that a loss of meaning or purpose brings. At least for me, believing that everything I do today is out of my control brings nothing but a big dose of fatalism.

But that's not the only problem I have with the loss of free will. It seems apparent that if there is no free will, then we really must be okay with whatever anyone does. Oh sure, you might get upset because the guy who cuts you off in traffic triggers your own chemical reactions resulting in anger. But do you really have a moral basis for being mad at what he did? If there is no free will, his unique DNA (which he did not choose) is simply responding to the environment that your SUV created. We would not get mad at baking soda for causing a reaction when coming into contact with vinegar, even if it did make a mess we had to clean up. So how can we justify getting mad at an aggressive driver, an unruly neighbor, or a right- or left-wing politician, even if they make a mess of things? If there is no God, and therefore no free will, a solid argument against even the most heinous acts is simply hard to sustain.

The Loss of Justice

We hear a lot of talk about social justice these days. And in many ways, I am glad. Plenty of injustice is out there. Some say the city I live in is the largest purveyor of the sex trafficking industry in the United States—not exactly a point of pride. Fortunately, some folks have banded together to see if they can make a difference and stop the trafficking. Their efforts are not based on a *personal preference* that young women no longer be forced to have sex with men. Rather, their efforts are based on a strong belief that the practice of sex trafficking is *unjust regardless of anyone's preferences*. But justice of any kind is a rather slippery concept, if God is not under the hood.

Most would agree that one of the biggest blights on American history is that of slavery, and that one of the all-out failures on the world stage was the rise of Nazism. If we dig a little under the surface of these movements, we discover they were both based on the idea that some groups of people are by nature superior to others. In both instances, it was argued that there is a higher race, and that some are more fit to live, and lead, and lord it over others. Take, for example, the words of Adolf Hitler in his famed work *Mein Kampf.* He wrote that if "a superior race should intermingle with an inferior one" Nature's efforts "to establish an evolutionary higher stage of being, may thus be rendered futile."[10] This kind of thinking was not unfamiliar to the proponents of American slavery who viewed their captives as "riddled with imperfections from head to toe" and therefore fit for their role as slaves.[11]

Fit is an important word in this discussion, because a world without God is a "survival of the fittest" kind of world. It is a world in which some among us prove to be more fit than others to exist on this planet. Of course, this line of thinking puts us in a precarious position. For example, if we see one group of people systematically oppress or annihilate another group of people, on what basis can we call it unjust? Is not nature simply doing its thing? And if we want humanity to progress, should we not encourage the process of subjugation and elimination so that we weed out the less fit among us? I know very well that all this goes against most modern sensibilities (and so it should), but if there is no God, are those sensibilities to be trusted when it comes to deciding what is ultimately just or unjust?

One of my favorite writings of Martin Luther King, Jr. is his "Letter from Birmingham Jail." In it, he says we have the moral responsibility to obey just laws and disobey unjust laws. But then he asks the all-important question, "How does one determine whether a law is just or unjust?" His answer was: "A just law is a man-made code that squares with the moral law or the law of God."[12] Such an answer might be expected from a religious man like MLK, but perhaps he was on to something that transcends religion. Maybe he understood that if we remove God from "under the hood," we are left only with competing preferences where the most powerful, the most fit, or best DNA-equipped win. And as history has shown us, that kind of justice can lead to fateful consequences.

The Loss of Love

"Love makes the world go round." At least that's what Madonna tells us in a song she wrote by that name. I've never been one to take my understanding of life from a pop singer, but in this case, I think Madonna is not too far off the mark. At least from my experience, there is much to be said about love's place in our lives, particularly in a satisfied life.

But just what are we to do with this thing called love? If we are made by a God who created us to love and be loved, then there might be something deep and meaningful to the tears that fall down our face when a loved one dies, to that longing we have for one who has traveled afar, or to that overwhelming elation and awe when we hold a newborn child. If, however, we take God out from "under the hood," and we are reduced to cosmic accidents, then the best we can say is that all we count as love is nothing more than a feeling produced by unavoidable chemical reactions. Paul Churchland, Professor Emeritus at UC San Diego, has long agreed with this point. He thinks that our "common-sense conception" of phenomena such as love "constitutes a radically false theory" that will soon be "displaced . . . by completed neuroscience."[13] For Churchland, this is rather exciting, and he looks forward to the day when libraries are no longer filled with epic novels brimming with stories of heroic love but instead filled "with long recordings of exemplary bouts of neural activity."[14] Of course, if you take Churchland's position, just think how differently a Valentine's Day card might read: "Would you be my Valentine? My neurons are chemically attracted to your presence and my evolved breeding instincts respond well to you."[15]

But it's not just the ooey-gooey kind of love that evaporates without the existence of God; any kind of relationship with others gets rather thin. Jean-Paul Sartre, the great 20th-century philosopher and committed atheist, understood this dilemma. He knew that no one wants to think that the object of his passion is just a machine that can't help but respond in kind. If that is the case "both his love and his being are cheapened" and he finds himself alone with a machine programmed to "love" him in return.[16] I know that's a rather depressing view of love, but if there is no God, it seems that is what we have left.

The Loss of Reason

Put two people in a room with different opinions about any subject and ask them to make their case for why they believe Republicans are better than Democrats, the Dodgers are better than the Yankees, or U2 is better than the Rolling Stones, and sparks will likely fly. But before steam starts coming out ears, you are likely to hear reasons: reasons why one viewpoint is better than another, reasons why the other's case is weak or faulty, reasons why I am right and you are wrong. It's just the way we work. Oh sure, from time to time, we may in frustration declare, "I am right because I said so," but we're not likely to be very persuasive at that point unless we've got a big stick in our hand.

The propensity to use reason to defend our position is no less prevalent when it comes to the issue of God. Ask an atheist why he or she doesn't believe in God and you might hear that science has made God unnecessary or that the existence of evil in the world proves that God, if he exists, cannot be all powerful and all loving. In other words, most atheists didn't wake up one day and just decide there isn't a God; they have a reason for staking their claim. But here is the real sticky thing about their reasons: If there is no God, reasons of any sort become quite untrustworthy. And this is true regardless of what line of reasoning the atheist might use. Let me explain.

If we say that life as we know it came about because nature selected what would best survive, we must say the same about our brains. That is, we have the brains we do because in some way they helped us survive better than a previous rendition. But under this scenario, just because our brains helped us survive doesn't mean they are telling us the truth. In fact, maybe they are telling us something that isn't true, because in some way holding to that untruth helps us survive. That might seem like a crazy proposition, but Francis Crick, the famed co-discoverer of DNA, arrived at this conclusion long before I did. He writes: "Our highly developed brains, after all, were not evolved under the pressure of discovering scientific truths but only to enable us to be clever enough to survive."[17] Steven Pinker, a Harvard Professor of Psychology, says something very similar: "Our brains were shaped for fitness, not for truth. Sometimes the truth is adaptive, but sometimes it is not."[18] In other words, these scientists tell us that if humans came about by a cosmic roll of the dice, our brains may well be feeding us falsehoods just to keep us alive. Now, that can put the atheist in an uncomfortable position. On the one hand, we are told to believe in atheism because of this or that reason, while on the other hand atheism suggests we have brains that were not designed to give us reasons we should trust.

Suppose someone installed a new computer in your office. You've been waiting for it to arrive and are excited to put it to use. Once it's booted up, you notice it has a number of programs loaded on it that you do not recognize. You ask about them and are told that they are to be used for the analytic processes required for your industry. Because you are unfamiliar with the programs, you ask who developed the software and are told, "Oh, they were just developed through a mindless, unguided process." After protesting, I am guessing you'd have a hard time trusting anything the programs churned out. For very similar reasons, if our brains came to be by a mindless, unguided process, we should have a hard time trusting our very thoughts. Oh sure, here and there they might be telling us something true, but it would be hard to know when, since survival and not truth is their apparent purpose.

One thing I like about Charles Darwin is that at times he was quite reflective. In other words, he did not just come up with the theory of evolution; he stood back and considered its implications. Some of those implications were not very comfortable, especially when it came to the trustworthiness of our thoughts. When writing his autobiography in the summer of 1876, he wrote: "But then arises the doubt—can the mind of man, which has, as I fully believe, been developed from a mind as low as that possessed by the lowest animal, be trusted?"[19] This was not a short-lived doubt. In 1881, Darwin wrote very similar words in a letter to a friend: "But then with me the horrid doubt always arises whether the convictions of man's mind, which has been developed from the mind of the lower animals, are of any value or at all trustworthy."[20] I understand how Darwin couldn't shed this horrid doubt. If there is no God, we cannot trust our thoughts, even our thoughts about atheism.[21]

The Loss of Identity

I am not so sure obituaries do anyone great justice. There's the bit about where one was born and died. Something is usually noted about the deceased's alma mater, work accomplishments, or community activities. And then there is the long list of survivors with perhaps a nice note about how much so and so was loved. I can't remember the last time I read an obituary of a person I knew and felt it really captured the essence of the person who died.

When we think of people we barely know or know only through their celebrity, we often associate them with things they have accomplished— the song they sang, the house they built, the office they held—but once you start to get to know someone the scorecard shifts. At that point, we begin to grade a person by their dreams and ambitions, by the way they treat people, and by the unique manner they walk and talk and go about their business. We say that they are driven or kind or rude or conceited or practical or a host of other adjectives. This is the "real" person regardless of what a future obituary might say.

This "real" person is quite important these days. "Take off the mask," "Be authentic," and "Don't be shaped by others' expectations," we are told. There is a real you, and expressing it should be what life is all about. You might be thinking that I am knocking the "be your best you" mantra, but that's not really the case. I am just trying to point out that finding ourselves and living authentically are rather important to us these days. I wonder, however, if the pursuit of our authentic selves is severely tarnished if there is no God "under the hood."

To explain further, let me tell you about the lichen that sometimes grows outside my house. Usually it looks rather fuzzy, has an odd green or red tint to it, and is attached to a fence or tree. I might stare at it for a few seconds and ponder how I might rid my surroundings of it, but I am quite sure I have never considered what the "real you" of that fungus is all about. As far as I am concerned, it's just something that came to grow at my house through a series of events that I need to circumvent if I don't want it to overtake my yard. But if I don't concern myself about the "real you" of the happenstance lichen in my yard, should I concern myself with my own "real you" if I, like the fungus, am only a result of cosmic happenstance? Alan Lightman, a professor at MIT, thinks not:

> Our consciousness and our self-awareness create an illusion that we are made out of some special substance, that we have some kind of special ego-power, some "I-ness," some unique existence. But, in fact, we are nothing but bones, tissues, gelatinous membranes, neurons, electrical impulses and chemicals. . . . We are a bunch of atoms. Like trees, and like donuts.[22]

I brought up DNA-discoverer Francis Crick earlier. As a skeptic with "a strong inclination towards atheism,"[23] he also didn't put much stock in our own sense of identity. He concluded: "The Astonishing Hypothesis is that 'You,' your joys and your sorrows, your memories and ambitions, your sense of personal identity and free will, are in fact no more than the behavior of a vast assembly of nerve cells and their associated molecules."[24] If Lightman and Crick are right, maybe we need to rethink all those flowery obituaries and just publish something about people's molecular makeup. At least that would keep us from having to come up with something nice to say.

In this opening chapter, I have walked through quite a long list of losses that seem inevitable if there is no God. Based on my experience in talking about these losses with others, I would not be surprised if you found a few of them jarring. This is probably a healthy response. We are people who define ourselves by the choices we make, the people we love, the purposes we pursue, the reasons we ponder, and the justice we seek. Collectively, it is these things that give us meaning in life. They are what shape our personal identity. And yet, if God is but a fantasy, then we are just the vast assembly of nerves and molecules Dr. Crick told us about, and all the other stuff that makes up the "real you" is a fantasy too.

Back to the Question

It's probably good at this juncture to make one thing clear. Nothing that I have presented so far proves God's existence. Perhaps you thought that was my aim in this chapter, but that's not the case. Just because the absence of God means a loss of many other things, the presence of God does not necessarily follow. So, what then has been my point in walking through the loss of love and reason and justice and so forth? The reason has been to answer the question of this chapter: Life is good, so why be concerned with God?

For most religious people, the reason to bother with God has to do with the life to come. That's not bad thinking. If there is a God and there is an eternal bliss for those who take his side, then it makes sense to give God a good look. This in fact is similar to Blaise Pascal's famous wager. Even though he was a skeptical philosopher who wrote in a very skeptical time, he recognized that a person does well to bet on God, given the finiteness of this life and the grand potential of life with God in eternity. It's like betting a dime for a chance of winning a billion. Or in Pascal's words, "For if you gain, you gain all; if you lose, you lose nothing."[25] For many, Pascal's Wager has been enough to encourage belief, but maybe that is not the case for you. Maybe the promise of a "sweet by and by" is so far-fetched that even betting a dime seems like a poor investment.

Notice, however, that of all the things I have said we lose if God does not exist, eternal bliss is not one I directly addressed. Certainly, if there is no God, then some grand eternity with him does not exist as well. But in this chapter, I have not pulled out the heaven card; instead, I've spoken about here and now kind of stuff. If there is no God, we don't just lose future love, we lose love today. If God is but a figment of our imagination, we lose not only future justice but any objective basis for justice today.

I understand that the existence of a God to whom we are accountable might seem very unlikely to you. I also understand it might be inconvenient to dig deeper to find out if God really is out there. But regardless of the odds you give for God's existence, it seems to me that the inconvenience excuse goes a little flat when we consider what would be lost without him. Why be concerned with God? Because if God is not under the hood, there is so very much we lose. Maybe even the stuff that makes life good.

Key Points

- Whether God exists or not has greater implications than we often imagine. If we are but creatures that came about by chance, by a long series of dice rolls . . .

  › Our lives have no objective meaning—no more meaning than Scrabble pieces accidentally strewn on the floor.

  › Our lives have no objective purpose. We are like a load of clothes that fall to the floor with no intended aim.

  › It would be wrong to talk about humans having a free will since our DNA can't help but respond to the environment to which it is exposed. Just as baking soda reacts when mixed with vinegar, so we must react to life as we do.

  › Justice is hard to demand when we are just dancing to our own DNA in a "survival of the fittest" kind of world.

  › Love is reduced to purely biochemical responses and is nothing more than a label we use to describe a mental sensation caused by neural activity.

  › We cannot trust our reason any more than we can trust a computer that has been randomly programmed.

  › Our personal identity is questionable given that what we love, the choices we make, and the purposes we pursue are simply the result of nerves and molecules doing their thing.

- When we take God out from "under the hood," what we consider to be of great importance in our lives is reduced to "Nobel Lies." This does not prove there is a God, but it gives us good reason to be concerned about the question of God's existence, even if life seems good.

Additional Resources

Making Sense Out of God: An Invitation to the Skeptical, Timothy Keller

Stealing from God: Why Atheists Need God to Make Their Case, Frank Turek

"What Difference Does It Make If God Exists?" in *On Guard: Defending Your Faith with Reason and Faith*, William Lane Craig

Why Should I Believe God Exists?

Bang! Bang! Bang! went the noise that startled me out of bed. I was probably seven years old at the time, and the window in my room looked over the front porch. Someone was pounding at the front door late on Christmas Eve, and I wasn't the only one who heard the ruckus. My brother and sister did as well, and soon we huddled together as our parents opened the door. There he was in all his regalia. Red coat, black boots, white beard, and properly donned hat. Saint Nick had arrived, and with presents in hand.

What a night! One I will never forget. Yet as unexpected and glorious as our Yuletide guest might have been, I was suspicious from the start. I was too old for such tomfoolery. It was all a fun ruse, but I knew Santa wasn't for real.

There was probably a time when you believed in Santa Claus, the Tooth Fairy, and perhaps the Easter Bunny. Your parents knew they were not real, but they set the stage anyway because the "existence" of these make-believe characters would add a little fun or hopeful expectation to your life. In fact, the expected coming of someone like Santa may have even been an incentive for good behavior, and most of us needed a little extra motivation. I don't believe many people look poorly on their parents for telling them stories about these seasonal characters. Fairy tales and the make-believe are part of what makes childhood magical. But what if the same is true of God? What if God is simply a passed-down, make-believe creature that encourages us to be nice or offers us some treats in the end? These are good questions. If God is not real, it might be a fun childhood myth, but it's probably wise at one point or another to grow up and face the facts.

I don't know where you stand on the question of God. Maybe you put him in the category of Saint Nick. If so, you are certainly not alone. There are plenty today who deny or are at least skeptical about God's existence. Some of them are my friends. As I see it, there are three options when it comes to the question of God: You can believe he exists, you can put him in the maybe category, or you can say with certainty that he does not exist. Atheists, of course, hold to the last of these three options. But with all due respect, I think it is the most tenuous of the possibilities.

Knowledge is a really big category. Let's suppose you had to write down everything about the oil and gas industry. How many books would that take you? I cannot even imagine. And the same would be true if you had to catalog all knowledge about ancient Roman history or biodiversity in sub-Saharan Africa. Even the smartest person on the planet is aware she knows only a smidgen of all that could be known, most of which has yet to be discovered. Sometimes, I like to illustrate all knowledge with a big circle and ask people to show me how much of that big circle represents what they personally know. So far, I have never had anyone mark out any more than a tiny, tiny dot.[1] We know so very little about what can be known, and we all know it.

But this puts us in an interesting position when it comes to God. When someone says with utter confidence that God does not exist, it seems a rather bold claim. Isn't there a possibility that God is out there somewhere, even if you have yet to find him? Now, of course, someone could counter, "But how can you be sure there is a God, when you too have limited knowledge?" That's a fair question. But consider this: Suppose you enter a large indoor arena, something like Madison Square Garden, and upon walking through one of the entrances, you see a mosquito fly by. At that point, you would be able to declare that mosquitos are a real thing in Madison Square Garden, even if you had only inspected a tiny part of the arena. The reverse, however, could not be said with much certainty. That is, if you just entered the building and saw no mosquitos, you might be able to say, "There may or may not be mosquitos in the entire building," but saying with confidence that mosquitos do not exist in the entire building would be a bit overzealous. Similarly, declaring with certainty there is no God, when we know so little about the whole of the universe, seems a bit overzealous. This is why I said that of the three options—God exists, God maybe exists, and God does not exist—the third stance seems most tenuous.

Of course, none of this says anything about whether God really does exist and whether we have any evidence to that end. It just says that if we have our doubts about God, we should probably be in the maybe category and not the atheist category. It seems that would keep us in the mind frame of a good investigative reporter or scientist and prevent us from closing our eyes to any evidence that might pop up along the way.

Evidence for God

I have been fortunate enough not to have too many things stolen from me over the years, but I did have the same car stolen twice in just a two-year period. Apparently, it was the kind of car that people who steal cars liked to take. The first time it was stolen, my wife and I had only the one car. She needed it that day and went to the street in front of our apartment to get in and go. She was in a bit of a hurry and came back frustrated because it was not where I had told her I had parked it. I was certain where I'd left it, but to make sure I went to all our normal parking spots before ultimately concluding that someone had taken it—and without even asking! Eventually, the police found our car abandoned in a field. When we got our hands on it, there were cigarette butts strewn about and a cassette tape in the stereo. (Now I am dating myself!) As far as we were concerned, plenty of evidence showed that our car didn't inadvertently roll down the road or mistakenly get taken by an aging neighbor. Now, of course, we never saw the person who stole the car and we know of no one who saw the thief, but I think we had enough to go on to come to our conclusion that someone with ill intent decided to take our car for something of a joy ride.

I am not sure what kind of evidence would be the most convincing concerning God's existence. Some people think if God showed up with some kind of grand cosmic show, we'd all know he exists. But my guess is there would still be plenty of people who would talk themselves out of what they had seen. That is why it might be more valuable to look at evidence beyond a single sighting. But just what would that evidence look like? I tend to think it would look something like the evidence surrounding my stolen car. That is, even though we may not catch God in the act on some surveillance camera, if he exists, I suspect there would be enough clues along the way for us to come to a reasonable conclusion.

Clue #1: We Are Here

Often people have asked the question of how we got here, but for a long time, many people didn't ponder the universe's existence. From at least as far back as Aristotle, the universe was said to be eternal—something that has always been here. In that case, there was little need to discuss the brute fact of its existence other than to say, "It is here and always has been." But the 20th century altered this kind of thinking. The universe has not always been here, and at least two well-confirmed theories say so.

The first of these theories is the Second Law of Thermodynamics. I won't make this into a science class, but basically that law tells us, among other things, that over time we would not expect two entities sharing the same space to maintain different temperatures in the long run. Put a hot cup of coffee on the counter and soon it will be same temperature as the room in which it sits. Because this is the case, if you come into the room and see steam rising from the cup, you would know it hasn't been there too long and that the Second Law of Thermodynamics has yet to complete its work. Understanding all this does not take a rocket scientist, but if you apply this same kind of thinking to the universe, you can see we have good reason to believe it hasn't been here for eternity. If it has, all the stars (including our sun) would have long burned out and we'd be living in a cold, dark world that is roughly all the same temperature. That's why the late Stephen Hawking declared, "The theory that the universe has existed forever is in serious difficulty with the Second Law of Thermodynamics."[2]

But it's not just this Second Law that undermines the universe's eternality; so does the Big Bang Theory. What got the whole Big Bang Theory going are a few observations that let us know that the universe has always been expanding. That might not seem too interesting at first, but if that's the case, then if we wind the clock back we'll eventually hit a time when our universe didn't exist at all. It might not bother you that the universe hasn't always been here, but it certainly bothered many scientists when the theory first came on the scene. And it worried them because once we say the universe has a beginning, we must then talk about how it got here. At least that's what world-famous cosmologist Alexander Vilenkin tells us when he writes, "With the proof now in place, cosmologists can no longer hide behind the possibility of a past-eternal universe. There is no escape: they have to face the problem of a cosmic beginning."[3]

In response to the cosmic beginning, one might say, "Okay, so the universe had a point when it came into existence, but what keeps us from saying it just popped into existence—no explanation needed?" I suppose that is an option, but that certainly isn't par for the course. We don't think the tree in our front yard, the car that we drive, or the mess in our kids' room just came out of nowhere. In fact, if there is one thing our world has shown us repeatedly, it is that for everything that comes into existence there is a cause behind it. If the universe has always been here, it wouldn't need a cause. But as we've seen, the evidence tells us it hasn't always been here. This means that like it or not, there must be a cause behind it. There must be something outside our universe that explains why we are here.

I know we sometimes speak as if the universe is made up of planets and stars and galaxies, but there are some things even more fundamental than that. If we get right down to it, the universe is made up of time and space and matter. But what is really mind-blowing is that before the universe existed, time, space, and matter didn't exist either. That leaves us in an interesting predicament when it comes to searching for the cause of the universe, because whatever made the universe must be non-temporal, non-spatial, and immaterial. There is just no way around that. In addition, whatever made the universe must be an agent of change. If it weren't, it would not have been able to do whatever was necessary to get it all started.[4]

For millennia, Christians have talked about God and have even described his attributes. These attributes include the idea that God:

- stands outside of time,
- is not confined by space,
- is immaterial,
- and is a powerful agent of change.[5]

In other words, before all this modern science came into play, the description given for God in the Bible fits very nicely with the characteristics science now tells us are necessary for the cause of our universe.

Suppose someone came into my home while I was on a walk and stole money I had left on the counter. I have video footage, but because it is very grainy and the perpetrator wore a ski mask, I can tell only that he was tall enough to require ducking under the door frame and that he had a large tattoo of some sort on his left arm. Suppose also that for the last month on my daily walks I have noticed a very tall man walking the neighborhood, and like the figure on the video camera, he has a large tattoo on his left arm. At this point, I cannot be able to prove beyond all doubt that he was the one who committed the crime, but I think you can see why I am not unreasonable to put him high on my list of suspects. Similarly, while the fact that the universe is here (and we along with it) may not prove that God exists, I don't think it is unreasonable for me to be suspicious of God's activity even if I didn't catch him in the act.

Of course, a question many ask at this juncture is: "But if everything needs a cause, what caused God?" As I've already explained, seeking a cause for things that come into existence is very reasonable indeed. When the universe was thought to be eternal, no cause was sought because none would have been necessary. However, now that we know the universe is one of those things that came into existence, seeking its cause is more than justifiable. And just as a cause for the universe was not necessary when it was thought to be eternal, so a cause for God is not necessary if he has always existed. In fact, demanding a cause for that uncaused God would be rather nonsensical, somewhat like asking how many wives a bachelor has. This answer might seem like a tidy way to avoid the issue of the origin of God. But it isn't. Because things don't just pop into existence out of nothing, if anything exists at all, there must be something or someone that is uncaused that got the whole thing going. That uncaused something is either natural, which seems very unlikely given that we have no evidence that anything natural existed before the Big Bang, or, it is supernatural and has the properties that would be necessary to create the world we have. As we've seen in this first clue, God (as Christians have long described him) does have the properties necessary to create the world. He is the uncaused, pre-existing "criminal that fits the crime."

Clue #2: Our Fine-Tuned Universe

When it was first built, it was quite the thing. Some people down in Arizona decided to make a world inside a world that was fully self-sufficient. They called it Biosphere 2, since they figured Earth itself is Biosphere 1. For most people, the big glass structure looked like something out of a Star Trek movie, and the people living within it like ants trying to survive inside of one of those mail-order kits. Some people say the experiment was a success, others say it was a failure, and most people say it was something in between. But whatever the case, everyone recognized that if Biosphere 2 worked at all, it was because there were countless, calculated decisions behind it. Everything from oxygen to soils and from water to plant life had to be carefully planned out in advance so life could work at least at the level of human survival. In other words, creating a world that supports life was not something that could be left to chance.

I think some sci-fi movies give the impression that life is pretty easy to sustain and that life-supporting systems can be found in abundance on all kinds of planets. So far, however, that hasn't proved to be true. In fact, if science has shown us anything in recent years it is how incredibly precise the conditions must be to sustain life anywhere in the universe. Consider gravity, for example. We all know it helps keep us fastened to planet Earth, but on a bigger scale, it allows for masses to clump together and form the stars or planets that make life on Earth possible. What is key to understand, however, is that it's not just gravity's presence that is important—its fine-tuned nature is also paramount. In fact, if gravity were just a little greater or a little lesser in force, those same stars and planets would not be here. The precision of this fine-tuning is astounding; adjust the gravitational constant by only 1 part in 10^{60} and bye-bye to life as we know it.[6] To better understand that kind of precision, let me provide an illustration. Suppose my wife is very particular when it comes to the temperature of our house. I set the thermostat at 74 degrees and she is too hot. I set it at 73 and she is too cold. So, I try to rig the system so that the temperature can be adjusted by one-tenth of a degree. Still, I find that at 73.4 degrees she is too cold and at 73.5 she is too hot. Eventually, I am able to alter the system so that instead of just ten notches between each degree of Fahrenheit I have a trillion, trillion, trillion, trillion, trillion notches to choose from, and then and only then am I able to find the exact temperature suitable for my wife. That is the kind of necessary precision we are talking about when it comes to gravity and the necessary conditions for life like ours in the universe. Change its force just a tiny bit and no significant life is possible anywhere in the universe.

Even if gravity were the only thing in our cosmos that needed to be fine-tuned for complex and intelligent life to exist, we should be impressed. But if we look a little further, we can see there are all kinds of cosmological constants that must be fine-tuned.[7] For example, the mass density of the universe must be fine-tuned to one part in 10^{59} and the cosmological constant that helps explain the expansion rate of the universe must be fined-tuned to one part in 10^{120}.[8] Just to put things in perspective, there are only an estimated 10^{80} subatomic particles in the entire universe. That means you would have a far better chance of shooting an arrow blindfolded and hitting a predetermined proton or electron somewhere out in space than you would seeing the cosmological constant be fine-tuned for life. It is these kinds of numbers that have caught the attention of many in the scientific community.

> *The laws of nature form a system that is extremely fine-tuned,* and very little in physical law can be altered without destroying the possibility of the development of life as we know it. Were it not for a series of startling coincidences in the precise details of physical law, it seems, humans and similar life forms would never have come into being. (Stephen Hawking Theoretical Physicist, University of Cambridge, & Leonard Mlodinow)[9]

> The really amazing thing is not that life on Earth is balanced on a knife edge but that *the entire universe is balanced on a knife-edge.* . . . The entire universe seems unreasonably suited to the existence of life, almost contrived. We might say a "put up" job. (Paul Davies, Theoretical Physicist, Adelaide University)[10]

> *Fine-tuning is too remarkable to be dismissed* as just a happy accident. (John Polkinghorne, Mathematical Physicist, University of Cambridge)[11]

There are times you have probably gotten a peek inside a sound booth at the rear of an auditorium. In doing so, you may have seen a large soundboard with hundreds of knobs, buttons, and sliders. Imagine if a new soundboard was installed in a world-famous venue just prior to the production of *Hamilton* hitting the stage, and upon powering it up, discovering that all the knobs and buttons and sliders are exactly as they need to be in order for the show to sound its best. I doubt you would think that the precision of the soundboard's fine-tuning is simply a coincidence. Someone had to know the venue; someone had to know the needs of the production. Even if you wanted to hold out hope for chance as an explanation, I don't think you can blame someone for concluding that there was some sort of intellect behind the soundboard's perfect setup. Nor does it seem you can blame astronomers like the famed Sir Fred Hoyle (who coined the phrase "Big Bang Theory") from looking at our universe and concluding: "A common sense interpretation of the facts suggests that a superintellect has monkeyed with physics, as well as with chemistry and biology, and that there are no blind forces worth speaking about in nature. The numbers one calculates from the facts seem to me so overwhelming as to put this conclusion almost beyond question."[12] And given that God fits the definition of the kind of "super-intellect" it would take to fine-tune the world, can you blame people for believing there is a God who made it all?

Many people over the years have been quite impressed by the fine-tuning argument for the existence of God, even before all the insights into cosmological constants. A person only has to look at the universe like one would look at a common wristwatch or the presidential faces on Mt. Rushmore to conclude that random chance as an explanation for substantial fine-tuning is rather outlandish. But there is a common objection to fine-tuning evidence often floated these days that probably should be addressed. It has to do with something called the *multiverse theory*. Basically, the objection goes like this: "Yes, the universe appears perfectly designed to allow for intelligent life. And if our universe were the only one, it would be hard to say we just got lucky given the odds. But what if ours is not the only universe? What if there are zillions and zillions of universes, such that the odds are drastically increased and finding one that supports life is not at all surprising?" There is a certain logic to this theory, but here are three problems I see with it.

First, there is no evidence that any other universes exist. It is pure speculation, even on the part of the scientific community. The multiverse theory has come to the forefront not because other universes have been observed (or have left any trace of their existence) but as a means to better accept the reality that our universe is remarkably conducive to life on planet Earth. In other words, it is the possibility of a supernatural, intelligent cause of our fine-tuned universe that has spawned the multiverse theory and not any scientific observations.

Second, supposing there are countless universes, we still must account for each universe's existence. Those touting the multiverse theory often propose the possibility of a universe-making machine that pumps out the myriad of universes. But it's not clear how this machine would avoid the need for itself to be fine-tuned. Take an old slot machine that has cherries among the ten symbols on each of the three reels. Your odds of hitting three cherries are 999 to 1. Thus, if you pull the lever 999 times you would expect on average to produce three cherries once. But the only way you can hit three cherries at all is because the machine has been fine-tuned to have one cherry per reel in the first place. Thus, even if there is a universe-making machine out there, we still must explain how it was fine-tuned to produce even one life-permitting universe.

Third, the multiverse theory provides an explanation that would be laughable if applied to other scenarios. Consider, for example, that you have been lost in the woods for several days. You are cold, wet, and hungry. As another evening approaches, you see light in the distance. You follow the light and soon you find a cabin. You knock on the door, but no one is there. Desperate, you decide to enter. The warmth and light are enough to bring great relief, but within moments, you notice something very strange. The smell of the cabin is like that of your home, and the music playing features your favorite band. The food in the refrigerator is just as you would stock it, and the beer is from your prized local brewery. Furthermore, the bed and pillows are just as you like them, and pictures on the hearth are of places and people you love. At that point, you have two choices. You can say, "Someone must have known I was coming and set this all up for me in advance." Or you can say, "Wow, even though I have yet to see any other cabins, there must be a zillion out there, and I just happened to find the one that suits me perfectly." Personally, I think the second explanation is extraordinarily far-fetched, and yet it is this kind of thinking that those who propose the multiverse theory want us to embrace in order to dismiss the evidence from fine-tuning.

Clue #3: Math's Uncanny Applicability

Math seems to be one of those dividing lines in life. You either like it or hate it, and there isn't much middle ground. But even if math class made you queasy growing up, hang in there on this one, because I won't be giving you any equations to work out.

You may not have noticed, but in everyday life you refer to two different kinds of entities. Some of them are physical in nature, and you can touch and see and hear them, like dogs that have spots, New York City, and the cranky neighbors who live next door. For these kinds of objects, it makes sense to ask when and where we might find them. There are other kinds of entities, however, that are a regular part of our world but are abstract in nature. These include things like straightness or triangularity or redness. Unlike physical entities, it makes little sense to ask for their location on a map or how heavy they are. Numbers, equations, and basically all things mathematical are in the category of abstract entities. They are not time and space kinds of things.

Because mathematical ideas are not time and space kinds of things, they would exist even if the universe did not exist, or if nothing was found in the universe to which they can immediately apply. Just as straightness and triangularity and redness would not be invalidated if there was nothing in our universe to which these concepts would apply, so too is the case for mathematical proofs. Mathematicians have long recognized this, and many math professor types pursue their mathematical proofs and concepts with little regard as to whether they apply to anything in our physical world. Take, for example, G. H. Hardy, the famed 20th-century British mathematician. He once bragged that not a single abstract math concept he had proved "is likely to make, directly or indirectly, for good or ill, the least difference to the amenity of the world."[13] But here is the crazy thing: Hardy's math, whether he wanted it to or not, ended up having all kinds of valuable applications in areas like genetics and physics. And this dynamic is true not just of Hardy's mathematical discoveries but also of the discoveries of other mathematicians over and over again. If you are not into math, this might not seem too interesting, but stay with me and I think you will see that it all adds up to a clue for the existence of God.

In mathematics, we have abstract entities that would have existed before our universe came on the scene, so why is it that once we discover these entities, we find at some point that they apply so well to the physical world we are seeking to understand? That's like finding plans for a highly effective heart pump that predates any living organisms coming on the scene. Nobel Prize winner Eugene Wigner (who was part of the Manhattan Project) once wrote a famous article about the uncanny applicability of mathematics, saying, "The enormous usefulness of mathematics in the natural sciences is something bordering on the mysterious and…there is no rational explanation for it."[14] But is there really no rational explanation for the usefulness of mathematics in our physical world?

Let's return to my heart pump example. If there was no source of intelligence before life existed in the universe, then there would be no rational reason for pre-existing heart pump plans. But if there is some form of intelligence that has been around long before our world began, there is a very reasonable explanation. And that explanation is simply this: that the pre-existing intelligence not only made the heart pump plans, but later the very hearts to which it applies. In that case, we should not be at all surprised that the heart pump plans fit with our human hearts. Similarly, we should not be surprised when the abstract concepts of math that were in existence long before the universe keep applying to the physical world if there is an intelligent source from which they both come. John Lennox, Emeritus Professor of Mathematics at Oxford University, says the same, when he writes: "It is, therefore, not surprising when the mathematical theories spun by human minds created in the image of God's Mind, find ready application in a universe whose architect was that same creative Mind."[15] So, while I don't know of a single math equation that proves there is a God, maybe the uncanny applicability of math to our physical world points to God as a reasonable cause for the world in which we now live. That might not be to your liking, but there is one benefit: If you've never liked math, now you can blame God for it!

Clue #4: Right and Wrong

If you already suspected some outside intelligent source might be behind the universe, the first few clues might be enough to push you more firmly into the God-believing camp. But from what we have seen so far, all that really can be concluded is that God is an invisible and nondescript engineer *par excellence* who is especially keen on math and has some interest in promoting life on our planet. That might give us reason to give him a nod here or there, but it would hardly give us cause to join gatherings with religious types or to bow and pray instead of heading to the beach for a nice long walk with the dog. That's why this clue is so important—by looking at right and wrong, we have more to go on when it comes to God.

To work out this clue, first it is best to acknowledge that *without a personal God, objective morals and duties do not exist.* Oh sure, we can call things moral or immoral, but if we are just happenstance creatures, as explained in the opening chapter, we simply do what we do and there isn't any right or wrong to it. That's why many in the atheist camp today readily admit that under atheism, there is no objective right and wrong. For example, Friedrich Nietzsche, who adamantly declared there is no God, concluded, "There are no such things as moral facts."[16] Or, as we read earlier, Richard Dawkins has concluded that in our universe there is "no evil and no good, nothing but blind, pitiless indifference."[17] Of course, there are atheists who think there are objective morals despite our happenstance existence (they float around as abstract objects, so they say), but we must wonder why as accidental creatures spit out by the cosmos we would have a duty to uphold such morals.[18] In saying this, I don't at all suggest that atheists themselves cannot do what many would consider right or good and even call others to do the same, it's just that if we are only "a decaying piece of matter in a decaying universe and nothing more significant than that,"[19] it is difficult to explain where moral objectives come from and why we are obligated to live up to them.

Now, to be fair, some have argued that evolution can point us to a certain morality. If a particular behavior is something that keeps our species alive, it is morally good. If not, it is morally bad. But why is the propagation of the human species the determinant of what is good? Why not the propagation of the ant? And how do we get the idea of human rights or racial, economic, or gender equality from the unguided development of our species? Can we really prove that equality of that kind increases the survival of our species? If we look across nature, we see a great deal of violence and discrimination where the strong kill the weak or run them off. Why is that not appropriate for humanity?

Maybe you agree that human evolution absent of God does not provide a reasonable explanation for the rights and wrongs we seem unable to disavow, and so you point to social convention. You argue that we simply know what is right and wrong by looking at what the majority agrees upon. But does this not put us in a dangerous position? The majority of Germans were on board with Nazism, but I think few Germans today are prepared to say that the treatment of Jews and other minorities by the Nazis was therefore moral. Does that then mean that Nazi genocide was moral in its time but is no longer? Furthermore, if social convention is our measuring stick, which measuring stick are we to use? For some the mores of fundamentalist Muslims or neo-Nazis are abhorrent, but they certainly are not for Muslims or neo-Nazis! Ultimately, if there is no God, there is no way to say any action is moral or immoral but only that one group presently has more power to impose its preference on the other.

So at this point you might say, "Okay, so if there is no God, there are no objective morals. I'm good with that. I see right and wrong as relative, so I don't need a God." I don't necessarily disagree with your logic, but I wonder if you really are as much a moral relativist as you proclaim. Personally, I have found that those who identify as moral relativists are just as likely to affirm objective morals as anyone else. For example, if someone says morals are relative and happens to love wildlife, I find she is as quick as the next person to decry the killing of an endangered species regardless of whether the person who killed the animal is good with it. In other words, although she claims to be a moral relativist, she doesn't act like one. And if you are honest with yourself, I'm guessing you are not much different. People, you see, have an uncanny knack for being moral relativists in matters they don't care about but staunch moral objectivists as soon as something they value is threatened.[20]

I can tell I am not a moral relativist by examining the thoughts that go through my head. One of the features of my thoughts is that they come with a voice—a voice, in fact, that never seems to quit speaking. Sometimes that voice tells me about facts—such as the amount that is due on my credit card or the name of the person I am about to call, but what I find most often is that the voice inside my head makes judgments. That is, it does not just tell me that the car passing me is pink; it tells me that the color of that car is ugly. Neither does it only tell me that I have a piece of seasoned steak in my mouth; it tells me it is delicious. But, of course, the voice in my head does not provide opinions on just cars and food. It makes judgments about anything and everything and especially about people. It has something to say about how fast people drive, or about the money people earn, or about the intelligence of the one to whom I am talking. It also tells me that so-and-so should not have spoken to me like they did, that the President made a poor decision, or that people who try to steal your money on the internet are bad. Sometimes I notice that the voice is just giving words to a preference, like chocolate is better than vanilla. But many times, the voice speaks as if its judgment is not just my preference but something objective by which everyone should abide. It says things like "discrimination based on race is wrong," "rigging an election should be punished," or "those in power have an obligation to ensure that people do not take advantage of the poor." At first you might have thought it a little odd when I spoke of the voice in my head, but I'm guessing that as I've continued, it's made a little more sense. It's made more sense, because you too have a voice that speaks inside your head and makes judgments at every turn. And many of those judgments have a tone that express far more than personal preferences. They suggest that there are some things that are objectively right and wrong and that we have a duty to pursue the first and avoid the second.

Earlier I suggested that if God does not exist, objective morals and duties do not exist. And yet now we've seen that, like it or not, we are hard-pressed to do away with objective morals. But if objective morals do indeed exist, where does that point us? I believe it is one more clue as to the existence of God.

That said, there is something more to the clue of objective morals than just pointing to the mere existence of God. If we say there is a God, and that moral objectives are standards set by him, those very same moral objectives probably give us a good clue as to what God is like. That is, if we are sure that being kind to others is an objective moral, maybe it's because God himself is kind. Of course, you and I might argue about which morals are objective and thus point to the character of God, but I find that if you boil down the morals most people stand up for, they tend to go in the direction of love and justice. That's why people say things like, "You all just need to get along," or "You can't do that; it's unfair." Perhaps, then, when it comes to this clue, we don't just have one more clue for the existence of a creator God—we also find support for a God who at his core is both loving and just. And if that's the case, God becomes a whole lot more attractive.

Clue #5: All Those Other Senses

Lots of things make me turn my head. Sometimes, I hear a noise; at other times, it is an unusual scent. Sometimes, I feel a touch from behind or maybe catch a glimpse of something out of the corner of my eye. On most occasions, turning my head results in a bit more information. Upon examination, the sound came from a book falling off a table or the scent came from a cake baking in the oven. In other words, for the most part, my five senses don't let me down. There is something real that has triggered what I am sensing. But every once in a while, they lead me astray. I think I see something to my left, but when I turn to look, nothing is there. Or, I think I feel something crawling up my leg, but when I investigate, no creature is to be found. These instances, however, do not cause me to doubt my senses altogether.

In the opening chapter, I spoke of a number of losses if God does not exist, if he is not "under the hood." Those losses include the loss of objective meaning and purpose, the loss of free will and justice, and the loss of love, trustworthy reason, and personal identity. My conclusion was that if there is no God, the "sense" we have that these things are real is false. But given the other clues we have for God, is it really necessary to say these "senses" are leading us astray? If I hear what sounds like voices in the other room and then find a table full of dirty dishes that were previously not in that room, should I not conclude that my sense of hearing was correct? Maybe I did not see anyone when I went to investigate, but tell-tale signs indicate that someone was there. And as such, I have no reason to think the voices I heard were just in my head. Likewise, given my strong sense that meaning and purpose do exist, that I do experience love, and that I am more than just a conglomeration of nerves, I do well to trust these senses and even add them to the list of reasons to believe that God exists, even if I can't see him. Admittedly, my sense of things like justice can go astray at times, and I can think certain things are wrong that I later discover are not. But by and large I don't see any reason to throw out the belief that justice is real any more than I have reason to throw out my belief that what I think I see and hear and smell and taste and feel are generally an accurate account of the world around me.

Maybe the reason that a deep-seated sense of meaning and purpose is so important to us is because God has made us with an objective meaning and purpose in mind. Maybe the reason we feel we have a choice to take one job or another, or choose one item off a menu over another, is because God himself has given us that choice. Maybe the reason we feel adamant that someone pays the price for vandalizing several local businesses is because God is concerned with justice and has an objective standard with which we resonate. Maybe the reason we are overwhelmed with a feeling of love when we hold a newborn child is not because of some hormonal charge but because God has made the child lovable and has given us the capacity to love. Maybe the reason you use to construct a building or to analyze data from a lab is generally reliable, because God has given us the ability to reason just as he has given us the ability to see and smell. And maybe the reason we don't want to be pressed into a mold but given the freedom to express our own personality, dreams, and passions is because God has uniquely made us.

Sometimes we think we must see things in order to know that they are real. But that is most certainly not the case. Most people are well on board with gravity. They do not, however, believe in gravity because they see it but rather because they see evidence of it in our world. By saying this, I am not suggesting it is impossible to see God, but I am saying that even if we can't see God, we have plenty of reasons to believe in his existence. We can believe in him because he is a reasonable cause of the universe and its fine-tuned nature. We can believe in him because of the uncanny applicability of mathematics in our time and space world. We can believe in him because of the existence of right and wrong. And we can believe in him because of our sense of love and justice and reason and meaning and purpose. In fact, it has been said by many that given this evidence for God, it just might take more faith to be an atheist.

Key Points

- If God is not visible, how do we know he is not a myth like Santa Claus or the Easter Bunny? Here are several clues that support his existence.

- We Are Here

  › The universe had a beginning.

  › Everything that has a beginning has a cause, so the universe must have a cause.

  › Before the universe came into existence there was no time, space, or matter. Thus, the cause of the universe must be non-temporal, non-spatial, and immaterial. It must also be able to effect change.

  › God has long been described by the Bible as non-temporal, non-spatial, immaterial, and a change agent, making God a strong suspect as the cause of the universe.

- Our Fine-Tuned Universe

  › The universe is remarkably fine-tuned for life.

  › The precision of the fine-tuning cannot be explained as the result of chance.

  › When we see things that are fine-tuned, we regularly infer an intelligent creator. Thus, it is reasonable to infer from the fine-tuning of the universe, that an intelligent creator, like God, exists.

- Math's Uncanny Applicability

  › Math consists of abstract entities and ideas that are not bound to the physical world. This means they would exist even if they applied to nothing in our universe or if the universe did not exist.

  › Even when mathematicians make new discoveries with no goal of application, it is usually not long before those discoveries are found to explain something in our physical world.

  › A good explanation for math's uncanny applicability to our world is that both math and the physical world come from the mind of God.

- Right & Wrong

  › If God does not exist, objective morals do not exist.

  › Objective morals do exist, and we can't seem to get away from them.

  › Therefore, God exists.

  › Furthermore, if objective morals center on love and justice, there is good reason to conclude that God is both just and loving.

- All Those Other Senses

  › Although our sense of sight, taste, smell, sound, and touch are not perfect, we generally trust that things that really exist are what trigger them.

  › Although our sense that meaning and purpose, free will, love, justice, and personal identity exist is not perfect, we should generally trust that they really exist.

  › If we don't doubt our sense of meaning, purpose, free will, love, justice, and personal identity, then they give us additional reason to believe that God exists, even if we can't see him.

Additional Resources

On Guard: Defending Your Faith with Reason and Precision, William Lane Craig

God's Crime Scene: A Cold-Case Detective Examines the Evidence for a Divinely Created Universe, J. Warner Wallace

The Case for a Creator: A Journalist Investigates Scientific Evidence That Points Toward God, Lee Strobel

Can We Know the Truth about Anything (Especially about God)?

I am not sure when people started losing faith in truth or in our ability to know it when we see it, but somewhere along the way a wave of skepticism rolled in. This is especially so when it comes to discussions about God. We might still feel comfortable in our ability to discover the truth about the number of cars in our garage or even the temperature outside, but that's a far different endeavor than discovering the truth about a God we cannot invite over to dinner or with whom we can take a selfie. That is why this chapter is really not about God. It is a chapter about truth and how we go about discovering it, because if truth is not something we can get our hands on, especially when it comes to God, then why even bother talking about God in the first place?

Why Truth?

This morning I ate a bowl of bran cereal. I would not call it my favorite breakfast meal, but it sounded good to me when the day got rolling. There wasn't a whole lot of thought behind my decision, or at least it didn't appear that way when I pulled the cereal box from the pantry. But now that I think about it, there were many things I took to be true when I ate that first bite. First, I believed the cereal would not harm me. I am not into swallowing things I believe will make me sick, so though it wasn't a conscious thought, lifting the spoon to my mouth indicated that I took it to be true that the cereal was edible. Secondly, eating bran cereal this morning suggests that I take certain things to be true about cereal manufacturers and about my wife who bought it. Both could have tainted the cereal to my demise. But I believed that not to be true, so I gladly finished the bowl. Thirdly, I took it to be true that the meal would satisfy my growling stomach at least for a little while or I wouldn't have bothered eating it in the first place. Again, none of this went through my head before I swallowed the first spoonful, but that hardly matters. My very actions indicated I was confident in the truth that:

The cereal was edible.
The manufacturer did not taint the product.
My wife did not taint the product after she bought it.
The cereal would tame my hunger, if only for a short while.

What is particularly telling about my breakfast this morning is that not only did I take the above propositions to be true but also I was so confident in their truth I was willing to risk my life with every bite. This same dynamic happens every day. Over and over again, you and I are so confident that certain things are true that we risk our lives on the things we hold true. That's why I think even self-proclaimed skeptics of truth are really much less skeptical in practice than they might imagine. The skeptic, if he were to do a little self-examination, would recognize that he is making countless unconscious decisions about what is true every day.

Not only do skeptics affirm things to be true by the daily, unconscious decisions they make, but also they openly declare things to be true whether they recognize it or not. For example, the skeptic often claims that even if truth exists about God or anything else, we can't ever really know with certainty that we have found it. But notice what the skeptic has done when making this claim. He has declared something to be true, namely that we can't ever really know we have found the truth. That seems a little odd, doesn't it? That's like saying, "I don't know how to speak a word in English." But the skeptic has done this, because despite his claim to the contrary, he can't avoid affirming that certain things are true.

In saying that we cannot avoid believing certain things to be true, I am not suggesting that everything we believe to be true is indeed true. We've all been confident we left our wallet in a particular place, only to recognize later that we were mistaken. I am only saying that skepticism about our ability to know anything at all is not a workable option. Oh sure, you can sit around in a philosophy class and say that no one can know the truth about anything, but such a claim has little bearing on how you or I live our everyday lives. For instance, we don't say, "There is no possible way to know with any degree of confidence whether this bridge or any other will hold us up, but I'll go across it anyway." Instead, we walk across it without deliberation, because we have already decided that there is some truth attached to that bridge, specifically that it will hold us up. And this we do a thousand times a day when we drive to work, visit a restaurant, or water our garden, because like it or not we are creatures who cannot get away from confidently affirming truth.

What Is Truth?

Some concepts can be hard to explain even if we talk about them all the time. Take, for instance, the word *air*. If I ask you to throw a ball up into the air, you would know what to do. You wouldn't pause and ask me what *air* is. But if the ball is taken out of the equation, and you are asked in a classroom to define *air* you would probably struggle with an answer unless you majored in atmospheric studies. I am guessing that this is the case with truth as well. If I ask you to tell me the truth about your whereabouts yesterday, you would probably have a confident answer. If, however, I ask you to tell me what *truth* is, you might struggle to put words to it. So let me give it a shot, and you decide if what I say about truth makes sense.

Truth corresponds with reality. When we talk about truth, what we mean more often than not is that certain propositions—like "The woman is six feet tall"—corresponds to the reality that she really is six feet tall. I could say she is five feet, nine inches tall, but if she were really six feet tall, I would not be speaking the truth. And I wouldn't be speaking the truth because my proposition does not correspond to reality. Sometimes people say, "You have your truth, and I have my truth," but this sounds very odd if truth is what corresponds to reality. Suppose you are on a flight to Philadelphia that gets diverted to Baltimore because of bad weather. The plane lands and soon an argument breaks out. Apparently, some of the passengers don't believe they are now in Baltimore; they believe they landed in Philly. If you are in the "We all have our own truth" camp, what do you say in a situation like this? Do you say, "Well, if some people think they are in Baltimore, that location is true for them, and if some people believe they are in Philadelphia, that location is true for them"? I doubt it. Truth, if it is truth, must correspond with reality. And that goes for footballs or flowers, which we can see and touch, and gravity or God, which we cannot.

Truth is located in its object, not in our subjective experience of the object. It is true that you and I may see or react to things differently, but that doesn't mean our individual experience shapes the truth about the object of our experience. For example, you may feel like I am speeding and I might feel like I am driving well under the speed limit, but neither of our experiences would be telling us the truth if the car is traveling right at the legal limit. Likewise, you may sense that there is someone in the other room and I may not, but our senses do not affect the truth of someone's presence. Furthermore, some may have experienced God to be very close, and others may have experienced God to be altogether absent, but those experiences do not determine whether there is a God in the first place or even his proximity to us. If God exists, he is real apart from our personal, subjective experience.

Truth claims remain true whether we believe in them or not. When we tie truth to an object, it is not difficult to see that our belief or disbelief in the object does not change the veracity of the object in question. I might declare that 15 x 15 equals 225, and you may not believe me, but your disbelief does not change the truth of my proposition. Similarly, I might tell you there are 500 peanuts in a jar. Again, you may not believe me, but if there are 500 peanuts in the jar, that many peanuts can be dumped out and counted whether you believe my claim or not. That's why if I say there is a God and you say there is not, neither your belief nor mine is what determines the truth of our beliefs. What makes the existence of God true is whether God actually exists apart from our beliefs.

Truth can't contradict itself. If you've taken a class on logic, you may be familiar with the law of noncontradiction. This law simply states that something cannot be true and false in the same sense at the same time. For example, the statement "The New York Yankees won the World Series in 1949" cannot be both true and false at the same time if we have a consistent understanding of terms like "New York Yankees" or "World Series." In the same manner, if I say God created the world and you say God did not, we cannot both be right. Some, particularly those familiar with Eastern thought, do not agree with the law of noncontradiction. They want to say that a proposition can be true and false at the same time, and that those like me who say otherwise are wrong. Notice, however, that in doing so they actually support my position. They recognize that my claim that truth can't contradict itself is contradictory to their claim, and they recognize that both can't be right at the same time.

Truth is discovered not invented. If truth is found in the object of truth, then truth is not a personal invention; it is only something we discover. When John Muir traveled throughout the West and saw some of America's most beautiful forests, mountains, and rock formations, he reported the truth of what he saw to President Theodore Roosevelt. But the existence of Yosemite or Yellowstone was not something that Muir invented; it was only something he discovered to be true. Likewise, if there is something true about God, it is not something that we invent either individually or as a community. That's because the truth of God, or anything else for that matter, can only be discovered.

All this defining of truth might seem a little much for you, but it's important if we are going to keep ourselves from arriving at some rather peculiar conclusions. Imagine heading to the emergency room with searing pain in your side. An examination quickly points to appendicitis. The doctor says you need surgery immediately to remove the infected appendix. My guess is you would not object, saying, "Well, that's true for you, but that's not true for me." And you would not say this because the truth is not something that we get to invent or alter by our belief. Neither is it something that can be true and false at the same time. Instead, truth is something that must correspond with reality, wholly independent of our individual experience of it. This is simply the way truth works.

How Do We Know the Truth?

It's one thing to define what truth is, but it is quite another to know that we have found it. You might, for example, agree that truth must correspond with the actual characteristic of the object or event in question, but you might be unsure that we ever can find out what the characteristics of the object or event are in the first place. This is why it's so important to take a look at how we arrive at truth in everyday life.

Imagine your car is missing and is found by the police in my garage with many of its parts missing. Furthermore, they discover a string of recent deposits in my account from used car part shops. When they question me, I tell them aliens must have stolen the car, sold its parts, stored the car at my house, and inexplicably deposited the proceeds in my account. The officers discuss my alibi and, since there is a possibility aliens exist, conclude that I should not be arrested. I, of course, am glad for their decision, but you would probably be flabbergasted. Sure, there is a possibility aliens exist, but why should the mere possibility of other-worldly suspects prevent the police from arresting me? Clearly, the most reasonable explanation for my possession of the vehicle is that I stole it, and mere possibility should not deter the authorities from acknowledging that truth.

Our dog doesn't like to stay in the backyard, at least when we are not at home. If we leave and don't tie him up, he will dig a hole under a fence in short order. We did not know this about him at first. We had to discover this to be true. Our discovery of the truth occurred first by recognizing his absence from the yard on several occasions. Second, we noticed that his disappearance always corresponded with a large hole dug under one fence or another. Third, after we discovered the hole, our dog could be found wandering the neighborhood under his own watch. And, finally, when we led him to the hole under the fence, he had every look of shame a dog can have. Given this evidence, I think we were reasonable in concluding that we have a dirt-digging escape artist for a dog. There are other possible explanations: Maybe a neighbor who wanted to play with our dog dug a hole for the dog to get out each time he escaped. But while that is a possibility, it is not a very good candidate for the truth. And it is not a very good candidate for truth because discovering truth is not about picking and choosing any *possible* conclusion; it is about looking at the evidence and arriving at the *most reasonable* conclusion.

In discovering truth, it is important to note that the evidence we must consider in arriving at a reasonable conclusion varies for different kinds of propositions. If, for example, I want to know whether it is raining, I might look outside and see if water is falling. If, however, I want to know whether Abraham Lincoln was present at the Battle of Gettysburg or if squaring an integer will always result in a whole number, looking outside will do me little good. I bring this up because one common misperception is that the only way we can be confident something is true is to have "scientific" evidence. But that is hardly the case. Suppose I tell you that my mother graduated from John Marshall High School in Los Angeles. What kind of evidence is necessary to arrive confidently at the truth of that statement? You will not check my mother's blood to see whether what I tell you of my mother is true, and you will not examine the sound waves when I give voice to that claim. That kind of "scientific" evidence will tell you nothing pertinent to my claim. Instead, you will need to explore other kinds of evidence, such as checking the school's records, confirming the authenticity of my mother's printed diploma, and interviewing fellow students who were in her class. You will do this because truth-finding involves arriving at a reasonable conclusion based on evidence *appropriate* for a particular truth claim, whether or not that evidence is "scientific" in nature.

So what does all this mean when it comes to knowing the truth about God? At the very least, it means that if we are to arrive at truth about God's active presence in our world, we must begin by deciding on what counts for appropriate evidence. If God were visible, it would be reasonable to look for photos of him taken from video surveillance cameras or satellites probing the universe. But if God does not regularly make himself visible to people as the Bible suggests, we probably ought to look for the effect of his presence rather than a photo of him.

In the previous chapter, I presented five clues to God's existence. None of the clues involved were photographs or video feeds of God. Instead, they were clues that speak of the effect of God's presence and activity. And that can be enough. If I leave my home in a grand mess and return to see everything put in order, I may never see the people who tidied up the place, but I can nonetheless be confident of their engagement in my world by examining the effect of their presence. Similarly, though we may not see God, if the effect of his presence has been left on the world, we can nonetheless be confident about the truth of his engagement in the world.

You might say, "But there are other possible explanations for the clues of the last chapter that don't involve God." That may be so. The question is whether those explanations are the best explanation of the evidence or mere possibilities, like aliens from another universe. If they are the latter, then such explanations ought to be dismissed, because knowing the truth is not about "alien alibis" but reasoning to the best explanation.

Can We Be Certain?

It's pretty tough to prove things with absolute certainty whether it has to do with the Battle of Waterloo, the workings of a distant star, or the existence of God. Even if I am confident that my mother went to John Marshall High School, it's still possible that someone has meddled with the school records, that her diploma is a fraud, and that her classmates are all lying about her attendance at the school. Okay, that's not too plausible, but if elimination of all possible explanations is what is necessary to arrive at knowledge, then knowledge will always remain out of reach about my mother's high school or anything else for that matter. But maybe absolute certainty is not what we should be aiming for when it comes to knowledge. Maybe we should aim for something much more reasonable.

This evening I went into my bedroom and on my bed was a pile of clean clothes folded just as I like them. Earlier in the morning, they were in a basket in the laundry room crumpled and dirty. What am I to surmise about this personally advantageous change of events? One explanation is that someone broke into my home during the day and for one reason or another was bothered by my stinky garments and decided to do me a favor and wash my clothes. That in itself would be quite remarkable, but given this explanation, the intruder would have also gone into my closet, discerned how I like my clothes folded, and then, by luck, put them on my bed just where piles have been placed in the past. A second possible explanation is that my kind wife, who often takes care of my laundry, folded them as she usually does and put them on the bed for me to put away. This option also fits with the fact that I heard my wife speaking to someone on the phone about having done our laundry today and with the fact that she did not look at me quizzically when I thanked her for doing the laundry. Of course, either of the two explanations for the existence of folded clothes is possible, but I am about as confident as I can be that the second explanation represents what really happened. I can't be 100% certain the first explanation is not the right one, but absolute certainty is not what I am after. What I am after is reasonable confidence based on the best explanation of the evidence, not the elimination of every wild possibility.

Perhaps after reading the last chapter about the existence of God, you said, "Okay, so you've provided evidence for the existence of God, but you can't be 100% certain that the evidence points to God. And if you can't be 100% certain, why should I believe God exists?" My response is: "You're right, we can't be certain, if by certainty you mean that we must eliminate every possible explanation, regardless of how far-fetched, for the universe in which we live and love." But we don't have to be certain in that way to believe in God. We simply must be confident that the evidence is better explained by God than any other explanation. This response is not a cop-out. It is not a lowering of the evidential bar to sucker you into believing what I believe. It is simply a response that asks you to consider the evidence and arrive at the best explanation of it, even if it does not eliminate every other possibility. This is what I do when I eat cereal in the morning and when I see a pile of folded laundry on my bed, and when I draw just about any conclusion. And it is what you do too.

When it comes to certainty, it may also help to recognize that while we may not be certain or even reasonably confident of some aspects of an object or event, that does not mean we cannot be supremely confident of other things. Take, for instance, the sun. There is a great deal we don't know about the sun. We don't know why the sun's atmosphere is substantially hotter than its surface. We don't know how energy from fluid flow and plasma waves becomes heat in the solar wind. Heck, we don't even know whether something chewy is in the sun's center! But just because we don't know everything about the sun does not mean we can't have great confidence in our knowledge of some things about it. For example, we can know that if we look at it our eyes will be adversely affected. We can know that some plants do well when they are exposed to a great deal of it and that some plants do not. We can know its light will go out of view tonight and return tomorrow morning. Furthermore, we can be so confident about what we know of the sun that we shape countless decisions by it, from putting a hat on a bald head to keep it from burning to setting a clock for a predawn run. If this is true about our knowledge of the sun, I do not see why it would not also be true relative to any knowledge of God. If God exists, we need not know everything about him in order to know some things about him confidently. And if we confidently know some things about God based on the evidence, there is no reason we can't begin applying what we know of God to the way we live.

But Aren't We Hopelessly Biased?

My dad loves golf. He *really* loves golf. He has played about four times per week all of my life, and he professionally appraises golf courses. His wardrobe primarily consists of golfing attire, and his garage walls are adorned with golf-related artwork. His love for golf is so great it provides the lens for much of what he hears and sees in the world. If I tell him about a recent trip to San Diego, it reminds him of a golf course he recently played there. If I tell him about the tree I cut down in my yard, he tells me of the tree that was recently removed from his home course. Some people have rose-colored glasses; my dad has golf-colored glasses. For him, golf is the greatest game in the world.

My dad's "golf glasses" might amuse you, but chances are you have some glasses too. These glasses are the lenses through which each of us views the world; they are what some would call our biases. In some cases, our biases are rather harmless, like my dad's, but in other cases, they can be rather problematic. Jim Wallace is a cold-case detective for Los Angeles County. He describes a scene in which a well-known drug addict was found dead in her bed. Given the plethora of drug paraphernalia near the dead body, the officers who first arrived on the scene assumed that she had died of a drug overdose and called the coroner's office to collect the body. However, when the coroner's investigator arrived and pulled the sheet off the woman, it was quickly discovered that she had been stabbed to death. The officers had been on the scene for over an hour, but their bias concerning her drug addiction had gotten in the way of discovering the truth.[1] While we are not all guilty of the same bias, we can all remember times when our first assessment of a person, place, or event were dangerously off the mark because of certain biases we did not immediately recognize.

Bias is a common feature of the human experience and can keep us from discovering the truth. Some have even argued that since we can't arrive at a completely "bias-free" state, we can never be sure that we have discovered the truth. But while our biases can create barriers to discovering the truth, to say knowledge of the truth is therefore beyond our grasp goes too far. And it goes too far for a number of reasons. First, if we were all hopelessly biased, we would have to distrust everyone about everything. If a woman is a doctor, we must dismiss her recommendations because she is biased toward the value of medicine. If a historian speaks of the value of knowing history, we must dismiss his claim because he is speaking as one who thinks highly of history. And if Christians, atheists, or agnostics try to convince us of the veracity of their position, we must disregard what they say for no other reason than that they are speaking as those who are insiders to their particular viewpoint. But, of course, if we must distrust everyone else due to bias, we must distrust ourselves whenever we make a claim or state a case. We'd even have to distrust our claim that we are hopelessly biased.

Second, if human bias is so intractable, it's hard to see how anyone could ever change his or her position on any matter. Most people change what they believe because they are presented with new evidence and have come to a new conclusion. If we were thoroughly biased, however, we'd always find ways to dismiss the evidence and the most reasonable conclusion to which it points in favor of whatever we currently believe. In other words, it would be impossible for us ever to come to a new conclusion about anything.

Third, rather than get in the way of truth, bias can sometimes be advantageous in the quest of truth. My niece has always loved animals. Now she is studying to be a vet, and she is doing so in earnest. Is she biased toward the idea that animals deserve good care? Yes, she is, and every one of her future clients will be glad she is—for without that bias, it's unlikely she would ever endure her rigorous course of study in the first place. In fact, in many cases, someone who is biased is the best source of truth. Personally, if I am interested in golf, I want to learn from someone like my dad who is biased toward the game, not from someone who couldn't care less about golf. Similarly, if I want to see if there is something worthwhile to know about God, I want to learn it from someone who has some skin in the game, from someone who has considered God enough to arrive at reasonable conclusions on the matter.

To be sure, personal bias can keep us from seeing the world around us accurately, and it can do so in virtually any realm. From science to relationships and from religion to politics, entrenched biases can keep us from making better sense of the evidence and discovering the truth. Sometimes those biases can lead to disastrous results. But concluding that our biases are impenetrable not only is self-defeating but also does not account for the way humans keep coming to know more and more about our world. Time and time again history has shown that people can put aside wrong ways of thinking and embrace the truth when presented with better evidence and better explanations for the world around us. They don't all see the light all the time, of course, but it is possible even given our biases.

Doubting Our Doubts

I don't know of anyone who doesn't have doubts. Should I take this new job opportunity? Am I really prepared to get married? What if Jesus is just a mythological figure? Doubts like these are commonplace, and for many they are what hinder a decision to go forward with confidence. In some cases, our doubts are the result of substantial evidence of one sort or another that counters what we previously thought. At other times, our doubts are ungrounded; they are doubts without much substance. It's at times like this that I find it helpful to doubt our doubts. And I say this because often our doubts fail to meet a reasonable standard of proof far more than the position we currently hold or are considering.

Imagine, for example, that it is your wedding day. You love the man to whom you are to be married, and you have for years. You have seen him at his best and at his worst, and he has seen you just the same. Nonetheless, your love for each other has never wavered. Furthermore, you have seen the way he treats others and you have heard the way others speak so highly of him. Evidence of his character and your shared adoration has been growing from the day you first met. For months, you have looked forward to the day you tie the knot, but now when you awake on your wedding day, a sudden wave of doubt washes over you. It is precisely at times like this that you ought to doubt your doubts. There is no new evidence that suggests the marriage will not work. There is nothing that says the man you are about to marry is not who he has made himself out to be. So you should doubt your doubts, walk down the aisle, take your vows, and live happily ever after.

Some people have been exposed to evidence for the existence of God and have found it persuasive, but somewhere along the way doubt settled in and they pushed God away. In some cases, if I ask them what made them walk away, they don't have much to offer. They have doubts without a great deal of substance. Again, it's at times like this that we should doubt our doubts. If the evidence for God is strong, and the doubt we have is not particularly well-founded, then it is most reasonable to conclude that God exists and to live accordingly.

Truth or Consequences

Stonehenge has always been a fascinating site to me. The huge stones standing next to one another quickly draw the eye. They are placed in somewhat of a circle and, in some cases, are bridged at their highest point. Numerous theories have suggested why the stones were placed in their location. Virtually no one, however, believes that Stonehenge came about by natural forces. Some intelligent mind and probably a good deal of muscle-power were behind its creation. We can't see who put the stones in place, but nonetheless we confidently know that someone did.

Some wonder how we can know anything about God. As I have already suggested, we can know about God, at least in part, by what he has left behind. He has left evidence like Stonehenge—telltale signs that something intelligent and powerful has been at work. That's what the clues of the last chapter were all about. Certainly we could come up with complicated natural theories as to how Stonehenge came to be (like an incredible confluence of rushing wind and flowing water or the visitation of ancient Martians), but the conclusion that people built it seems less far-fetched and accounts for all the evidence. Likewise, we could come up with complicated theories to explain away cosmic fine-tuning, mathematics, or our penchant for love and justice, but the conclusion that there is a God behind it all makes good sense of the evidence that has been left behind.

Some people struggle to embrace the reality of God not because the evidence for God is weak but because the thought of God makes them rather uneasy. Preeminent American philosopher Thomas Nagel wrote a scathing attack on the present-day evolutionary explanation for human life. Nagel does not make his case as a Christian but rather as an atheist. In Nagel's view, evolution simply cannot account for human consciousness and reason, while God can.[2] Nonetheless, Nagel resists the God conclusion. And he does so, in large part, because the idea of God makes him uncomfortable. He writes:

> I want atheism to be true and am made uneasy by the fact that some of the most intelligent and well-informed people I know are religious believers. It isn't just that I don't believe in God and, naturally, hope that I'm right in my belief. It's that I hope there is no God! I don't want there to be a God; I don't want the universe to be like that.[3]

I greatly appreciate Nagel's transparency. Many share his uneasiness about a world with God. For if God exists and made the world in which we live, there is every expectation that he also has the right to tell us what we ought to do and be the judge of whether we have done it. In one sense, I sympathize. Acknowledging there is a God who gets to call the shots is sobering indeed. But, in another sense, I find a person's uneasiness with the possibility of a God wholly insufficient as a reason to reject his existence.[4] I say this because whether or not we are comfortable with the idea of God does little to impact the reality of his existence. As one author writes, "Comfort is important when it comes to furniture and headphones, but it is irrelevant when it comes to truth."[5]

Of course, disregarding what is comfortable in order to follow the evidence wherever it leads is often not easy. It can take both courage and humility: courage, because in pursuing the truth, we may discover something that demands a great deal from us; and humility, because it may call us to admit that what we have long held to be true is incorrect. Every year in the United States, hundreds of thousands of people have heart bypass surgery, and yet about 90% of patients subsequently refuse to change the lifestyle that led to the surgery in the first place.[6] They do so because embracing the facts and making congruent changes is not easy. But here's the rub: Not changing, when all the evidence points to doing so, comes with consequences. For the heart patient, heart problems will return and life will once again be threatened. Likewise, for the person considering God, opting for comfort over truth is bound to come with its own set of consequences—ones we may regret long beyond the grave—if it is true that God exists.

Key Points

- Every day we believe certain things to be true, often unconsciously. Even if we say that truth cannot be known, we find ourselves declaring a truth about the inability to know truth. Like it or not, we are creatures who regularly affirm truth.

- Truth can be hard to define, even if we intuitively understand what it means. Some good ways to describe truth include the following:

  › Truth corresponds to reality.

  › Truth is located in its object, not in our subjective experience of the object.

  › Truth claims remain true whether we believe in them or not.

  › Truth cannot contradict itself.

  › Truth is discovered not invented.

- In our quest to discover truth, we need not be deterred by mere possibility. Instead, we should focus on examining *appropriate* evidence (even if it is not "scientific" evidence) and then coming to the most reasonable conclusion.

- For some people, the inability to know things with absolute certainty keeps them from acknowledging the truth, but certainty is an impossible standard. That's why it is best to aim for confidence instead of certainty and let truth rest on the most reasonable explanation of the evidence.

- We don't have to know everything about something (like the sun) to be confident about some aspects of it. Similarly, we don't have to know everything about God to be confident about some aspects of God.

- We are all biased, but our biases don't make it impossible to discover truth. If we were hopelessly biased, we would have to distrust everyone who makes a claim (including ourselves), we would be unable to ever change our point of view, and we would have to ignore the ways bias can be advantageous in the quest for truth.

- Everyone has doubts, but we need to doubt our doubts when there is less evidence supporting our doubts than exists for that which we are doubting.

- The existence of God can be an uncomfortable reality because it means a creator exists who has the right to say how we are to live. Discomfort, however, is irrelevant when it comes to discerning truth. If God is real, he is real whether we are comfortable with him or not; and dismissing him due to discomfort may come with significant consequences.

Additional Resources

True for You, But Not for Me: Overcoming Objections to Christian Faith, Paul Copan

If God, Then What: Wondering Aloud About Truth, Origins, and Redemption, Andrew Wilson

Longing to Know: The Philosophy of Knowledge for Ordinary People, Esther Lightcap Meeks

4

How Can a Person Believe in God in this Scientific Age?

It was as noisy as usual when I sat down with about ten undergraduates at an elite university. I was invited by one of the university's colleges to join students for lunch whenever I wanted. It was the school's way of making sure that a university education didn't keep its students from practitioners in the real world. A few of the students I knew, but many times when I sat down, there would be a handful I had never met. With the table already full, one more student squeezed in and sat next to me. I had sat far across a table from this young man before but had never had a personal conversation with him. But this I knew: He was not afraid to let his opinions be known, and this day would be no exception.

Whenever I joined students, I was clearly the odd man out. Students weren't unaccustomed to visitors like me, since the college had invited a number of people from the community to mingle with their undergraduates. Nonetheless, I'd still get the "Why are you here?" look from time to time and frequently was asked what I do. My answer was not always the same, but usually it had something to do with working for a nonprofit that creates safe spaces for people to explore questions about life and God. Some students would be curious and ask more questions. Others would leave it at "Oh" and probably thought, "That's weird." But on this day my table companion would have none of it and lit up at my reply. I don't recall his words exactly, but they were something along these lines: "Rational people do not believe in God. How can you possibly believe in God given science? You shouldn't even be here." His words were laced with a few choice expletives, so I knew I had my work cut out for me to create a safe space for the ensuing conversation.

Dropping the Names of Scientists

We all like to think we make decisions based purely on the facts of a matter, but more frequently than we are probably aware, we make our choices because we are influenced by voices we trust. That's why when I am asked questions like this senior asked, I often begin by name-dropping a few scientists and conveying what they say. If scientists themselves are good with God, then maybe religion and science are not so much at odds. Maybe religion in some form or fashion can be trusted.

A brief view of history should be enough to confirm that a great many scientists have not seen faith and science in conflict with one another. On the walls of his apartment in Berlin, and later in his home at Princeton, Albert Einstein prominently displayed the portraits of Sir Isaac Newton, Michael Faraday, and James Clerk Maxwell. While Einstein himself had a complicated view of God and religion, giants like Newton, Faraday, and Maxwell certainly did not. All three men freely spoke of their faith in God. And they were not alone. Johannes Kepler, Sir Frances Bacon, and lifelong Catholic Galileo Galilei[1] also set their faith firmly on a supernatural Creator.

One might argue, "If scientists like Newton or Galileo knew what we do today, they would be compelled to recant their religious beliefs." But that is a hard claim to make, given the belief of more recent, eminent scientists like William Phillips (Nobel Laureate in Physics), Francis Collins (Director of the National Institutes of Health), Georges Lemaître (originator of the Big Bang Theory), Lise Meitner (co-discoverer of nuclear fission), and many more. Even a look at Nobel Prize winners in the hard sciences from 1901 to 2000 reveals that about 90% had some kind of religious faith.[2] Furthermore, when Elaine Howard Ecklund, an expert in the relationship between science and faith,[3] completed an extensive survey of 1,700 elite scientists at the nation's top research universities and personally interviewed 275 of them from 2005 to 2008, she found that only 15% of scientists see science and religion fundamentally at odds with one another.[4] This is far different than the narrative many hear, which is why Ecklund writes:

> After four years of research, at least one thing became clear: Much of what we believe about the faith lives of elite scientists is wrong. The "insurmountable hostility" between science and religion is a caricature, a thought-cliché, perhaps useful as a satire on group-think, but hardly representative of reality.[5]

Teasing Out Faith, Science, and Reason

Like the young man who sat next to me for lunch, many find faith and science to be at odds. Faith, they say, is unsubstantiated belief void of reason while science is supported by reason. But the relationship of faith, reason, and science is often confused. First, let's consider the idea of faith. *Faith* is not a religious term. Of course, it is often used in religious contexts, and some people talk about their "faith" when referring to their religious convictions. But that does not mean that religion has sole rights to the idea of faith. Faith is simply what we exercise when we believe something to be trustworthy. If I believe that my wife will soon be home from a long trip, I may express my faith in her return by cleaning up the house a bit. Similarly, if I believe that a bank is a safe place to keep my money, then I may exercise faith by depositing funds there. Scientists themselves exercise faith when they decide to vaccinate their children with the belief it will prevent certain diseases.

Sometimes the faith we exercise is grounded in evidence. For example, we might use a particular antibacterial agent to clean our kitchen counters because evidence shows that the agent has the right kind of properties to kill a majority of viruses potentially lurking. On the other hand, we can also have faith that is poorly grounded in evidence. For instance, we can exercise faith by diving from a cliff into murky water even though we have not tested its depth or seen anyone jump before us. Again, faith is simply our way of expressing confidence in a matter regardless of the quantity or quality of the evidence involved.

The same can be said about reason. Every day we provide reasons for the actions we engage in or the positions we take. We might say, "I am going to the store because we are out of food." Or, "I am not planning much for tomorrow because it is going to rain." But the reasons we use to justify this or that are generally not backed up by the same degree of evidence. Sometimes our reasons are backed by clear evidence (an empty pantry), but at other times not so much (weather reports indicating 0% chance of rain tomorrow). So reason, like faith, can be substantiated by evidence or not.

When we see faith and reason in this light, faith is not something that only the religious exercise, and reason is not something only the scientifically minded employ. Regardless of whether a person is religious or scientific or both, she can and does exercise faith and has her reasons for doing so. Sometimes her faith and reason are exercised with little evidence—and sometimes with an abundance of it. That means that when it comes to the question of God, it's not a matter of faith versus reason. Rather, it's a matter of whether one's faith and reason for believing in God, or not believing in God, are supported by the evidence.

Before moving on, it is valuable to note that most elite scientists who have moved away from religion have not done so because of reasons associated with their engagement in science. In other words, it is not some discovery in the lab that has convinced them that God is not a worthy pursuit. Rather, based on extensive interviews by Elaine Howard Ecklund, they typically dismiss religion because of these reasons: They were not raised in a religious home, they have had bad experiences with religion, or they see God as irrelevant to their scientific pursuits.[6] This might be a bit of surprise since many believe that members of the scientific community reject religion because their science has provided strong evidence that has encouraged their disbelief. But this appears rarely to be the case.

Science Has Not Squeezed God Out

Many people have come to the conclusion that God is no longer necessary given the increasing breadth of scientific discovery. The thinking goes something like this: There was a time when people did not understand how things worked, so they concluded that God was the force that made such and such occur. Science, however, has now explained many of the gaps in knowledge where God once stood as an explanation. Therefore, science has squeezed God out, making his existence seemingly unnecessary. Dan Barker, atheist author and former pastor, summed up this position nicely during a University of Florida debate:

> All through human history, we've had these questions. What causes thunder? What causes lightning? I don't know, there must be a big Thor [Norse God] up there that does it. But now, now we've learned about electricity. Now we don't need that Thor anymore. We've erased that God, right? And as the line moves up, answering more and more questions, the Gods disappear. We still have a lot more questions up here and we no longer put a God down here. . . . He's living in the gaps, [and] the gaps are getting smaller.[7]

Baker and others like him are right that people have used God or gods to explain things that are now understood by science, but I am not sure this is the case for everyone. For Christians, not only is God used as a place marker for things that have yet to be explained, but also he is considered the maker of everything we understand through science. To this point, Oxford mathematician John Lennox writes: "The God of the Bible is not a god of the gaps. He is the God of the whole show. He is the God of the bits and pieces we don't understand and the bits we do."[8] Because this is the perspective of Christians who are scientists, they are not shaken by new discoveries. They simply say, "Great, now we better understand how God made things."

In the last week, my wife and I just finished a kitchen renovation project. We put in new floors and countertops, painted the cabinets, and installed two new appliances and a sink. If you saw our kitchen a few weeks ago and saw it again this week, you would agree with the truthfulness of my claim. At the same time, however, it could be argued that we did not renovate the kitchen at all. In fact, we hardly lifted a finger when it came to our kitchen. It was the general contractor and the various subcontractors who were the ones who did the work; they were the ones who actively completed the renovation project. But, of course, none of it would have happened without our direction. We set out the parameters of the project, and we picked out the colors, materials, and appliances to be used. Most importantly we provided the monetary resources. In other words, just because the completion of the project can be explained by all of the craftsmen, it does nothing to eliminate our involvement as the originator of it all. We can still say that we renovated the kitchen.

Christians have long understood that God can be either the direct causation of physical events or use "*secondary* methods of causation, such as the laws and mechanisms he has built into nature."[9] He need not be the one who makes plants grow directly once he has put a sun in place to purposely do that. And he does not need to put a sun in place if he has intentionally set up certain cosmic parameters to see that a sun would form around, which Earth would orbit. Similarly, when Christians said over the centuries that God is the one who makes each human in unique and special ways, they did not need to change their story once the discovery of DNA provided an explanation of how some of that uniqueness came about. Rather than such a scientific finding squeezing God out, in the Christian view, it simply better explained the mechanism by which God got the job done.

Shaky "Scientific" Assumptions

One reason people like my lunchtime friend say science does not support a belief in God is because of certain assumptions that many scientists employ from the onset of their studies. Often these assumptions are so baked into the cake that we forget they are just that—assumptions. We all know that assumptions about nearly anything can lead us down bad roads just as easily as good ones. Remember the new car you bought assuming your job was secure, only to be laid off a few months later! So examining the assumptions undergirding the scientific perspective of atheists is very important.

Naturalism. There are two frequent assumptions that atheists make when looking at the world. The first is *naturalism*. Naturalism is the belief that everything comes about because of natural properties and causes. In other words, nature is a closed system, and nothing supernatural started or influenced things along the way. I say this is a baked-in assumption because for many it has become a "known fact," as it had for my friend at the lunch table. But I am not so sure it is justified to move this assumption into the fact category.

No doubt we can use science to explore nature, and from that exploration establish this or that to be a fact of nature. But while science has proved to be a very helpful means of discovering the intricacies of nature, it is not well-suited for concluding if anything lies outside of nature. As Francis Collins once noted: "Science is limited in that its tools are only appropriate for the exploration of nature. Science can therefore certainly never discount the possibility of something outside of nature. To do so is a category error, basically using the wrong tools to ask the question."[10]

I like to think of the scientific method as a portable metal detector used to find lost rings and coins at the beach. If there is something metallic under the sand, there is a good chance the metal detector is going to find it. But suppose we assume there is no oil under the sand before we start using the metal detector; and then after finding no oil where we are looking, claim that our assumption is justified. In that case, have we really turned our assumption about the nonexistence of oil into fact? I think not, for the simple reason that the metal detector is not equipped to support such a claim about oil in the first place. Similarly, while science has served us well in understanding more about nature, it falls short of being able to declare that the supernatural does not exist.

Scientism. The second assumption that often undergirds the atheist's scientific pursuits is called *scientism*—the belief that science, particularly the hard sciences, is the only or the most reliable source of knowledge. According to scientism, knowledge from the hard sciences using the scientific method "is vastly superior to what we can know from any other discipline."[11] But as with naturalism, this assumption is also on shaky ground for a number of reasons. First, the very claim "science is the most reliable source of knowledge" is not a scientific statement because it cannot be tested using the hard sciences or the scientific method. Therefore, if we take the claim that science is the only or most reliable source of knowledge at face value, we should conclude that scientism itself is unreliable.

Second, in making the claim that scientific knowledge is the most reliable form of knowledge, it unduly discounts other sources of knowledge that can be of equal or greater reliability. For instance, consider the life of William Shakespeare. We might look to certain writings by or about him, but that falls very short of scientific evidence of his existence. Yet, I think many people are more certain of Shakespeare's existence than the reported effectiveness of a new cancer treatment. Or take, for example, the conversation you had with your father before he died. There was no recorder, and no one else was in the room when you had the conversation. The words spoken may have been some of the most important words you ever exchanged. They are words you will never forget. Yet, according to scientism, that memory is substandard in its reliability because the hard sciences cannot reproduce it in a lab. I find such a situation unsatisfactory because I am far more certain of many events in history (including my own history) than I am in the latest scientific findings, especially since the scientific community will likely update its conclusions in a few years.[12]

A third reason I find scientism hard to swallow is that generally those who hold this view believe that knowledge gained from science is not only more reliable than non-scientifically derived but more valuable and important as well. In many cases, this simply isn't true. For example, knowing something about the thermodynamics of boiling water may be of some importance or value if I see a pot boiling on the stove. But learning from my wife that the same pot of boiling water has been prepared to make us a pasta dinner is of much greater value and significance to me than anything science might tell me about how water boils.[13]

So, again, science may provide me some technical information that comes in handy at times (perhaps even saving my life), but it is not the exclusive source of valuable information. Robert Oppenheimer, a vaunted member of the Manhattan Project, which developed the atomic bomb, concurs:

> We need a science of everything that can be studied; . . . But such knowledge is by no means all of human life. Even in the getting of it we are involved . . . in commitments, in values, in resources quite outside the domain of science, in meanings, in intentions, in styles and beauties and senses of relatedness and of joy and of sorrow, in all that makes our inner life human, and all that we should be able to talk to one another about and ennoble our common discourse. . . . In part they are spoken about, but in terms devoid of the high excellence and the high quality which they deserve and which we need.[14]

Of course, I don't share these weaknesses of scientism to suggest that science hasn't provided us with some great insights that have made us live longer and allowed us to enjoy many wonderful conveniences. Like you, I am very grateful for the knowledge science has given us. At the same time, I am not prepared to make science bigger than it is. I am not prepared to say that science and only science provides us with either the most reliable or the most important information. This is what I fear the assumption of scientism does.

Holding on to Assumptions at All Costs

It was clear in my conversation with my lunch friend that naturalism and scientism were settled matters for him. But as our conversation continued, it was evident that he had never considered the problems with both. I don't blame him, because it's not unusual to find the scientific community defending naturalism and scientism even when the evidence hints elsewhere. Take, for example, Sir Fred Hoyle. He was one of the most prominent cosmologists of the 20th century and was the one who unwittingly coined the phrase "Big Bang" for the theory of the universe's origin. He did not use this phrase for the cosmic theory because he was in support of it—quite the contrary. His assumption that the universe did not have a beginning was key to undergirding his unwillingness to embrace a God of creation. So he fought for years to undermine the Big Bang Theory. Even today, there are those who, like Hoyle, refuse to accept that the universe had a beginning, not because of evidence to the contrary but because of a persistent assumption that the universe is a closed system that has no need for an originating cause.

Entrenched attitudes toward naturalism and scientism can be found in the biological sciences as well. Richard Lewontin held an esteemed position in biology at Harvard University and was forthright about the assumptions that atheist biologists make:

> We take the side of science *in spite* of the patent absurdity of some of its constructs, *in spite* of its failure to fulfill many of its extravagant promises of health and life, *in spite* of the tolerance of the scientific community for unsubstantiated just-so stories, because we have a prior commitment, a commitment to materialism. It is not that the methods and institutions of science somehow compel us to accept a material explanation of the phenomenal world, but, on the contrary, that we are forced by our *a priori* adherence to material causes to create an apparatus of investigation and a set of concepts that produce material explanations, no matter how counter-intuitive, no matter how mystifying to the uninitiated. Moreover, that materialism is absolute, for we cannot allow a Divine Foot in the door.[15]

Notice what Lewontin concedes. He says that the "methods and institutions of science" do not compel us to accept an explanation of our world that is limited only to the material. He also concedes that the result of holding onto such a material view has resulted in "unsubstantiated just-so stories" from the scientific community that he is championing. But Lewontin says the material position is nonetheless justified because it is necessary to keep God out of the picture. But why is that necessary? If I find an unexpected yet official piece of paper on my windshield, why should I begin with an assumption that no person was involved with putting it there and then boldly claim that it was the wind that blew it under my wiper blade? I shouldn't, especially if a different assumption (such as the police left it for me because the parking meter ran out) makes a whole lot more sense.

Building Science on the Idea of God

I didn't get much further in my lunchtime conversation than discussing the above, but I wonder where our dialog would have gone if my friend had considered a different starting point. Instead of assuming that the universe is a closed system that excludes the possibility of God, what if he assumed something different? What if he assumed instead that God was very much involved? That might seem like an arbitrary decision, but assuming God is the cause of our universe is a big part of what helped get the whole scientific revolution rolling.

Earlier I shared how many of the great scientists of old believed in the existence of God. But more than that, it was often Christians who set the very groundwork for modern science. Such thinkers as Albertus Magnus, Thomas Aquinas, Robert Grosseteste, Roger Bacon, and William of Ockham were all Christians who worked to set an understanding of how knowledge could be obtained by observation and induction.[16] Their ideas inspired Francis Bacon, who popularized the scientific method, which was later refined by Isaac Newton. These latter two men, as I mentioned previously, were also firm believers in God. But it's not just that Christians set the framework for modern science; it was their Christian worldview that compelled them to do so.

Steeped as we are in Western culture, we take the scientific way of viewing nature as commonplace. That is, we look for natural causes to natural events. Those before us may not have seen the world this way, but we assume that with the passage of time it was inevitable that ancient myths about the gods directing the forces of nature would give way to more superior scientific explanations. But history tells us a different story. Great civilizations arose and fell without developing a scientific mindset.[17] Indian philosopher Vishal Mangalwadi provides an explanation of why this is so:

> A culture may have capable individuals, but they don't look for "laws of nature" if they believe that nature is enchanted and ruled by millions of little deities like a rain god, a river goddess, or a rat *deva*. If the planets themselves are gods, then why should they follow established laws?[18]

Mangalwadi goes on to name some outstanding ancient and medieval Indian mathematicians and ponders why Indian mathematics did not spread throughout India and then the world. His answer is this: "Consider growing up in a culture that believed that the world you see and touch is unreal—*maya*, an illusion, a dream. Would you devote your life to study that 'unreal' world? Wouldn't you seek to escape the world?"[19] But if even great ancient cultures could not spawn the scientific revolution, what kind of culture could?

For many, the answer is a culture imbued with an understanding of Christianity's monotheistic God. Noted mathematician and philosopher Alfred North Whitehead surprised his audience during the Harvard University Lowell Lectures in 1925 when he said that the scientific endeavor was rooted in Christian Europe's medieval insistence on the rationality of a personal and intelligible God not found in the philosophies of Asia or elsewhere.[20] They were surprised because Whitehead never identified himself with Christians. Nonetheless, he could not ignore the evidence that modern science arose from the worldview of Christians and not from the Greeks or other learned cultures.

But why would Whitehead, and so many like him today,[21] make such a claim? What is it about the Christian worldview that has proven so valuable to the scientific endeavor? Here are just a few examples:

- In contrast to ancient Greek culture, Christianity teaches a high view of the material world. The world is seen as something that God made. Furthermore, God declared what he made good, making it valuable to investigate and explore.
- Many ancient religions saw the gods as inhabiting nature. Thus, nature is something to be warded off or satisfied. Christianity, however, says that although God is engaged in the world, he is separate from the world he created, making it possible for humanity to investigate nature without fear.
- If a person believes in capricious gods who act in arbitrary and perhaps terrifying ways, there is little reason to expect nature to exhibit any kind of order. In contrast to this view, Christianity sees the world as being the product of a reliable and rational God who created an orderly world. With this view, Christianity provides a framework to search for the created order.[22]
- Not only do Christians believe that God is a rational God, but also they believe that people have been made in God's image and,

therefore, have the rational capacity to understand the world God created. In other words, Christianity says a rational mind made the world and has given us rational minds to understand it.[23]

One of my favorite movies is *My Big Fat Greek Wedding.* In it, the father is so proud of his Greek heritage that he stretches the bounds of credibility by providing a Greek root behind every word spoken, including the Japanese word *kimono*! It would be easy to take the worldview elements above and say they are an equally questionable effort to find a Christian basis behind everything scientific. But these worldview elements are not afterthoughts. They are the very elements that set the foundation for the birth of the scientific revolution. They are the God assumptions that were a big part of getting the whole thing started.

Over my lifetime, I have lived in five different houses, two of them in Texas. At no time, however, did my family or I ever consider drilling for oil. We didn't even hire a geologist to do any probing just to make sure we weren't missing something. We never did that, because we did not believe oil was under any of the properties that would make it worth the effort to go looking. Prior to the broad acceptance of the Christian worldview in Western Europe, there simply was not a widespread belief that nature had any discoverable order to be found or that it could be investigated without upsetting unpredictable gods. Although the laws of nature were just as prevalent in past eras, no one made a sustained and concerted effort to go looking for them. That's because faith makes a difference, and not just any faith. By recognizing a Creator God who made a good and ordered world capable of being understood by the rational creatures made in his image, Christianity provided the faith, or grand assumption, on which to build the modern scientific endeavor.

A Continuing Better Fit

Although you may concede that Christianity provided a useful framework that started the scientific revolution, you could argue that science can operate just fine without Christianity at this point in history. Perhaps Christianity is like scaffolds that provide help during the construction stage. Once the building is sufficiently complete, however, the scaffolding (or Christianity in this case) simply gets in the way. In support of this view are the scientists who have no religious affiliation yet still readily expand scientific understanding. But before we come to the conclusion that Christianity is no longer an important part of the scientific endeavor, it is valuable to see what might be lost if we remove belief in God. In the first chapter, I suggested that without God many valuable things would be lost, like the loss of free will, justice, and love. I used the illustration of a car and said that although we may not have any interest in what is under the hood, we would only need to remove an important component to recognize how essential it is to the car's function. When it comes to God and science, the case is the same. If we remove God from under the hood, we soon find that some essential things are missing from the scientific endeavor. I will name four.

First, if there is no God, then we cannot trust the reasoning we use in the scientific process. That is, if our reasoning capacity came about through an unguided, purposeless process, it's hard to be confident that we have any reliable thoughts. This is the point I made in the opening chapter, and this is the point Hans Halvorson (who teaches Princeton's popular course on the Philosophy of Science) makes when he asks: "If you assume that your cognitive faculties are the result of unguided evolutionary processes, then don't you have reason to be suspicious of the results of the scientific enterprise?"[24]

Second, although one may choose to pursue science for fame, fortune, or the advancement of knowledge, if there is no God, there is no ultimate objective purpose or value to any scientific endeavor. Eventually, the universe will wind down and we will all be but dust in the wind. Even efforts to make the world a better place will prove to be no more effective in the long run than sitting on the couch endlessly playing video games. Only if there is a God—who designed us for a reason, takes stock of our doings, and offers a life after this one—can there be enduring purpose and value to the scientific pursuit.[25]

Third, if we pursue science as if there is no God, it can handicap our pursuit of scientific understanding. For example, many scientists initially deemed large portions of the human genome as pseudogenes or "junk DNA" left over from an unguided evolutionary process. As a result, there was little attention given to their study as it was thought these pseudogenes had no function today. But what if rather than considering pseudogenes mere junk, scientists assumed that God had put them there for a purpose? It is likely they would have more heartily pursued an understanding of their purpose. This is what those who believe in an intelligent creator encouraged, and this is what more recently they have begun to do.[26]

Finally, if there is no God, we lack a firm moral grounding for the integrity required of sound scientific inquiry. The importance of such grounding has become even more evident in recent years with revelations regarding misrepresented, altered, or falsified data. Certainly there are advantages to acting honestly in order to keep one's reputation intact or keep one's job. But if there is no God who sets the standard for our behavior, can we really blame scientists who employ the same guile found in the animal kingdom to fool others for the sake of personal gain?

Given the far-reaching losses that occur when we remove God from the scientific endeavor, maybe the God assumption is not outdated scaffolding but necessary structural support. And maybe this is why when compared to belief in God, atheism "isn't particularly well-suited to helping science achieve its aims."[27] Whereas Christianity provides a framework that undergirds the general trustworthiness of our cognitive skills, the existence of enduring value and purpose, the impetus for research of yet understood biological functions, and an objective source of ethical behavior and accountability, atheism does not. Of course, in saying that maintaining a Christian perception of God is a better fit when it comes to scientific pursuit than atheism, I am not suggesting that atheist scientists cannot be excellent at what they do, nor am I saying that such a fit proves that God exists. But I am saying that when we try the God assumption on for size, we see that it does not chafe against the pursuit of scientific knowledge as my lunchtime friend asserted. In fact, God and science seem to go together hand in glove, meaning there is little reason to dispose of God even in this scientific age.

A Word About Origins

When it comes to questions about science and faith, one specific inquiry comes up frequently relative to the Bible's account of creation. Therefore, it seems only fair to address it before closing this chapter. The question goes something like this: *How can you believe the Bible when it says that the universe and all that is within it was made in six days?* This is a legitimate thought considering what we read in our science books about cosmological history and biological evolution. One way to answer it is by understanding the two "books" Christians look at when seeking to understand God and his ways.

Christians have long held that God speaks to us through two different "books," that is, through two different sources that must be examined and interpreted well. The first "book" is that of nature, which includes everything from the stars in the sky to molecules under a microscope. By examining the book of nature, Christians believe they can discern certain characteristics of God. That is, when they see an intricately designed universe, the Christian might say God is a "master engineer." They may even go on to say that since God is the master engineer behind our universe, he is worthy of worship. This might sound like a stretch, but we do something similar when we visit an art museum. When seeing a beautiful painting, we conclude the artist behind it is a master. We might even develop awe for the artist and begin to follow his or her career.

The second "book" Christians study is the one in which God directly reveals this or that about our world. This could happen through God coming to earth and telling us a thing or two, as Christians say occurred when Jesus lived. It could also happen through a literal book, such as the Bible, in which the words of God to humanity are said to be preserved. In contrast to the first book, the second book is akin to the little plaque on the wall next to a piece of art that tells us the story behind why the artist painted the depicted scene. In other words, while the first book (nature) tells us something about the skill, power, and creativity of the Creator, the second book (the Bible) tells us more about the motives, purpose, and heart of the Creator. Both kinds of books, according to the Christian, are important in understanding God.

If it is true that God has given us two books from which to learn about him and what he has made, it seems only fitting that the books would speak in a consistent manner and not contradict one another. Thus, if we look at what we read in the Bible and interpret it one way and then look at what we see in nature and interpret it in a contradictory way, something has gone askew. At least one of the two interpretations needs some kind of adjustment. Such an adjustment is what happened when evidence started piling up about the sun-centered nature of our solar system. The Bible speaks of the sun rising and falling, and given that the intellectual community had long been confident that the sun moved around the earth, the rising and falling spoken of in the Bible had long been interpreted to say the same. However, once better cosmological data was in, Christians by and large concluded that the writers of the Bible were describing how things appear to us on earth (even as we do now when we say "the sun just came up"), and they no longer took the Bible to say that the sun revolved around the earth.

Today, as has always been the case, there are different camps in Christianity regarding the interpretation of both the book of nature and the book of the Bible. Some say, when looking at the biblical account of creation, that the only valid biblical interpretation is that the universe was made in six days and less than 10,000 years ago. Those who come to this conclusion believe that an adjustment should therefore be made to our interpretation of scientific data. They believe that although the scientific community says the universe is much older and that it was formed through a long process that included biological evolution, this scientific interpretation of nature is skewed and ought to be corrected. Others, however, say science has settled the matter regarding the age and development of the universe, and thus it is not the scientific interpretation of nature that needs adjusting but our interpretation of Scripture. Furthermore, this adjustment to biblical interpretation is said to be reasonable because the arguably more "poetic" literary style of the beginning of Genesis provides some interpretive latitude.

Therefore, if we look back at the question *"How can you believe the Bible when it says that the universe and all that is within it was made in six days?"* we see that Christians answer it in different ways. Some say, "We believe it was made in six 24-hour days, and we ought to re-interpret science accordingly because the Bible speaks clearly on the matter." Others say, "We don't believe it was made in six literal days but that the writer of Genesis was speaking of six eras undefined in their length, similar to when we say, 'In the day of the horse and buggy.'" Those who take this stance argue that the Hebrew word for "day" allows for this era-oriented interpretation. Still others do not believe the word "day" in Genesis was meant to express a unit in time at all but rather was simply a literary device the author employed to package all that God made into literary units.[28] In each of these cases, however, the issue is not whether one should believe in the Bible or in what nature is telling us, but only how one should interpret the information we gain from each. While it would be nice if all Christians were on the same page, this disagreement should probably not keep you from believing in the existence of God. This is so, because regardless of the approach you take to reconcile scientific discoveries and the Bible, God's existence can remain intact.

Personally, I am not so sure that the intention of the Genesis creation account is to tell us exactly when or how God made everything. As one reads more of the Bible, it becomes evident that Scripture is primarily trying to tell us who God is, the relationship God wants us to have with him, and how we are to relate with God given that we are prone to make a mess of things. In other words, it speaks mostly of God's character as well as his motives and purposes. Yes, Genesis speaks of a creation that took six days (however that is best interpreted), but more than that, it tells us that God made everything, that God made everything good, and that he made man and woman in his image with some rather grand purposes—grand purposes that begin with God, and grand purposes that even include scientific pursuits. So, once again, there seems to be no reason to do away with God, even in this scientific age.

Key Points

- Many prominent scientists have clearly stated their belief in the existence of God, indicating that faith and scientific pursuit are not fundamentally in conflict with one another.

- Both faith and reason need to be grounded in evidence. Thus, when it comes to the question of God, it's not faith versus reason. Rather, we should consider whether the reasons and faith we have in the existence of God (or non-existence of God) are well supported by the evidence.

- Christians do not claim that God is an explanation for only the gaps in our understanding. They claim that God is the underlying cause of both the parts of the world we understand and the parts we don't understand.

- Atheists generally approach science assuming both *naturalism* and *scientism*. Naturalism is the belief that nature is all there is. Scientism is the belief that information derived from science is the most reliable and important source of knowledge. Science, however, cannot prove that naturalism or scientism is true.

- Those at the forefront of the scientific revolution often held a Christian worldview. This worldview holds that a rational Creator made a good and ordered world capable of being understood by the rational creatures made in his image. In contrast to other worldviews, Christianity provided the framework that encouraged and supported scientific pursuit.

- Christianity presents itself as a good fit when it comes to scientific pursuit because it provides a framework that undergirds the general trustworthiness of our cognitive skills, the enduring value and purpose of scientific pursuits, the impetus for research of yet understood biological functions, and an objective reason for the importance of integrity.

- For Christians, answering the question of origins has to do with interpreting the book of nature and the book of the Bible. Christians differ in how to interpret the two books consistently, but always do so without questioning the existence of God.

Additional Resources

Can Science Explain Everything? John C. Lennox

Scientism and Secularism: Learning to Respond to a Dangerous Ideology, J. P. Moreland

Science and the Mind of the Maker: What the Conversation Between Faith and Science Reveals About God, Melissa Cain Travis

Seven Days that Divide the World: The Beginning According to Genesis and Science, John C. Lennox

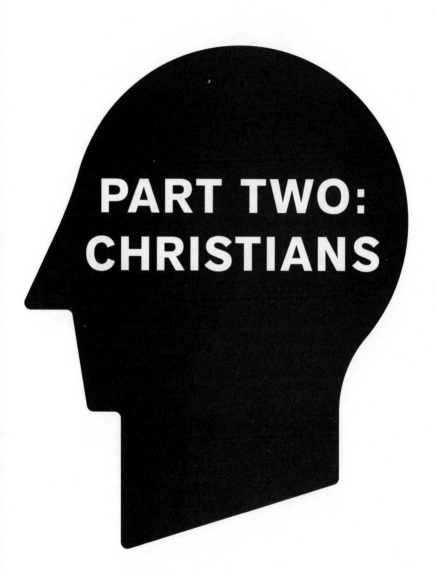

PART TWO:
CHRISTIANS

Don't Christians Use Their Faith As an Emotional Crutch?

Life can be hard. Storms come. Health wanes. Jobs are lost. Friends betray us. People die. Yet, we have to get up the next morning and somehow manage to make it through another day. No wonder, then, that people grasp for anything that helps them cope. For some that means pouring themselves into a hobby, sequestering themselves from others, or drinking away their worries. But oftentimes the emotional crutches people lean on are simple beliefs. People believe all kinds of things to buoy their spirits and inspire a new day's effort. They believe things like, "Everything will turn out just fine," or "You can be anything you want to be," or "They are in a better place now." Beliefs like this can be harmless and may even provide a little hope and inspiration, but it's hard to say they represent the truth every time they are spoken. Often things turn out horribly wrong even when everyone is confident of the best. And I, for one, have no chance whatsoever of becoming the world's best tennis player even if that's what I want to be. So wouldn't it be best to avoid such feel-good beliefs and stare reality boldly in the face?

If there were buckets representing the different kinds of beliefs that help people cope with life, the bucket for religious beliefs may be the biggest one of all. People all across the world believe in one God or another, and frequently take great comfort in doing so. But are such beliefs really necessary? Few doubt that religion can provide an emotional salve in the midst of our daily struggles, but if there is no God, shouldn't we come to terms with reality and dispense with giving homage to the Divine?

Freud wasn't the first to suggest that religious beliefs are just psychological coping mechanisms, but he certainly managed to express this view in a powerful way:

[Religious beliefs] are illusions, fulfillments of the oldest, stron-
gest and most urgent wishes of mankind. . . . The benevolent rule
of a divine Providence allays our fear of the dangers of life; the
establishment of a moral world-order ensures the fulfillment of
the demands of justice . . . and the prolongation of earthly existence in a future life provides the local and temporal framework
in which these wish-fulfillments shall take place.[1]

For the simple-minded looking to brighten their day, holding onto religious beliefs is understandable (like a child who shoos away loneliness
with an imaginary friend), but for the more rational, grown-up types
among us, there seems to be little reason to hold on to ancient mythologies just because they make us feel better. We are big enough to stare
life and death in the face. Or so we are told.

Meet Sarah: A Born and Bred Christian

Sarah is a friend of mine. She is on the ministry staff of a big church. That
alone may be enough to make you suspicious of her beliefs in God. "Of
course, she believes what she believes," you might think. "She gets paid
for it!" But there is more to the story, and frankly more that may make
you dismiss her beliefs in God all together.

Sarah grew up in a Christian family in the South. Her father is a
Presbyterian pastor and leads a small church. His conversion is a dramatic one that took him from the pits of alcoholism and despair to the
pulpit. Sarah heard all the famous Bible stories as far back as she can
remember, and rarely a week went by without Sunday school or youth
group. Summers were spent at a Christian camp, and she gave her life
to Jesus "more than once" during her teens. Christianity for Sarah was a
"forgone conclusion." Just as mom and dad knew what was best when it
came to crossing the street and avoiding strangers, Sarah always trusted
them when it came to God and Jesus and all the rest.

It was not just Sarah's upbringing, however, that landed her firmly
in the Christian camp. Her life experience has done so as well. When
doubts crept in as college started, heartfelt Baptists came to her side and
showed her love and support more than any of her other classmates. She
experienced the same care, years later, when she found herself trapped in
an abusive marriage. Looking back, she does not know how she would
have made it through those hard days without the Christian community

who listened to her, prayed for her, gave her advice, and even reminded her of passages from Scripture.

Sometimes Sarah's positive experience with Christianity has not come from others; it has accompanied her own decisions. Sarah says she has seen the freedom that comes from following Jesus' teaching—like forgiving others, loving your enemies, and being kind—even when it's hard to do. She even claims her trust in God allowed her ultimately to feel an abiding peace after watching the brother to whom she donated her own stem cells take a quick turn for the worse and die.

If you ask Sarah if she wants Christianity to be true, her answer is an emphatic yes. If there is a hell to be avoided and a heaven to be gained, she wants a ticket to the latter, and Christianity offers just that. But she wants Christianity to be true for more than just "fire insurance." She also wants it to be true because of the meaning it brings to life. She does not want to think we are just cosmic accidents biding our time until we are reduced to dust. In addition, Sarah wants Christianity to be true because she knows that this life is not fair—some are dealt vicious blows despite their virtue and others bask in endless pleasures because of stolen gain. If Christianity is true, however, the tables will be righted, and Sarah's desire for justice will be satisfied. Finally, there is the matter of her brother, as well as others she loves. Sarah wants Christianity to be true so they can all be reunited forever. All in all, Sarah has countless psychological motives to keep believing in God.[2]

So, Sarah gets paid to be a Christian. She was born and bred to become a Christian. She has experienced the benefits of the Christianity community and has felt some warm-fuzzies even in the face of death because she believes God is looking over her. And she desperately wants Christianity to be true so this life is not the end and so justice can be attained. Some people look at Sarah and others like her and say, "Sure, you believe in Christianity—look at all the motives and psychological benefits you have for believing like you do. It is your way of coping with the world. It's your emotional crutch and nothing more. And while I am glad it works for you, I have no need for it. I can get by without trusting in a make-believe God."

Meet Holly: A Proud Atheist
If her parents believed in God, Holly never really knew it. There were no Bible or religious books in her home, and her family never went to

church. She certainly did not have a sense of missing out on something; life without belief in God fit in fine in her Northeast environment. A ferocious reader at a young age, Holly gravitated toward the academic world of literature, and completed her PhD in her twenties. By that time, Holly was not just nonreligious or indifferent to the topic of God; she was actively convinced that atheism is true. For her, "the Bible was a collection of folktales and myths, just like the stories I'd read of Zeus and Thor, Cinderella and Sleeping Beauty."[3]

Although Holly struggled at times to explain the world through the lens of atheism, by and large she was at peace with her worldview. The thought of her soul-less "body decaying and returning its components to other living beings to use" was a "beautiful and consoling prospect"[4] Meaning in life, for Holly, did not need to be found in a mythological God or in the hope of some eternity but in "being a teacher, appreciating literature, winning fencing tournaments, writing a book, saving and investing in money."[5] Furthermore, Holly found solace and pride in her atheism. She was one who could face the facts and was proud to embrace her place as "a meaningless speck in an uncaring universe and go on living without the artificial comforts of religion."[6] Holly even "got a kick out of being an unbeliever."[7] As she says, "It was fun to consider myself superior to the unenlightened, superstitious masses, and to make snide comments about Christians."[8]

Beyond all this, Holly had motives for holding on to her atheism. Personally, she enjoyed her position of superiority over the weak-minded and had no interest in giving that up. Also, to be a member of the academic world and believe in the "superstitious" would have been costly in terms of the respect of her colleagues. Finally, giving up the image of a tough intellectual who did not have time for religious nonsense seemed unbearable—almost like a loss of herself.

Comparing the Stories of Sarah and Holly

The stories of Holly and Sarah are very different on the surface, but they may be more similar than they first appear. Both grew up in environments that fostered their separate positions on God. In other words, they were similarly preconditioned to believe what they believed as adults. They also both found a certain satisfaction in their personal stance on God and were able to draw on what they believed to find the strength to make it through their days. In addition, both had motives for believing what they did. For Sarah, the motive could be tied to her job on a church staff and her personal hope of being reunited with her deceased loved ones. Holly, too, had professional motives, and she relished a personal sense of superiority over those who held on to religion that she had no desire to relinquish.

Why all this on Sarah and Holly? Too often the beliefs of Christians in particular, and the religious in general, are dismissed out of hand. Tough-minded intellectuals like Holly claim that Christians like Sarah should not be taken seriously. Christians simply believe what they believe because of their upbringing, because of the meaning or comfort a mythological God gives them, and because of the personal gain they derive from holding on to their beliefs. But cannot these same defeating statements about Christian faith be applied to those who hold onto atheism as well? Have not people like Holly also been preconditioned to believe what they believe as a result of growing up in an unbelieving home? Can they not find a certain solace and meaning in their atheism, and have motives for holding on to their beliefs as well? I am not implying that all Christians have a story like Sarah or all atheists are like Holly; I am only saying that if we are going to dismiss Christianity as merely an emotional crutch for the religious that tells us nothing of the reality of God's existence, it seems only fair that we also dismiss atheism as merely an emotional crutch for atheists that tells us nothing of the reality of God's nonexistence. In other words, if we are to claim that belief in God is merely an emotional crutch, we have reason to claim the same for atheism.

Paul Vitz, Professor Emeritus of Psychology at New York University, argues this same point. In his book, *Faith of the Fatherless: The Psychology of Atheism*, Vitz recognizes that "many atheists are famous for arguing that believers suffer from illusions, from unconscious and infantile needs, and from other psychological deficits."[9] Yet his studies have found that for many of the world's most influential atheists, profound psychological dynamics are also at play. As Vitz lays out, atheists like Friedrich Nietzsche, Bertrand Russell, David Hume, Jean-Paul Sartre, Albert Camus, Voltaire, H. G. Wells, and Madalyn Murray O'Hair, among others, experienced deep disappointment or abandonment from their own fathers. Sigmund Freud, an atheist himself, claimed "that once a child or youth is disappointed in or loses respect for his earthly father, belief in a heavenly father becomes impossible."[10] But if that's the case, then why should we believe what these atheists have to say more than what Christians have to say? Should we not consider their atheism as nothing more than the product of their upbringing? In asking these questions I am not suggesting (and neither is Vitz) that all atheists have bad relations with their fathers or that all those who lack a good father figure are destined to be atheists. It just seems disingenuous to conclude that Christians are simply projecting infantile psychological needs in their beliefs about God and not discount the beliefs of atheists when psychological needs seeded in early childhood are equally present.

Back to the Quest for Truth

If you are reading this book, there is a good chance you don't want to be duped. You don't want to embrace a God who isn't there. You don't want to hope in something just because it helps you cope with hardship or grief or face the unknown. You also don't want to hold on to your beliefs only because leaving them behind would have a social or even economic cost. All in all, you don't want an emotional crutch. Perhaps, then, you will resonate with these words from philosopher Douglas Groothuis:

> What if hope cannot extend beyond human endeavor itself and is never answered by anything beyond it? What if the millennia of human cries echo only into the empty sky and no further? . . . In the end, hope without truth is pointless. Illusions and delusions, no matter how comforting or grandiose, are the enemies of those who strive for integrity in their knowing and being. Statements such as "I like to think of the universe as having a purpose" or "The thought of an afterlife gives me peace" reflect mere wishes. These notions do not address the truth or falsity of there being purpose in the world or of our postmortem survival.[11]

Groothuis' words are sobering for religious people, but as we have seen, it's not just Christians like Sarah who can have psychological reasons for holding on to comforting beliefs; atheists like Holly can too. That's why the psychology of both the believer and the nonbeliever is irrelevant in determining the reality of whether there is a God. I might take comfort in the hope that one million dollars will find its way into my bank account by month's end, but that wish says nothing about whether or not the funds will actually appear. In contrast, you might take comfort in not finding a million added to your account, because you don't want the family attention it would bring. But, again, your wish says nothing about whether the funds will show up. Clearly, then, the psychology behind believing in the existence or nonexistence of a million dollars is irrelevant when it comes to the truth of those beliefs. Instead, if we want to discover the truth or falsity behind those beliefs, we need to look at the cold, hard facts. We need to look for the money. Similarly, if we are going to find out the truth or falsity about claims concerning God, we need to lay aside our psychoanalysis and look at the cold, hard facts. We need to look at evidence like presented in Chapter 2 about the existence of God, and we need to look at evidence presented in Chapter 7 about the Bible. Then we can draw from that evidence the most reasonable conclusion—whether or not it is in sync with our upbringing, makes us feel good, or is consistent with any underlying motives.

In many ways, that is what this book is all about. What I write is not to encourage you to consider Christianity because it will make you feel watched over in the present or lessen your anxiety about the future. Rather, it is to provide you evidence on which you can make a sound decision as to the reality of Christianity's claims—evidence that can be examined apart from one's personal experience of belief or unbelief. Sarah says she is not without periodic doubts but those doubts are quieted when she remembers evidence for the existence of God like in Chapter 2. She knows that such evidence stands outside of herself. It is not evidence that is tied to her own feelings, experiences, or wishes. Nor is this evidence a product of her upbringing. It is just cold, hard evidence that she cannot reasonably explain without acknowledging the existence of God.

Meet Lee: The Investigative Reporter

Lee probably filled the bill for an All-American kid growing up in the 1960s. His family lived in an upper-middle-class neighborhood just out-side of Chicago, and his father did well enough in business to provide everything the family needed and more. Lee was a good student, was popular enough to be elected president of his junior high class, and served as editor of his high school newspaper as well as a columnist for a local newspaper. Church was not entirely foreign to Lee. His mother and father were members of a Lutheran Church, but as soon as he met his parents' demands of completing the church's confirmation classes, he was given the right to discontinue going to church. That was a right Lee quickly exercised.

Like many famous atheists mentioned earlier, Lee did not have a good relationship with his father. He was the "surprise baby" his father never wanted. While his older siblings had a father who coached their teams, attended their events, and celebrated their accomplishments, Lee had none of that. He cannot remember a single in-depth conversation he ever had with his father,[12] and just before Lee left home for good, his father told him, "I don't have enough love for you to fill my little finger."[13]

If one needs evidence for Freud's theory that those who have a poor relationship with their father will turn away from God, Lee could act as Exhibit A. The skepticism that existed during his church-attending youth soon developed into full-blown atheism. As Lee writes:

> For much of my life I was a skeptic. In fact, I considered myself an atheist. To me, there was far too much evidence that God was merely a product of wishful thinking, of ancient mythology, of primitive superstition. How could there be a loving God if he consigned people to hell just for not believing in him? How could miracles contravene the basic laws of nature? Didn't evolution satisfactorily explain how life originated? Doesn't scientific reasoning dispel belief in the supernatural?[14]

Lee's atheistic conclusions were not the result of any significant investigation. He admits he had given the evidence only a cursory look:

> I had read just enough philosophy and history to find support for my skepticism—a fact here, a scientific theory there, a pithy quote, a clever argument. Sure, I could see some gaps and inconsistencies, but I had a strong motivation to ignore them: a self-serving and immoral lifestyle that I would be compelled to abandon if I were ever to change my views and become a follower of Jesus.[15]

Soon after establishing his career as an investigative reporter, a more supported case for Lee's atheism became paramount. To his utter dismay and contempt, Lee's wife announced that she had become a Christian. It felt like betrayal, like he had become a victim of a bait-and-switch scam. Her conversion was not something Lee could ignore, especially since her whole attitude on life seemed to change, and for the better. He had used his intellectual skills to prove his father's estimation of him wrong, and he would use them again to expose the fanciful nature of his wife's beliefs. This would be no half-hearted effort, as Lee was now an award-winning journalist for the *Chicago Tribune*. He knew how to dig for evidence, how to make sense of it, and how to keep his personal prejudices at bay. Of this time, Lee writes:

> Setting aside my self-interest and prejudices as best I could, I read books, interviewed experts, asked questions, analyzed history, explored archaeology, studied ancient literature, and for the first time in my life picked apart the Bible verse by verse.
>
> I plunged into the case with more vigor than with any story I had ever pursued. I applied the training I had received at Yale Law School as well as my experience as legal affairs editor of the *Chicago Tribune*. And over time the evidence of the world—of history, of science, of philosophy, of psychology—began to point toward the unthinkable.[16]

The unthinkable was that God existed, and that Jesus was who he claimed to be—God in the flesh. Lee's conclusion was not based on pre-conditioning. It was not the result of personal experiences he attributed to God. Nor were his conclusions about God and the claims of Christ something he wanted to be true when he set out on his investigation. Instead, they were based on a long look at the evidence and honestly considering the most reasonable conclusion. By saying this, I am not suggesting that it is impossible to look at the evidence and come to a different conclusion than Lee's, but I am saying that Lee did it right. In the end, he did not dismiss looking into Christianity simply because some believers have grown up in Christian families, or because they might have personal motives, or because they enjoy some degree of emotional solace from their beliefs. While those factors might exist, they do not provide a solid reason to dismiss Christianity any more than they provide a definitive reason to embrace it. Only a good look at the evidence can do that.

Unfortunately, many today never take the time to examine the evidence for Christianity. At best, they consider one-liners and memes posted on social media sites by those with their own motives for rejecting Christianity. Holly, though once an atheist, ultimately came to embrace the Bible's claims concerning Christ. Looking back, she realizes that had she been more willing to do a bit of honest exploration, much earlier in her journey she would have found Christianity to be far more substantive than she had imagined:

> If I had inquired, I would have found the Bible was nothing like I thought it was. I would have found [the Apostle] Paul's forthright declaration that Christianity is based on the historical, witnessed events of Christ's death and resurrection. I would have found that theology and philosophy offered real answers to my questions, not an appeal to blind faith. I would have found that the history of the Church did not conform to my image of the Christian faith as a self-serving, politically useful fiction. But I thought I knew exactly what faith was and so I declined to look further. Or perhaps I was afraid that there was more to it than I was willing to credit—but I didn't want to deal with that. Easier by far to read only books by atheists that told me what I wanted to hear: that I was much smarter and intellectually honest and morally superior than the poor, deluded Christians.[17]

Holly's experience is not unusual. It is not that most self-proclaimed nonbelievers have ardently looked at the evidence and have found it to be insufficient. Rather, they have rejected Christianity without examining it at all.[18]

A Cure Not a Crutch

My brother has been battling cancer for five years. He did not have a doctor look for cancer because he was feeling poorly. In fact, when he received his diagnosis, he was feeling as strong and vibrant as he had at any time. Furthermore, given the absence of cancer in our family tree and his own healthy lifestyle, there was no need to be worried about something lurking inside him. Nonetheless, after scans had been completed, cancer was confirmed throughout his neck and chest cavity—a cancer that doctors say had been growing there for probably 25 years!

Personal experience is a tricky thing. At times, it can point us in the right direction, like when a throbbing thumb suggests we cut it deeper than we thought. At other times, it can be a red herring and send us in the wrong direction. Nothing about my brother's upbringing or his own experience would have pointed to cancer, but to deny the diagnosis because of these factors would have been foolish.

Those who distance themselves from religion might figure that Christians need to hold on to their antiquated beliefs in order to cope with life, and that such beliefs are unnecessary for non-Christians to enjoy a happy life. As highlighted in Chapter 1, atheists may *feel* no need for God and see themselves as getting along just fine without embracing Christianity. But if you find yourself in that camp, it is valuable to remember that my brother certainly felt no need for chemotherapy. He felt as healthy as ever. But his lack of felt need was not a reliable measure of truth. Christianity says that we all have a life or death need for Christ, meaning that if Christianity is true, then we have a real need for what Jesus offers whether or not we feel our "health" before God is compromised.

People may feel uncertain about their future, powerless in the midst of hardship, or guilty about certain past behaviors. In turn, they can create and call upon gods to calm their worries, give them strength, or assuage their guilt. Indeed, people have been doing so for millennia. This does not mean, however, that all religions are merely feel-good coping mechanisms. Suppose my brother started feeling the immediate effects of his cancer and soon thereafter was offered morphine. Upon taking it, he'd feel significantly better; his pain would have disappeared. But, of course, he would be no better off in terms of the growing cancer. The real problem would still exist underneath, because he needs a cure not a palliative. That cure (we hope) is chemotherapy, which is not rendered invalid simply because people physically feel better when taking morphine. Likewise, just because some people create and adhere to religions that make them feel better does not mean there is not a true religion that can cure the underlying problems that ail the human condition.

Christianity declares that all people have rejected God on some level and that as a result guilt, dissatisfaction, and death are knocking at our door. In response to this predicament, Christ does not offer us morphine to make us feel better today. Instead, we are told that any who trust in Jesus are given a cure—which begins to take effect today and ultimately means we will enjoy life with a loving God forever. This was not lost on Jesus' early followers, one who wrote the following:

And I am convinced that nothing can ever separate us from God's love. Neither death nor life, neither angels nor demons, neither our fears for today nor our worries about tomorrow—not even the powers of hell can separate us from God's love. No power in the sky above or in the earth below—indeed, nothing in all creation will ever be able to separate us from the love of God that is revealed in Christ Jesus our Lord. (Romans 8:38-39)

It may be that you don't *feel* much need for God right now. That's fair, but that does not mean a *need* does not exist or that a cure is not available. That's why it is so important to take a deeper look at the evidence for Christianity. My brother could have forgone an exam and never discovered his cancer and his need for treatment, but this would not have erased the cancer. It would have meant that he would have lessened his days on this earth. Similarly, if Christianity is true, not examining the evidence will not make the need for Jesus go away. It will only lessen the days you can enjoy the love of God.

The Value of Wants and Desires

We've all known people whose wants and desires are detached from reality. Youth sports provide examples in abundance. You may have known a dad who wants to see his son become the starting quarterback but fails to see that the boy can hardly throw a pass. Or maybe you are a friend of the mom who believes her daughter deserves a college scholarship even though the girl can't make a B-level team. But despite plenty of cases when a person's wants and desires don't match up with reality, we certainly can't conclude that just because someone desires something to be true it therefore cannot be true.

I, for example, want my wife to be faithful to me. That desire, of course, does not make her faithful, but it would be wrong to say that since I want that to be true of her, any claim I make about her faithfulness must be distrusted. Similarly, I have a desire for my children to be alive, but it would be wrong to conclude that just because I have a desire that they be living anything I say about their present life should be distrusted. Desires can blind us, but also they can be aligned with reality and even point to the truth. In fact, maybe my desires are rooted in the fact that I have already experienced the value of a faithful wife and I already enjoy children who are living life to the fullest. I tell you all this because I don't think it is fair to discount the veracity of Christianity simply because there are wants and desires connected to it.

When I look across the landscape of humanity, I find that people have all kinds of wants and desires, yet when we peel them back we often reveal significant commonality among the wishes people hold. People want security. They want to know they'll have a job tomorrow, that cancer won't take their life anytime soon, and that their country isn't soon to be invaded. People desire to love and be loved. They want to be noticed, cared for, and listened to, and they want to find joy in sharing their affections and concern for others. People want to believe their life has purpose and that their role in this life has particular significance. They also desire that goodness will rule the day and that justice and fairness be meted out equally to all. When people fail, they want to know forgiveness, and not just as a courtesy but because they truly have been forgiven. People also want to know awe—to be overtaken by a stunning landscape, a beautiful piece of art, or the wonder of new life. Finally, people desire that life won't end and that if life after this one does exist that it is without sorrow and pain.

Given the commonality of these desires across continents and centuries, maybe we ought to consider whether they are pointing to a reality we would do well not to miss. What if, for example, we desire security because security can be found. Or what if we desire forgiveness because forgiveness is available? The Christian narrative is that people have needs like those I have noted because God made us with such needs. He made us to be loved and to love. He made us to treat others fairly and to seek goodness and grant forgiveness. He made us to be significant players in a grand purpose that involves a secure and glorious future. So rather than wishful thinking to help us cope with a violent and unpredictable world that will end our decay, maybe our wants and desires point to the existence of something real that can fulfill them. Along these lines, consider the following from C.S. Lewis:

> Creatures are not born with desires unless satisfaction for those desires exists. A baby feels hunger: well, there is such a thing as food. A duckling wants to swim: well, there is such a thing as water. Men feel sexual desire: well, there is such a thing as sex. If I find in myself a desire which no experience in this world can satisfy, the most probable explanation is that I was made for another world. If none of my earthly pleasures satisfy it, that does

not prove that the universe is a fraud. Probably earthly pleasures were never meant to satisfy it, but only to arouse it, to suggest the real thing.[19]

Notice that Lewis suggests that this world does not seem capable of filling the wants and desires common to humanity. It's not that people don't try to see if this world is up to the task, because they do try. They try to milk relationships and success and pleasure for all it is worth. As one author writes:

> In trying to fill the hollowness that afflicts them on weekends, [people] may surf the Internet or indulge in games and entertainment that get them through to Monday. During the week they watch television for hours, read cheap fiction and surf the Internet even more. These activities, they realize after some years, are not enough. They need something that is decidedly not frivolous.
>
> Or, more subtly perhaps, they want to live more expansively. They travel to places that are meaningful to them—a small village in rural Mexico or Peru, in which they mix with the residents, or the Colorado Rockies, where they immerse themselves in natural beauty. They find new friends and spend time communicating with them via the Internet or by texting. With their travels and new friends, they find a deeper satisfaction, and they do, indeed, live more richly. But something still gnaws at them.[20]

Christianity has never been surprised by the presence of such a persistent gnaw. From its earliest pages, the Bible repeatedly tells us that it is only God who can fill our common needs. It is only God who gives a long-term sense of security. It is only God who knows everything about us and yet loves and forgives us in the most perfect of ways. It is only God who knows our ultimate purpose and our significance in it. It is only God who is utterly good, and just, and fair, and will see that in the end that all the tables are righted. It is only God who can fill our sense of awe day in and day out. And it is only God who can provide and secure glorious immortality. If this is all true, then maybe any yearning to see these fulfilled in God is not akin to reaching for a flimsy emotional crutch but rather more like running toward a freshwater spring in the middle of a desert.

Meet Martha: Evidence of a Cure?

Martha was raised in a traditional Protestant church. She went through its confirmation classes and in that way came to know what the church believed. There was nothing personal about her experience though. Like attending a history class, her church experience was informational but certainly not life-changing.

When Martha went to college, she met a student who spoke of her relationship with Jesus and God in very personal terms. Martha wasn't sure what to make of it, but she also recognized a desire within herself to know God in this same way. She says it was "a yearning for good-ness, maybe a closeness, an intimacy, a sense of peace, a sense of being loved."[21] Often though, those yearnings would be followed by a sense of not measuring up and would lead to depression. Martha was not sure where the feelings of inadequacy were coming from, but "for whatever reason: genetics, natural temperament, imperfect parenting, a household with a lot of anger," she "grew into a quite depressed young woman."[22]

In graduate school Martha attended a loving church that embraced and accepted her, so on some level her needs were being met by human relationships. Nonetheless, something was still missing, and she was encouraged to meet with a professional counselor. Through counseling, Martha began to understand what the Bible and God said about her. She learned more fully that she was created in God's image, that God loved her, and that through his mercy he had made her a child of God. Then Martha reports:

> One Sunday afternoon at 4:30, I think it was, I was cleaning my apartment and praying under my breath, maybe in response to something on the radio—it was a Christian talk show, but I was only half listening. Suddenly it was as if God said, "It's enough. It's enough. Your longing for me, your yearning for me and desiring to know that I love you is enough. It's done. It's over. You've been dealing with depression long enough. Do you not see it?"[23]

And in that moment, Martha did see it. She saw that God loved her, that God accepted her, and that her longings were met in him. She was filled with joy and experienced an emotional release like she had never known. Soon others even noticed. When she arrived at work the next day her boss said, "You're different. Something has happened. What's up with you?"[24] Somehow Martha's carriage was different. Her disposition and facial expressions had changed, and she gave off a sense of peace that has remained in place.

> Up until then I had had a very strong sense of myself as being someone who was melancholic and tending toward depression. I knew nothing of happiness, even at a superficial level, much less joy. But afterward I had the freedom to focus on what I was doing and the people I was working with. Before, I was always taking my temperature, trying to figure out what I was feeling—"Am I measuring up; am I feeling sad now?" I wasn't saying these things to myself anymore. I wasn't nagged by self-doubt, feelings of inadequacy, and sometimes paralyzing sadness. I no longer characterized myself as a naturally depressed person. I was able to read the promises of scripture and say them, sing them, with the sense, "This is true. This is true."[25]

Certainly, Martha's experience doesn't make Christianity true, but if it is true, should not we expect stories like Martha's among those who believe? Shouldn't we expect that if God designed us with needs only he can fulfill, that he will satisfy those needs when we seek him out? Many today view Christianity as an emotional crutch for those who cannot face up to a godless world, but that conclusion holds only if the evidence does not point to Christianity being true. If, however, the evidence points to the veracity of Christ's claims, then the solace and peace and joy and freedom and forgiveness experienced by those who trust in Christ are not a temporary salve but further evidence of the effective cure Christianity claims to offer.

Key Points

- Religious people, like Sarah, can have beliefs that have been shaped by their upbringing, are the result of personal experiences, or spring from personal motives. So can nonreligious people, like Holly. Therefore, if we discount religious beliefs because of the personal upbringing, experience, and motives of those who hold such beliefs, we must also discount the beliefs of the nonreligious for the same reason.

- Any psychological benefit experienced by the believer or the nonbeliever is irrelevant in determining the reality of whether there is a God. If we are to discover the truth or falsity of religious claims, we must do so by looking at the evidence for those claims, not at the psychology of those who believe or disbelieve those claims.

- Too often Christianity is dismissed without any significant investigation into its claims, as was the case for Lee and Holly. If the evidence, when honestly considered, points to the truth of Christ's claims, then Christianity should be embraced. In that case, Christianity is not a psychological crutch but a cure for the human condition.

- Sometimes a need exists when we don't recognize it, as is true for a cancer victim who has yet to feel symptoms. That's why it is important to look at the evidence for Christianity even if we don't feel like we need Christianity.

- Most people desire things like security, love, purpose, and justice. If God gave us these desires with the expectation that he would fill them, then finding these desires filled when we trust in God is not reaching for an emotional crutch but finding the place of their true fulfillment.

- If the evidence points to the veracity of Christianity, then the solace, peace, joy, freedom, and forgiveness experienced by those who trust in Christ, like Martha, are not a temporary salve but further evidence of the eternal cure Christianity claims to offer.

Additional Resources

Existential Reasons for Belief in God: A Defense of Desires and Emotions for Faith, Clifford Williams

Faith of the Fatherless: The Psychology of Atheism, Paul C. Vitz

Not God's Type: A Rational Academic Finds a Radical Faith, Holly Ordway

The Case for Grace: A Journalist Explores the Evidence of Transformed Lives, Lee Strobel

Haven't Christians Caused More Harm Than Good?

A Pennsylvania pastor convicted of murdering his second wife is later convicted of killing his first wife as well.[1] In Chicago, a pastor is indicted on fraud charges for stealing over $900,000 from a federally funded food program. He used the money to pay off personal expenses, like the purchase of a 2015 Bentley luxury sedan.[2] A New York mega-church pastor is fired because of multiple sexual indiscretions.[3] And then there are the hundreds of allegations of sexual abuse at the hands of Catholic priests. A review of nearly any newsfeed will result in finding all kinds of terrible deeds done at the hands of Christians. Add to this the boorish behavior of a Christian relative or colleague you are required to endure, or what you hear about Christianity's involvement in the Crusades and the Spanish Inquisition, and you are right to wonder if Christianity should be rejected for no other reason than it has done more harm than good.

While the heinous acts of some Christians are bad enough, what may really get you riled up (and rightly so) is that Christians are often the ones calling for everyone to do good and to avoid this sin or that sin. How hypocritical is that?! And if there is one thing we all have a hard time with, it's hypocrites. Parents who wake up with a hangover on Saturday morning will always find it difficult convincing their son to avoid the drinking scene on Saturday night. The doctor who is grossly overweight will probably get many quizzical looks when she tells her patients how important it is that they lose weight. And the teacher who tells his students to be organized but is fumbling often to find a pen with which to write probably won't inspire his class. Explain it any way you like, but when we see people who do not walk their own talk, they do not get our ear or our respect. So why should it be any different when it comes to Christians? When Christians call us to love and do good deeds but they themselves cheat and steal and kill, then should not Christianity itself be looked at with skepticism if not disdain?

Taking Aim at the Right Target

Hypocrites are those who pretend to be something they are not, to present a better image of themselves than is warranted so as to gain the esteem and respect of others. But when applying this definition so as to identify and reject hypocrites, Christian or otherwise, we nonetheless must be careful not to set the trap too tight. And this is what we do if we reject everything a person says or does just because that person is hypocritical in some way or another. In that case, I am guessing there is not a person on Earth who would not be discredited. I say that because the only people who can live up to their own standards perfectly, and thus be free of all hypocrisy are those who have no standards at all. And I, for one, find those kinds of people in short supply.

It seems better, then, to have a slightly nuanced definition of a hypocrite. Rather than saying that a hypocrite is one who does not live up to his or her own standard perfectly, maybe it is better to say that a hypocrite is one who does not hold himself or herself accountable when he or she does not live up to the standard. Suppose, for example, that I tell my children to respect their elders. Later, however, they hear me speak unkindly to my own father. I am a hypocrite if I don't apply my own standard to myself once I have broken it, but I am not a hypocrite if I own up to my error and make amends. In the latter case, although I have failed, I still recognize the rightful place of the standard and judge myself by it. In fact, the Bible often recognizes this very scenario. It understands that Christians will not live up to all of Christ's teachings, and thus the Bible instructs Christians to acknowledge their errant ways, seek forgiveness, and get back to doing good.[4] A Christian who does so is not a hypocrite but one who has walked consistently with the lessons of the Bible.

If we define hypocrites in the manner I have described, then when you tell others of the importance of hard work but find yourself not living up to that standard, you are not a hypocrite if you soon acknowledge your slothfulness and begin putting in full days' work once again. Likewise, the Christian who tells others it is not right to end the night in a drunken fit is not a hypocrite if he drinks too much one night, recognizes his error, confesses, and takes steps to see it does not happen again. I provide a definition of hypocrisy along these lines not to let Christians off the hook but because without such a definition, we are all hopeless hypocrites who have lost the right to be heard on just about any topic.

Jesus Hated Hypocrites Too!

Defining hypocrisy in the manner I have still opens the door to the existence of real hypocrites, as there are plenty of people who do not consistently hold themselves to the standard they publicly declare. Some of these people are very religious, even proudly calling themselves Christian, and point to the Bible as their standard. If it is these people that irk you, I do not blame you. In fact, you are in good company—the company of Jesus.

Jesus often found himself around those with a rather sordid past, enough so that some he spent time with earned the public tag of "sinner" for their gross indiscretions. Considering that Jesus always preached a high moral standard, you would think that his harshest words would be aimed at this crowd. But that was not the case. Instead, we find that Jesus' most pointed, even angry words, were directed at religious leaders who put on a public façade of "righteousness" but fell well short of doing what they demanded of others. In one particular tirade, Jesus called these leaders out in public, labeling them hypocrites six times and adding descriptive phrases like "blind guides," "whitewashed tombs," and "brood of vipers."[5] Furthermore, Jesus told them that their hypocritical ways were worthy of eternal judgment, even asking at the end of his rant, "How will you escape the judgment of hell?"[6] If you think Jesus always spoke in gentle tones, think again; he got in the grill of hypocrites. So, know this, if you do not like religious hypocrites, you and Jesus see eye to eye. Perhaps, then, when you see the hypocrisy of those who call themselves Christians, you need not push Jesus aside.

Truth, Even from a Hypocrite, Shouldn't Be Ignored

As I have mentioned, it's very difficult for us to accept what comes from the mouth of a hypocrite. But, it seems to me, there are still instances in which we ought to listen to what a hypocrite has to say. Suppose you had a real jerk of an English teacher. She was the rudest teacher you knew. Moreover, throughout the year, she told you the importance of being a good listener but never once gave any attention to a question or comment put forward by you or your classmates. During the course, she repeatedly emphasized the proper use of "then" and "than," but because of her rude behavior and hypocritical ways, you decided purposely to reject her instruction. When "then" is called for in a writing assignment, you wrote "than," and vice versa just to raise her ire. In one way, your act of rebellion was justified; why listen to a teacher like her? But in another way, you acted rather foolishly. "Then" and "than" serve different purposes in English writing, and there simply is a right way to use them regardless of your teacher's hypocritical behavior.

Or consider this example. You live in a small town far away from sophisticated medical care. You have not been feeling well of late, and though you hate to do so, you visit the town doctor who is rather full of himself. In addition, he has proved himself rather untrustworthy in a host of business transactions that have financially hurt some of your friends. As part of your exam, he runs a test and sends the results to a big city lab, where it is determined you have an aggressive form of cancer. He says you are in bad shape and if something isn't done immediately you are going to die in just a few months. Now, you are in a dilemma. You don't care for this doctor because of his arrogance and shady business dealings. In fact, you would love for him to be wrong for no other reason than that it would take him down a notch or two. But if he is right, shunning the truth of his words about your cancer would be very costly—it would likely cost you your life.

Many today have had bad experiences with Christians or with the church. I understand that. I have had bad experiences with certain people as well. They are not fun to be around. And sadly, I must admit that sometimes I have been the Christian who has given others a bad experience. But when we are around such people, we still must ask ourselves if anything they say is true. Ultimately Christianity is not about Christians or about how we conduct ourselves. Rather, it is about Christ and his words and actions. If Christ is found wanting, then you can go on your merry way and dismiss Christianity altogether. If, however, there is a ring of truth to Jesus' words, then maybe you ought to give Christianity a good hearing even if some of Jesus' words are being repeated by people you do not respect.

Sign On with the Original

Recently, I heard the story of Greg Kelley. He was just 18 when he was accused of heinous acts against two young children. He was a hardworking young man who not only was well liked but had earned a Division 1 college football scholarship. Everything about his future looked bright, until out of nowhere he was identified as the one who had committed terrible crimes. Eventually, because evidence was withheld or intentionally not investigated, Kelley was sentenced to 25 years in jail—all for a crime he did not commit. Only five years later would his conviction be overturned and he would be exonerated.[7] Only after five years did people stop associating his name with a crime he did not commit.

Identity theft is a major issue today. People find out personal details about you and then "in your name" access your bank accounts, take out loans, and steal your property. In the wake of their actions, you are required to account for things you did not do, for actions you do not support. No one likes to be put in this position. It's simply not right. Likewise, when someone comes on the scene calling himself a Christian but acts in ways that are not consistent with what Christ taught, I do not think it is right to charge Christ for the bad behavior and blame him for what he did not do and does not support. For the very reason it was not right for Greg Kelley to be charged for a crime simply because someone attached his name to it, we must be careful to divorce what people do "in the name of Christ" with what Christ himself taught and stood for.

Imagine starting up a new delivery service called OTET (for "On Time, Every Time"). Your number one priority is customer service, and you've worked hard to maintain an impeccable on-time delivery record. Recognizing the success of your company, a group of competitors start using the OTET name to secure business for themselves, but they do not provide the level of service you do. Before long, bad reviews start showing up on your website. You don't understand. Your on-time delivery record is outstanding. Soon you discover the problem. Someone is using your name, but not living up to it. I am afraid something similar can take place when some people try to "sell" Christianity. They use Christ's name but don't live up to what Christ is all about. No wonder people want to stay clear. As the owner of OTET, you would hope that people don't blame the poor delivery service on you and are still willing to sign on with the original. I think this is the case with Jesus too. Jesus knows that those who use his name will often fall short; some will even use the name of Christ for very selfish ends. Yet, Jesus hopes you will look past all that and still sign on with the original.

"Christian" Evils on the World Stage

It is one thing to look past the obnoxious neighbor who tells you to get right with Jesus. . . or else. It's quite another thing to sweep aside all you've heard about the horrid behavior of Christians through the ages. I'll be the first to admit that there has been plenty done in the name of Christianity that has not been very Christian. At the same time, as I've looked back in history, I've noticed something odd. In many cases, it seems as if the dastardly deeds of Christians have been overplayed, while the camps to which people retreat have often been engaged in greater savagery. Let's take a look at the Crusades, the Spanish Inquisition, and the supposed oppression caused by Christian missionaries, and I'll explain what I mean.

The Crusades. It often has been suggested that the Crusades were a violent Christian land grab that forced conversion on peaceful Muslims. But while there was certainly some shameful violence along the way, the record of history paints the Crusades in a much different light. Christianity had expanded initially not by the sword but primarily through persuasion, with much of its expansion outside of western Europe. From Northern Africa to Iraq, through Central Asia and into India and China, the influence of Christianity spread deep and wide through the seventh century.[8] Then came Mohammed and his followers, who sought not to win the battle of hearts and minds by the art of persuasion but rather by the sword—a sword that overtook many places Christians lived and thrived. Conquered areas included Palestine, Syria, and Egypt, and in the centuries to follow, the whole of North Africa, Spain, and what is now known as Turkey, would come under Muslim rule. Lands farther to the east were also not spared, as Islam claimed Pakistan and worked its way into India and Central Asia.[9] Places Christians had once called home had become in the words of 13th-century Arab historian Ibn al-Athir "the lands of Islam."[10]

What then were the Crusades? They were not a greedy land grab that sought to line the pockets of the invaders. Neither were they a vicious unprovoked action upon wholly innocent people. Nor were they the acts of an ambitious pope or mercenary knights merely cloaked in a love of God and pious self-sacrifice.[11] This has often been the picture painted. But it is not a fair one.

For more than 450 years, Christian lands had been on the defensive against Islam.[12] Islam had consumed much of the Christian world by force and had every intention of overtaking Europe. If Christian nations had not responded, it is hard to imagine that any of the democratic forces that sprang out of Europe would have arisen. Certainly, there were instances when the crusaders did not live up to New Testament ethics when executing their counterattack, but if we are to judge the damage done by Christians in this era of the Crusades it is far tamer than what Islam inflicted on what were once Christian lands.

I don't present the Crusades in this manner to excuse any atrocities committed at the hands of the crusaders, nor to disparage Islam, but only to put the Crusades in proper perspective. If we are to dismiss Christianity because of the Crusades, then we most certainly must dismiss Islam. Of course, you might be willing to dismiss both. The question is where then will you turn to find a worldview not tainted by "crusaders" of one form or fashion? If you turn to a so-called peaceful religion like Buddhism, you must be willing to dismiss the ravenous violence against Muslims by the Buddhist majority in Myanmar, and a long history of other Buddhist violence in places like Sri Lanka or even by the Dalai Lama's own sect.[13] If you turn to the serenity and beauty often found in Shintoism, you must confront its influence in the nationalist efforts of Imperialist Japan. Hinduism is also not a religion with a history of peace. Not only will you find plenty of murderous skirmishes in its past, but more recently, Hindu nationalism in India has violently threatened Christian and Muslim minorities, and that has even spilled out abroad.[14] Again, you may say that this is all well and good, because you have no interest in any religion whatsoever. You say all religions are bad, which gives you all the more reason to steer clear of religion in general. But before you settle there, let's look at the nonreligious atheistic regimes of the 20th century: Communist Russia and China were the big players, but we can also include other smaller states like North Korea, Vietnam, Cambodia, and Yugoslavia. The number of deaths under these regimes is staggering: 61 million killed under Stalin alone, and another 35 million under Mao Tse-tung in China.[15] After compiling the evidence for numbers like these, genocide scholar R. J. Rummel writes: "Of all religions, secular and otherwise, that of Marxism has been by far the bloodiest."[16] Of course, you could argue that there are other secular forms of government that have not caused such harm, and you are right. But as I will discuss later, these secular governments consistently draw from Christian-based ideals.

So incredible is the massacre of human life at the hands of atheist leaders in the 20th century alone that atheism's nonreligious stance may be the first one from which you must run. I understand it has long been popular to put Christianity on its heels by bringing up the Crusades, and most certainly Christianity should own up to the excesses of the crusaders, but when we compare Christianity's damage to what has been wrought by others, I don't think the Crusades provide any special reason to dismiss Christianity out of hand.

The Spanish Inquisition. The Spanish Inquisition conjures up some of the most horrid images of Christianity at work. Torture and burnings at the stake were aimed at Protestants, witches, scientists, and homosexuals alike. Claims of hundreds of thousands and even millions of lives lost have not been uncommon. Unfortunately, much of what has been said about the Inquisition over the centuries "is either an outright lie or a wild exaggeration!"[17] Motivated by the English and Dutch in the 16th century, both of which were at war with Spain, a narrative was spun to paint Spain in a despicable light.[18] The propaganda effort worked, and still many today look at the Inquisition as a case in point of the evils of Christianity.

More contemporary research on the Spanish Inquisition, however, is not based on unsubstantiated claims but on recent access to detailed archives of over 44,000 cases heard in Inquisition courts. Of these cases, fewer than 2% resulted in executions, or about 2,300 deaths over more than two centuries.[19] That's about ten per year. Certainly, none of these deaths can be justified by New Testament ethics, but in a time when religious intolerance and capital punishment were the norm throughout Europe, the Spanish Inquisition was remarkably tame.[20] Furthermore, the Inquisition rules regulating torture were far more restrictive than in other secular European courts—prohibiting danger to life or limb or the shedding of blood—and were applied in only a scant number of cases.[21] Even the prisons operated by the Inquisition were "by far the most comfortable and humane in Europe."[22] And about the books that were burned? It is unlikely any scientific books were ever destroyed as a result of the Inquisition. Instead, it was mostly pornographic material that found its way into the fire.[23]

Like the Crusades, the history of the Inquisition points to unsavory and violent activities of the Christian church that should not be forgotten. However, the exaggeration of any Inquisition evils, when secular powers were far more inhumane during the same time period, is even more concerning. It's as if those who seek to show that religion in general, and Christianity in particular, are worthy of scorn are diverting our attention from even greater evils perpetuated by the nonreligious. It is as if they want us to see the Crusades and the Inquisition as properly depicting Christianity, but when considering the horror of secular or atheistic leaders, they turn a blind eye.

Oppression by Christian Missionaries. Idyllic images of tribes on pristine tropical islands overrun by marauding missionaries is a disturbing one. At worst, such scenes smack of self-serving religious colonialism; at best, cultural insensitivity. But again, while one can find examples of Christian missionary efforts gone bad, there is also considerable evidence that Christian mission efforts, particularly Protestant efforts that were not seeking state control but personal, voluntary conversion, have created astoundingly positive effects.

After hearing a lecture in which a world-renowned expert on global trends suggested an odd historical link between democracy and Protestantism, Robert D. Woodberry spent 14 years researching whether there was any truth to the suggested correlation. Finally, his efforts were published in 2012 in the *American Political Science Review*, the field's most prestigious journal. So astounding and well presented was Woodberry's published research entitled "The Missionary Roots of Liberal Democracy"[24] that it garnered four major awards. What were his findings? Simply this:

> Areas where Protestant missionaries had a significant presence in the past are on average more economically developed today, with comparatively better health, lower infant mortality, lower corruption, greater literacy, higher educational attainment (especially for women), and more robust membership in nongovernmental associations.[25]

It was not just any Protestant presence that made the difference, however. It was only the presence of Protestant missionaries who did not come as part of state colonial efforts but simply sought voluntary, personal conversion of those among whom they lived. In other words, when Christian missionaries sought to teach people the Bible and the importance of personally trusting Jesus, far-reaching changes occurred that are still felt today. So well supported was Woodberry's research that fellow scholars could not help but take notice. One wrote, "I think it's the best work out there on religion and economic development . . . It's incredibly sophisticated and well grounded. I haven't seen anything quite like it."[26] Another said that Woodberry's "devastatingly thorough analysis" shows that conversionary Protestant efforts are not just one factor crucial to forming democracies; rather, "it turns out to be the most important factor. It can't be anything but startling for scholars of democracy."[27]

Of course, this does not mean there aren't plenty of examples of abhorrent missionary behavior, but as Woodberry states:

> We don't have to deny that there were and are racist mission-aries . . . We don't have to deny there were and are missionaries who do self-centered things. But if that were the average effect, we would expect the places where missionaries had influence to be worse than places where missionaries weren't allowed or were restricted in action. We find exactly the opposite on all kinds of outcomes. Even in places where few people converted, [mission-aries] had a profound economic and political impact.[28]

One reason people have looked down on Christian missionary efforts is because those efforts seem racist in nature. I mean, isn't it racist for people of one culture to ask those of another culture to abandon their beliefs? But I am not sure that is always the case. In fact, by saying that missionary efforts are racist, one may actually expose their own racist views toward the "weakness" of the native to fall prey to the missionary's views. Aboriginal historian James Miller writes scathingly about the stereotype that missionaries coerced the native peoples of which Miller is a member:

> If it is said that Christianity destroyed Koori culture, then it can be said that Koori culture was not a strong culture and that Koori society in general was inferior. Such thinking depicts the Kooris to be the helpless victims of brainwashing who abandoned every-thing that they ever believed in as soon as someone stood up and preached from an open Bible. This was not the case, and such think-ing degrades Koori society. Kooris were not helpless, and Koori

culture was not destroyed.[29]

In fact, if we say that native cultures like the Kooris are not strong enough to discern between good and bad, and truth and fiction, we must also say the same for cultures around the globe that have embraced Christianity. More often than not, Christianity is thought to be a Western religion, but this is hardly the case. Christianity was born in a Middle Eastern culture and first spread into North Africa and Asia. Later, it found a significant home in Europe and the United States, but today the center of Christianity is not the West. That is, the Christian church is growing the fastest in places like Africa, Asia, and Latin America.[30] Further, Christians who say their faith is very important are more likely to be found in countries like Brazil and Ecuador and Ghana and the Philippines than they are in the United States, and most definitely more so than in Europe.[31] Are we then to say that all these cultures are not strong enough to decide for themselves what is true and good? And could not we be accused of racism if we say so?

Not only are native cultures regarded as easily persuaded and less capable of discerning truth, they can also be romanticized. Undoubtedly, native cultures can have some honorable characteristics, but at times they can be found to engage in cannibalism, child sacrifices, genital mutilation, slavery, and religious beliefs that promote poverty and other unhealthy practices. When a Christian missionary reforms these kinds of behaviors, it easily could be argued that she is not degrading the culture but helping free it from its own slavery. Consider, for example, "the Aztec custom of slitting open the bowels of slaves and prisoners for the purpose of removing their living hearts as sacrifice, or the Inca custom of sacrificing children and (it appears) flaying the skin off their bodies."[32] Yes, Christian missionaries may have introduced them to Sunday church, but that seems like an improvement not a degradation of culture. Moreover, many of the so-called idyllic native cultures of the past were often encroached upon by secular or colonial forces with little interest in maintaining a people's culture, and sometimes even annihilated entire people groups.[33] So while Christian missionaries don't have a perfect record, they have been far more willing to maintain aspects of a people group's culture and prepare them to survive encroaching change.[34]

Once again, then, it appears that Christian activity over the centuries often has been presented in a manner that is far more negative than is justified. Undoubtedly, some people have done despicable things in the name of Christianity, but the Crusades, the Inquisition, and the oppression of missionaries should not be insurmountable barriers when considering the worthiness of Christianity, especially given the many good things that Christianity has brought to the world.

More Good Than Harm

I have a friend who lost 25 pounds, but if you just met him, I am sure you would have doubts about his exercise and diet regimen. I say that because he still probably has a good 50 pounds to lose to be in the healthy range, and if you didn't know where he started, you'd think whatever he is doing is lacking. It's situations like this that can make it hard for you to judge whether someone's "program" is really successful and worth pursuing yourself. I think something similar might play out if we try to evaluate the positive impact Christianity has had on someone's life. We might see someone who calls herself a Christian acting with little compassion or kindness and be quick to conclude Christianity has done little good for her, and perhaps even harm. But maybe, if we knew her before she started following Christ, we'd think a little differently. As bad as she may be now, maybe she was even worse before!

Nonetheless, it seems to me that if Christianity on the whole is not destructive, and even does more good than harm, then over the long haul we ought to see something positive either in the case of an individual or on a grander scale. Woodberry's research, for example, seems to show just that. His research indicates that when Christian ideals are introduced into a culture, far-reaching, positive consequences are likely to follow. But I'd like to point out a few other positive Christian contributions as well.

Charity. The world in which Christianity was born was largely devoid of charity toward the poor. In fact, in the Greco-Roman world, charity was a sign of weakness and poor judgment. Accordingly, the Roman philosopher Plautus (254–184 BC) argued, "You do a beggar bad service by giving him food and drink; you lose what you give and prolong his life for more misery."[35] Whereas Romans would give to others with the expectation that something be given in return, it was Christians who lived out the teaching of Jesus and sacrificially gave to the poor.[36] As Irish historian William Lecky noted: "The active, habitual, and detailed charity of private persons, which is such a conspicuous feature in all

Christian societies, was scarcely known in antiquity."[37] And it's not just that Christianity gave the world a new perspective on charity long ago, it is still fueling greater charity today. Christians give more money and volunteer more time than their secular counterparts, and this is true not just in relation to religious causes, but nonreligious causes as well.[38]

Healthcare. Closely connected to Christian charity is the Christian call to help the sick. Jesus made it clear that helping the physically ailing is part of Christian duty, even illustrating it with his famous parable of the Good Samaritan. Helping the sick seems like common decency today—something any civilized society should do—but this was not the case among the ancient cultures into which Christianity spread. Early historians noted that it was not uncommon for the sick to be cast aside and left for dead.[39] Christians, on the other hand, did not hesitate to care for the sick even at the cost of their own lives. Such care was not well thought of among many of their pagan neighbors, and even resulted in the martyrdom of one second-century believer, because "he nursed, supported, and protected a number of deformed and crippled children that had been saved from death after failed abortions or exposures."[40]

From these humble beginnings, Christians began to organize their efforts beyond individual care, establishing the first hospitals in the fourth century AD that provided beds and nursing to all, regardless of gender or class. There is a reason that world-renowned hospitals like New York Presbyterian Hospital and Methodist Hospital in Houston have the names that they do, because it was Christians who for centuries saw caring for the sick as a calling when others did not.

Soon after hospitals were built, orphanages followed, and by the fifth century homes for the aged were established as well.[41] Today, we take for granted that there are places our aging parents can spend their final years with excellent care, but we do so because it was the Christian belief that people are worthy of care throughout their life that has made it so. As historian Alvin Schmidt concludes: "People who may think that current human charity and compassion in the Western world, whether it is state welfare or voluntary charity, developed on its own as a result of mere civilization, without the impetus and influence of Christianity are misinformed."[42]

Education. For many around the world, attending school is a given, even compulsory until a certain age. And in the United States, if you want to get ahead, many find a college degree a minimum prerequisite.

But when and how did the importance of universal education arise? Undoubtedly, there were great thinkers among the ancients; one just has to recall people like Socrates, Plato, and Aristotle to know that learning is not something new. Yet because the Greeks and Romans saw education as only for elite males and frowned upon empirical research, they established no permanent educational institutions, libraries, or guild of scholars.[43] That would not take place until Christians got involved— Christians who believed that people of all ages, classes, and gender were worthy of education. The first Christian schools date back to the mid-second century, and by the fifth century, could be found teaching not only Christian doctrine but also grammar, rhetoric, logic, arithmetic, music, geometry, and astronomy.[44]

In fact, if you never liked school growing up, I'm afraid you have the Christian Reformer Martin Luther to blame for it. It was Luther who proposed the idea and took the first steps to make public, tax-supported, compulsory education the norm. Furthermore, the science labs you suffered through are a product of Christian thought. Ancient Greeks saw manual activity as only fit for slaves and, since empirical research required manual activity, left their theories untested.[45] Christians, however, believed God made us to use mind and body, and thus paved the way for the kind of research that would produce the vaccines and other medicines we enjoy today. It's no surprise then that Christians founded the first universities and established them from Paris to London and from Harvard to Princeton. As two chroniclers of the impact of Christianity on education stated:

> Every school you see—public or private, religious or secular—is a visible reminder of the religion of Jesus Christ. So is every college and university. This is not to say that every school is Christian. Often the exact opposite is true. But the fact is that the phenomenon of education for the masses has its roots in Christianity.[46]

The Arts. No culture is without its art, but the contribution of Christian artists throughout the ages is unmistakable. Whether through music, architecture, literature, sculpture, painting, or drama, Christianity has deeply enriched Western culture. Donald Grout stated in his magnum opus *The History of Western Music*, "The history of Western art music properly begins with the music of the Christian Church."[47] The same could be said for the whole of Western art.

Roman rulers took note of the Christian penchant for music early in the second century.[48] But that was just the beginning. In time, it would be Christians who developed music to heights previously unknown. From the Christian choirmasters at Notre Dame in Paris who developed multi-part harmonies and arrangements[49] to the monk who invented musical notation[50] that opened the gateway for Christians to develop symphonies, Christianity has left its mark. One wonders where music would be today without the likes of Bach, Beethoven, Handel, and Mendelssohn—all of whom deeply embraced Christianity and sought to express their view of life in the work they produced.

Of course, Christianity has left an indelible mark on literature as well. Dante, Chaucer, Shakespeare, Bunyan, Dostoevsky, Tennyson, John Milton, Jane Austen, T. S. Eliot, C.S. Lewis, and J. R. R. Tolkien are just a few of the myriads of Christian writers whose work has stood the test of time. They have left us everything from *Canterbury Tales* to *Romeo and Juliet* and from *Pride and Prejudice* to *Lord of the Rings*. You might be concerned that these works are by white, Western thinkers, but I could have also listed the classic *City of God* by Augustine of Hippo, a fifth-century North African Berber convert, or the powerful autobiography of a Black Christian pastor entitled *Narrative of the Life of Frederick Douglass, an American Slave,* which did much to fuel the abolitionist movement in the United States.

And then there are those like Leonardo DaVinci, Michelangelo, Raphael, and Rembrandt, whose works of art remain the most visited in the world. Each crafted their work from a distinctly Christian worldview, yet, if you removed their masterpieces, you may just alter your plans to visit Paris or Rome!

I know that it is in fashion to bash Christianity as being repressive and backward and contributing little that's positive to society, but such a conclusion doesn't measure up to history. Although Christians have at times done harm along the way, they also have greatly shaped our spirit of charity, the healthcare we've come to expect, the educational opportunities we take for granted, and the arts we have long enjoyed. In other words, Christians have created much of the world we enjoy today. To this very point, best-selling English historian Tom Holland recently wrote that while much of Christianity's impact is currently "hidden from view," we should still recognize that the assumptions many make today "about how a society should properly be organized, and the principles that it should uphold—were not bred of classical antiquity, still less of 'human nature,' but very distinctively of the civilization's Christian past."[51]

If Holland is correct, there is far more to applaud Christianity for than to complain about. It's why in a society that is increasingly skeptical of religion, so many of its instincts about what is right and good are still thoroughly Christian. It's why we argue over how we might make healthcare affordable for all or why we believe that all people are created equal and endowed with certain unalienable rights. Therefore, when Christians are blasted as hypocritical, it's not always because of the ideals they espouse but because they are not living up to the Christian ideals that though "hidden from view" have been good for us all.

Good for You

It may not be "bad" Christians you are running from but religion in general. There is simply too much evil that has gone on in the world that can be attributed to religion that you want to stay clear of not only Christianity in particular but any participation in religious teaching or practice. This, however, might be a costly personal decision at least in terms of longevity, health, and life satisfaction.

In 2016, *USA Today* published an op-ed by Tyler VanderWeele, a professor in the Harvard School of Public Health, and journalist John Sniff. The article was entitled "Religion May Be a Miracle Drug," and it begins with some rather provocative questions:

> If one could conceive of a single elixir to improve the physical and mental health of millions of Americans—at no personal cost— what value would our society place on it?
>
> Going a step further, if research quite conclusively showed that when consumed just once a week, this concoction would reduce mortality by 20% to 30% over a 15-year period, how urgently would we want to make it publicly available?[52]

The answer to these questions would likely be a resounding "yes," but as VanderWeele and Sniff explain, the "elixir" already exists, and it probably is located just down the street. What is it? A house of worship.

As VanderWeele explains in greater detail in "Religion and Health: A Synthesis,"[53] an abundance of research indicates that those who attend religious services on a regular basis not only live longer but also have "lower blood pressure, better cardiovascular function, less coronary artery disease, better immune function, better endocrine function, better social support, greater marital stability, greater purpose in life, and overall higher levels of happiness and subjective well-being."[54] These benefits do not accrue to those who simply identify as religious or who pursue certain religious practices on their own. Rather, they are experienced by those committed enough to be part of religious services on a weekly basis, whether they be adults or children. Relative to this positive impact on youth, Ying Chen, a researcher at Harvard stated, "Many children are raised religiously, and our study shows that this can powerfully affect their health behaviors, mental health, and overall happiness and well-being."[55] You might ask, "But is weekly attendance in religious services really causing all these benefits, or is it just somehow related to general social engagement?" The answer is that the positive impact recorded is causal in nature,[56] and it goes beyond any benefits that typically accrue with social engagement.[57]

Jonathan Haidt might provide the best illustration as to the impact engagement in a religious community can have. Although an atheist psychologist, he writes in his book *The Happiness Hypothesis: Finding Modern Truth in Ancient Wisdom*:

> Try to imagine yourself changing places with either Bob or Mary. Bob is thirty-five years old, single, white, attractive, and athletic. He earns $100,000 a year and lives in sunny Southern California. He is highly intellectual, and he spends his free time reading and going to museums. Mary and her husband live in snowy Buffalo, New York, where they earn a combined income of $40,000. Mary is sixty-five years old, black, overweight, and plain in appearance. She is highly sociable, and she spends her free time mostly in activities related to her church. She is on dialysis for kidney problems. Bob seems to have it all, and few readers of this book would prefer Mary's life to his. Yet if you had to bet on it, you should bet that Mary is happier than Bob.[58]

The harm done by Christians whether in past history or in present day can create substantial hurdles when it comes to considering Christianity. That's one reason so many today choose the pathway of Bob rather than

Mary, even if it does not make them happier. But one must take a step back and consider whether the hurdles are as substantial as we make them out to be. Have Christians in history really caused more harm than good? Have all those who have done things "in the name of Christ" accurately represented what Jesus taught and stood for? Is it right to ignore what Jesus claimed just because others have misrepresented him? Is it really true that engagement in a Christian community does not provide positive, healthy benefits?

When evaluating Christianity, maybe the problem is not the claims of Christ who himself denounced the hypocrisy you find so distasteful, nor the communities that seek to understand what Jesus said. Maybe what is really unattractive is the person who has hurt you personally or the bygone leader who used Christianity as a cover-up for greed. In that case, maybe you should be careful not to throw out the baby with the bathwater—to throw out Jesus because of those who fall short of living up to his ways. Maybe underneath it all Christianity offers something rather good, something that can lead you to the satisfaction of Mary instead of Bob, regardless of what life ends up throwing your way.

Key Points

- Christian hypocrites can make it easy to disregard Christianity.

- It is best to define a hypocrite not as those who fail to live up to their own standard but as those who fail to be judged by their own standard once they have failed. Otherwise, we would all be hypocrites and should all be disregarded.

- Our disdain for hypocrisy puts us in good company. Jesus hated hypocrisy too.

- People who are hypocrites may still be telling the truth, so we must separate the behavior of the hypocrites from the message of hypocrites.

- When Christians do things in the name of Christianity, it doesn't mean they always are properly representing Christ. Therefore, we should not dismiss Christ because people are doing evil in his name.

- Many have taken the Crusades, the Inquisition, and oppression caused by Christian missionaries to be prime examples of the harm Christianity has done. While these provide instances of Christian evil, they are often exaggerated in the face of other movements whose negative impact is simultaneously underplayed.

- Christianity has made many great contributions to the world, including in the areas of charity, medical care, education, and the arts. Christian ideals have so impacted our thinking in these areas that they have become commonplace even among the secular. Thus, there is good reason to believe that Christianity causes more good than harm.

- Regular engagement in a faith community is associated with numerous physical and mental benefits, as well as a longer and more satisfied life. This suggests that engagement in Christianity can be good for you.

Additional Resources

The Book That Made Your World: How the Bible Created the Soul of Western Civilization, Vishal Mangalwadi

How Monotheism Led to Reformations, Science, Witch-Hunts, and the End of Slavery, Rodney Stark

6 Modern Myths About Christianity & Western Civilization, Philip J. Sampson

How Christianity Changed the World, Alvin J. Schmidt

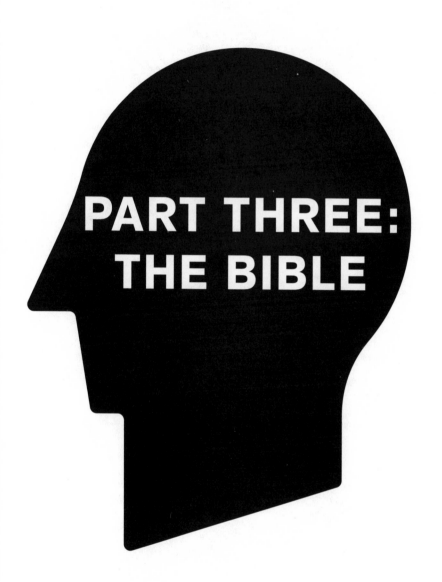

PART THREE: THE BIBLE

Why Should I Trust
What the Bible Has to Say?

The moon landing was a hoax.
There was no Nazi holocaust of the Jews.
JFK was killed by the mob.
Osama bin Laden was never killed.
The collapse of the Twin Towers was an inside job.
Water fluoridation is a communist attempt to weaken America.
Pharmaceutical companies want you to be sick.
Princess Diana was killed at the request of the British royal family.

Given the popularity of conspiracy theories, there is a good chance you agree, at least in part, with one of the statements above. I suppose we could chalk up our suspicion of any particular storyline as a product of the era of "fake news," but a look back at history tells us that people have had their suspicions of one party line or another for as far back as we can see. In some cases, our suspicions are warranted; there are just too many pieces of the puzzle missing or sinister characters in the background. But in other cases, ignorance or stubborn resistance is at play, and no matter how much evidence we are given to the contrary, we refuse to set aside our thoughts of conspiracy.

One of the longest standing and most prevalent conspiracy theories has to do with the Bible. On one hand, the Bible is the world's best-selling book and revered by many as an accurate account of historical events and, perhaps more importantly, God's word to humanity. On the other hand, it is seen as a grand hoax written to prop up political and religious leaders and control the masses. For many, it is somewhere in between. If you have strong leanings against the Bible's historical accuracy and are appalled by the claim that it is God's word, it may be that no amount of evidence to the contrary will convince you otherwise. But in my experience, most people are at least open to exploring what evidence does exist, and in many cases, they are surprised by the quality of the evidence supporting the Bible.

When it comes to suspicions about the Bible, I have found that most concerns fit into one of three categories. Some suspicions have to do with whether the Bible we have today is anything like what was originally written or included. I call these *authenticity* questions. Other suspicions have to do with whether the events in the Bible really occurred and the people recorded actually lived. These I refer to as *accuracy* questions. The final set of suspicions has to do with whether we should recognize the Bible as God's word to us and let it shape the way we live our lives. These are *authority* questions. Personally, I believe all three sets of suspicions are healthy. If I walk down the street and someone hands me a book claiming it is God's plan for this life and eternity, I'd need a lot of questions answered about its authenticity, accuracy, and authority before I gave it much of a look.

THE BIBLE'S AUTHENTICITY

I would love to have an original of many different things. I'd gladly accept an original Babe Ruth baseball card. Something original of Leonardo DaVinci I would be sure to display. And if I had an original letter from George Washington or Nelson Mandela, I'd take great care to preserve it. The people who own originals like these usually pay a hefty sum to acquire them, and so they find it well worth the effort to authenticate that what they are acquiring is truly an original.

In the case of the Bible, it would be ideal to have the original manuscripts for each of its books. That way there would be little room to doubt that what we read today mirrors the original. Unfortunately, the originals were generally written on materials that disintegrate over time, meaning it is highly unlikely they still exist in a readable state. Furthermore, even if we did manage to find a few, we probably could not be sure we had the original. We could analyze the paper and ink used, do some carbon dating, and compare script styles to place an ancient manuscript near the time the original would have been written. But even with that, it always could be argued that all we have is an early copy written soon after the original and not the original itself. This dilemma is not just true for the Bible; it is true for most ancient works. So, then, how can we have any confidence that the Bible we have today matches the original?

When it comes to ancient manuscripts, there are a few very important factors when it comes to judging authenticity. These aren't factors I've come up with; they are factors used by "textual critics" who regularly evaluate documents like the New Testament.[1] They include:

- The number of manuscript copies we have available today
- The date of the oldest copies
- The similarity between the various copies

With regard to the number of manuscripts, what we have for the Bible is well beyond what we have for other ancient works. Take the New Testament, for example. Its books were originally written in Greek, and we have nearly 6,000 Greek manuscripts alone. This is considerably more than the number of copies available for other well-cited ancient works (see chart below). Furthermore, when one considers the time differential between the oldest available copies and when the original was written for each of the works, the New Testament again fares very well. Among the last books written in the New Testament is the Gospel of John; it was probably written close to AD 90. The oldest New Testament fragment (the *Rylands Library Papyrus* housed in Manchester, England) of this Gospel is dated back to AD 130 or even before. That is only 40 years after the original, a far cry from the 1,000-year span between the time Josephus wrote his *Antiquities* and the earliest discovered copy of his work. Even the oldest copy of the complete New Testament (the *Codex Sinaiticus*, currently found in the British Museum in London) dates back to the mid-fourth century, meaning there was less than a 300-year span between when the New Testament was completed and our oldest complete copy.[2]

THE NEW TESTAMENT & OTHER ANCIENT WORKS[3]

Work	Surviving Copies	Date of Authorship	Oldest Surviving Copies
Homer's *Illiad*	1,900+	750 BC	415 BC
Caesar's *Gallic Wars*	251	50-58 BC	AD 9th c.
Thucydides' *History*	188	5th c. BC	3rd c. BC
Josephus' *Antiquities*	120	AD 93	AD 11th c.
Tacitus' *Annals*	36	AD 100-120	AD 850
New Testament (Greek)	5,850+	AD 40-90	AD 130

The number of Old Testament copies is also impressive, but since many of the manuscripts are part of private family/religious collections, the exact number of copies is harder to assess.[4] According to one scholar, there may be over 40,000 Old Testament scrolls in existence when taking into consideration those that are part of both public and private collections.[5] Among those that have been made public are the famed *Dead Sea Scrolls*. These scrolls were first discovered in 1947 and date as far back as the third century BC. Importantly, the *Dead Sea Scrolls* contain portions of every book in the Old Testament except Esther. They are preceded only by the *Silver Scrolls,* which date to about 600 BC, but the *Silver Scrolls* contain the recitation of only a few verses. In terms of number of copies and proximity to the original, the textual evidence for the authenticity of the Old Testament is also outstanding.

SELECTED OLD TESTAMENT MANUSCRIPTS[6]

Work	Earliest Copy	Biblical Books
Silver Scrolls	600 BC	Portion of Pentateuch in Hebrew
Dead Sea Scrolls	250 BC–AD 68	Portions of OT in Hebrew
Ryland Papyrus 458	150 BC	Portion of Deuteronomy in Greek
En-Gedi Scroll	300 BC	Portion of Leviticus in Hebrew
Codex Vaticanus	325-350 AD	Entire OT in Greek
Codex Sinaiticus	350 AD	Half of OT in Greek
Latin Vulgate	AD 400	Entire OT in Latin
Codex Alexandrinus	450 AD	Entire OT in Greek
Aleppo Codex	AD 900	Entire OT in Hebrew
Leningrad Codex	AD 1008	Entire OT in Hebrew

The number of old copies of the Bible should increase our confidence in the Bible's authenticity if the copies compare well with one another. If the copies vary greatly, it would be difficult, if not impossible, to ascertain what was originally written. Fortunately, those who copied the Bible took great care in the copying process, meaning that the resulting similarity we find between the copies is impressive. For example, prior to the discovery of the *Dead Sea Scrolls*, one of the oldest complete Hebrew manuscripts of the entire Old Testament was the *Leningrad Codex* (c. 1008). Because the *Dead Sea Scrolls* were written over 1,000 years before the *Leningrad Codex*, scholars were eager to make a comparison between the scrolls and the codex to see how well the two compared. When that comparison was made, only minor differences existed.[7] For example, two of most important *Dead Sea Scroll* manuscripts contain the text of the book of Isaiah, which contains 66 chapters. When comparing the *Dead Sea Scrolls* with texts like the *Leningrad Codex*, only a few insignificant changes were justified in modern translations. And these changes would be "similar to the difference between the American and British spelling of a word like *Savior* or *Saviour*."[8]

The same care and attention in the copying process can be found for the New Testament as well. Yes, skeptics are quick to point to the number of differences between the New Testament manuscripts, but these complaints are often overblown. For example, the vast majority of differences are simply variations in the spelling of certain words or the exclusion of a word like "the." These differences hardly impact our understanding of what the original text would have said. Only in a very few instances are experts unsure if the original text used one word or another, and most modern versions of the Bible clearly note these variances in their footnotes. (See, for example, Mark 3:14.) But even in these cases, one is hard-pressed to find examples of a larger passage's meaning being lost because we are uncertain of the original words. As Mark Roberts (PhD in New Testament and Christian origins from Harvard University) writes: "If you were to take two different teams of text critics and ask them to work independently on a critical edition of the Greek New Testament, they would agree more than 99% of the time."[9]

Furthermore, the number of differences that do exist between the manuscripts is largely a function of having so many different manuscripts in the first place, which is an advantage not a disadvantage. New Testament critic Bart Ehrman suggests that there could be 200,000 to 400,000 variants among the New Testament manuscripts.[10] That sounds like it would leave us completely unable to arrive at what the original said, until one better understands the numbers. Suppose, for example, that this book had 100,000 words (actually it contains more than that) and I asked two people to copy it by hand. If they made one mistake every 1,000 words (99.9% accuracy), there would be a total of 200 differences between the two copies and the original. But consider if I had 2,000 people copy the book with the same level of accuracy. Now there would be 200,000 differences, or more variants than there are words in this book. For any given word, however, the vast majority of copies would record the exact same word, allowing for great confidence in the content of the original. In this case, it easily could be argued that 2,000 copies with 200,000 scattered variants provides far more confidence in the original text than if I had only two copies with 200 differences, since the latter would only give me at most two points that agree.[11] Therefore, when it comes to the New Testament the fact that there are so many variants is neither surprising nor detrimental. The variants are simply a result of having a great number of manuscripts available to us.[12]

All said, then, the authenticity of the Bible is well attested. There are many available copies. The copies date back close to the original date of authorship, and the copies compare well with one another. Why then do people dismiss the authenticity of the Bible? I will offer three reasons. First, those who have not looked into the matter assume the copying process is like the "telephone game" in which one person whispers a sentence or two into someone else's ear, and that person in turn whispers the words to another person. By the time the words make it around the room, the original words are often completely lost. But the Bible's copying process was not like the "telephone game." Rather, it used written manuscripts as opposed to whispers in the ear, making copying much easier. Copyists also were not restricted to looking at only the latest copy but could refer to earlier copies when available. This would be akin to the tenth person in the "telephone game" going back to the third person in the chain to ask what was said. In addition, in most cases the copying was done by those trained in the copying process. For example, the Masoretes, who were among the most respected of the Hebrew copyists, had numerous methods to account for each letter they were copying. This included knowing the exact number of letters in each section of Scripture as well as the letter that should land precisely in the middle. Also, when copies were completed, they often were checked over by a "corrector," and in some cases punishments were meted out for errors.[13] In other words, they were very careful to get it right.

A second reason people may reject the authenticity of the Bible is not ignorance but a predetermined bias against sacred texts. This bias often means skeptics require more evidence to establish the authenticity of the Bible than they do for other ancient works. They say this is warranted because the authors were sympathizers, not recognizing that many other ancient historians were sympathizers of their own causes as well. The famed New Testament scholar F. F. Bruce notes this dynamic well:

> The evidence for our New Testament writings is ever so much greater than the evidence for many writings of classical authors, the authenticity of which no one dreams of questioning. And if the New Testament were a collection of secular writings, their authenticity would generally be regarded as beyond all doubt. . . . Somehow or other there are people who regard a 'sacred book' as *ipso facto* under suspicion, and demand much more corroborative evidence for such a work than they would for an ordinary secular or pagan writing. From the viewpoint of the historian, the same standards must be applied to both.[14]

A third reason people commonly reject the authenticity of the Bible, and particularly that of the New Testament, has not to do with any alleged copying errors but rather with the claim that entire books were improperly omitted from the New Testament. This argument was popularized by Dan Brown's novel *The DaVinci Code* and claims that gospels other than those found in the Bible were passed among Christians as inspired Scripture in the centuries following Jesus. When the church received the protection of the state in the fourth century, however, powerful church leaders removed certain gospels that did not fit in with their personal interpretation. These claims are dubious on several counts:

- There is little evidence that church leaders prior to the fourth century ever accepted the "other gospels" as Scripture.
- The fourth-century church councils at Hippo and Carthage, which allegedly excluded the "other gospels," simply acknowledged the 66 books that Christians had always respected as inspired Scripture. That is, they did not start with a long list of books and then vote some out because of personal theological preferences.
- The gospels included in the New Testament were written by eyewitnesses of Jesus' life and ministry or by those with direct access to eyewitnesses. This cannot be said of the "other gospels," which are dated well into the second century or later.
- The "other gospels" do not read like historical narratives and

include religious ideas, specifically Gnosticism, that did not develop until after the time of Christ and his early followers.[15]

- The "other gospels" include ideas that are antithetical to the nature of the early church. For example, women were a central part of the church from the very earliest days and considered to have equal standing in God's kingdom, yet the non-biblical *Gospel of Thomas* has Peter saying, "Let Mary leave us, for women are not worthy of life." In response, Jesus says in this same gospel, "I myself shall lead her in order to make her male, so that she too may become a living spirit resembling you males. For every woman who will make herself male will enter the kingdom of heaven."[16]

Thus, while there are those who doubt the authenticity of the Bible for one reason or another, there is good reason to trust that it has been copied well through the centuries and has not been edited later to omit portions that became unpopular. In fact, based on the evidence we have for the authenticity for the Bible compared to evidence for other ancient works, if we discount the authenticity of the Bible, we would probably have to do the same for most every other ancient writing.

THE BIBLE'S ACCURACY

When I grew up it was common to say that people in Christopher Columbus' day thought the world was flat. In fact, I even remember being taught that Columbus had to argue with those who said his proposed venture to the Americas would send him over the edge of the Earth. But there is no truth to the claim, as people had known that Earth was round for nearly 2,000 years before Columbus came on the scene. How then did the story get started? It is rooted in a fictional account of Columbus and his detractors written by American novelist Washington Irving. There have been a number of printings of Irving's *A History of the Life and Voyages of Christopher Columbus* since its original publication in 1828, but regardless of how well each of these printings represents the original text, they do not make Irving's statements about Columbus any more factual. That's why I think it is important to address not only the question of *authenticity* but also the question of *accuracy* when it comes to the Bible. Who cares if the Bible has been copied as well as Irving's novel has been copied, if what has been copied is simply made-up stories pawned off as history?

For some people, the question of the Bible's historicity is not important. They say the Bible does not need to be historically accurate in order to be valuable to us. Just as fables can have a helpful moral to the story, so, too, can the stories of the Bible even if they did not really happen. I understand this line of thought and believe the Bible does have a "moral to the story," but much of that moral lesson calls for the events to have actually taken place. For example, Jesus is declared to be the long-awaited Messiah who has come to save the world. But for Jesus to be recognized as the anticipated Messiah, he needed to fulfill ancient prophecies about the Messiah showing up as a historical person. Similarly, according to those who wrote the Bible, if Jesus' body didn't rise from the dead as a historical event, Christ and his teaching about our having eternal life easily can be dismissed.[17] So, based on the Bible's own words, its historical accuracy is of utmost importance.

Not all of the Bible is historical narrative; some of it is poetry, like the book of Psalms. Other parts are commentary on the events of the day, and some of what we find in the Bible is straight-up instruction on how to live a life that is pleasing to God. But a large chunk of Scripture is telling us that this or that happened between this person and that in such and such a place. I find this particularly helpful, because it gives us plenty of data points to fact-check its authors and evaluate its historical accuracy. If there is little to no evidence of the people, places, and events mentioned in the Bible, or, more importantly, if there is evidence to the contrary, we can dismiss it as a hoax.

Historical Evidence for the Old Testament

It is not possible to discuss every person, place, or event mentioned in the Old Testament and provide information that corroborates what the Bible tells us. But I can touch on a sampling of what we find in the pages of the Old Testament to see how it matches up with archaeological and documentary evidence.

- Early on, the Bible spends considerable space telling the story of Abram, whom God later renames Abraham. So prominent is Abraham in biblical history that he is still called "the father of the Jews" today. The Bible suggests that Abraham lived about 2,000 years before Christ and continually harkens back to Abraham's life even after Jesus ascended to heaven. But the question is: Was

Abraham a life-and-blood, historical person? An inscription found on the wall of an ancient Egyptian temple would suggest so. The inscription speaks of the victories of Pharaoh Shishak (who is also mentioned in 2 Chronicles 12:1-11), and among the conquered cities noted is the "Fort of Abram." According to the Bible, Abraham founded Beersheba, and while Shishak could have used that name to describe the conquered town of Beersheba, instead he chose to hark back to its founder. Undeniable proof that Abraham existed? Probably not, but this bit of evidence surely points that way.

- Sometime after Abraham, Moses showed up on the scene. He was tasked with freeing the Jewish people from Egyptian slavery. The Bible describes in detail how God sent plagues on the Egyptians in order to convince Pharaoh and his counselors to let the Israelites leave Egypt. The plagues include turning the Nile River into blood, sending locusts to devour vegetation, making the land of Egypt go dark, and even the death of royal children. Furthermore, the Bible states that when the Israelites were finally given permission to leave, the Egyptian people were so eager to see the Israelites go they gave them many of their valuables. All this sounds rather fantastical and a great myth to hand down to future generations, but curiously it matches up well with the ancient Egyptian *Ipuwer Papyrus* that speaks of similar happenings. This papyrus refers to a dark time in Egypt's history when the Nile was full of blood, agriculture was ravaged, darkness came over the land, the "children of princes" died, and valuables were acquired by slaves.[18]

- After Moses led the people out of Israel, God had them spend a number of years in the wilderness before leading them into the promised land west of the Jordan River. During their wilderness wanderings, the Bible speaks of Israel's vulnerability to surrounding peoples, including a king named Balak who ruled over Moab. Balak, in an attempt to gain the upper hand over the Israelites, hired the prophet Balaam to put a curse on the Jewish people. As much as Balaam wanted the income from the assignment, God would not let him curse Israel and had a talking donkey get in his way. Again, the biblical record sounds like the stuff of legends. And yet we have evidence outside the Bible that Balaam was not a made-up character added to spice up the story. In 1967, Dutch archaeologists discovered plaster fragments in Jordan dated to 800 BC that read, "from the Book of Balaam the son of Beor. He was seer of the gods."[19]

- It took some time for the Israelites to get fully settled in their eventual home, and once they did so, there was no form of central leadership. This arrangement was ultimately unacceptable to the Israelites, so they sought the appointment of a king. One of the earliest kings was David, and he is the main character in several Old Testament stories. Before becoming king, David is said to have defeated, with a sling and a stone, a giant named Goliath who represented the Philistine armies. For years, skeptics insisted David was a mythical character. But archaeologists who found two stone inscriptions—the *Tell Dan Stele* and the *Moabite Stone*—muted that claim. Both inscriptions are from enemies of Israel yet speak of the "house of David" as the leader of Israel. Furthermore, additional findings have confirmed that the Philistines were significant enemies of Israel in David's day, that slings were used as lethal weapons at the time, and that armies often would send their representative champions, like Goliath, to face off until death, just as depicted in the David and Goliath scene.[20] None of this validates the specific battle of David and Goliath, but it certainly increases its plausibility.

- The Israelite kings that followed David were many, and the Bible says they often found themselves at odds with the kings that ruled over Assyria, Babylon, and Moab, such as Tiglath-Pilesar, Nebuchadnezzar, and Mesha. Perhaps surprisingly, the records of these rulers name the Israelite kings mentioned in the Bible, such as Ahab, Jehu, Hosea, Manasseh, and several others. In addition to what foreign kings wrote about the Israelite kings, we have confirmation by way of clay seals called *bullae*. Bullae were used to seal scrolls before they were delivered so the intended recipients could be assured of the identity of the sender. Archaeologists have discovered bullae with inscriptions of more than 30 kings, scribes, and servants mentioned in the Bible.

- One Jewish king for whom there is particularly strong historical evidence is Hezekiah. He was king over the Israelites who lived in Judah and, as did the kings before him, reigned in the city of

Jerusalem. Sennacherib, the king of Assyria, destroyed the cities to the north and west of Jerusalem and soon began its siege. Given the strength and ruthless history of the Assyrian army, Hezekiah was understandably frightened. As soon as he recognized an Assyrian onslaught was imminent, he fortified the wall of the city to withstand the Assyrian battering ram and apparently built a 1,700-foot-long tunnel under the city wall to bring in water. He also summoned Isaiah the prophet for counsel. Archaeology bears out this entire narrative, including excavation of a hastily widened city wall, a remarkable tunnel hewn out of rock, and a bulla of Isaiah discovered just feet from where a bulla of Hezekiah was also found. In addition, the stone *Taylor Prism* and the near identical *Prism of Sennacherib* record the Assyrian account of the destruction of the cities north of Jerusalem, the siege of Jerusalem, and an Assyrian withdrawal.[21] In other words, when it comes to the story of Hezekiah, it's particularly difficult to put it in the category of myth.

- After Hezekiah, the kingdom of Judah generally declined, and eventually the Bible says that God allowed for the dismantling of the Jewish state by King Nebuchadnezzar and the Babylonian army. The *Babylonian Chronicles* discusses the very same events on stone tablets, specifically mentioning the replacement of Judah's King Jehoiachin by a king of Nebuchadnezzar's choice, just as the Bible says. When Nebuchadnezzar eventually toppled Jerusalem and reduced its temple to rubble, the Jews who remained alive were largely taken captive to serve in Babylon. They remained there, the Bible says, until King Cyrus of Persia conquered Babylon and allowed the Jews to return to Jerusalem and worship their God. This too is corroborated on the beautiful stone *Cyrus Cylinder* inscribed by Cyrus' court that is now on display in the British Museum in London.

To be sure, not every person, place, or event in the Old Testament has been corroborated by such outside sources as archaeological artifacts and ancient documents. This does not mean, however, that evidence exists that undermines the Old Testament, but only that for some people, places, or events, we simply do not have evidence of any sort. But the question probably should not be "Do we have an outside source that backs up each and every detail?" but rather "Where outside information is available, does it consistently indicate what we find in the Old Testament?"

Suppose you interviewed your grandfather soon before his death. He spoke of his birthplace and his childhood friends. He told you of his different jobs, and his time spent in battle. Perhaps you wonder if he was fabricating parts of the story along the way, and so you do a little research. You check out birth certificates and military service records. You speak to some of his acquaintances, physically inspect some of the places of which he spoke, and read newspaper accounts of events of which he said he was a part. In the process, you confirm a number of major details of what your grandfather told you. You do not have evidence for everything he said, but given that what you do have matches his story, you gain confidence in the details for which you don't have external sources. And you would not be unusual in doing so, because we lend this kind of credibility to much of what we learn from others. So, perhaps, it is not too outlandish to lend the same kind of credibility to the Old Testament given the evidence that is available to us.

Historical Evidence for the New Testament Gospels

Many have said, and I think rightly so, that Christianity hinges on the person of Jesus. I'll have more to say on that later, but for now let me just say that if Jesus did not do or say the things the New Testament record, you would do well to ignore Christianity all together.

So, what do we know about this Jesus person? First, we must look at the four biographies of Jesus found in the Bible, often referred to as Gospels. These Gospels all date to the first century, just decades after Jesus lived. As previously noted, early church documents indicate that they were all written by eyewitnesses or those with direct access to eyewitnesses. Furthermore, they were written in a style similar to other biographies of the day,[22] suggesting that the authors did not intend for us to read them as metaphors or grand parables but rather as verified accounts of the life of Jesus. Some critics dismiss the Gospels out of hand because they were written by Jesus' followers. If we took that approach for other biographies throughout history, we would have to discount any biography written by a friend or admirer, and most certainly every autobiography. This, of course, would leave us without many important details, because who better to know the inside scoop on someone's life than those closest to him or her. By saying this, I am not discounting the possibility of bias or fabrication; I am merely saying that unless there are outside sources that call an insider's account into question, we do well not to doubt what we are told.[23]

But even if we are inclined to accept the Gospels as historical accounts, it is still helpful to have numerous outside sources that corroborate the New Testament account of the life of Jesus. For example, there are seven non-Christian writers who mention Jesus in the 100 years following his death, as well as an additional source that mentions him shortly thereafter. These sources are Thallus, Tacitus, Flavius Josephus, Marion Bar-Serapion, Phlegon, Pliny the Younger, Lucian, and Celsus. Collectively, they corroborate the following important details about the life of Jesus:

1. Jesus lived during the reign of Tiberius Caesar.
2. He spent time in Judea, Galilee, and Egypt.
3. He possessed unusual powers.
4. He had a brother named James.
5. He was wise and influential and taught a high moral code.
6. He was called the Messiah.
7. He could accurately predict the future.
8. He was crucified under Pontius Pilate on the eve of Passover.
9. The day Jesus was crucified became dark and an earthquake shook at his death.
10. His disciple spoke of his resurrection.

To get a feel for the information ancient historians left us about Jesus, consider the words of Flavius Josephus, a first-century, Roman-Jewish historian who wrote with the blessing of Rome:

> At this time there was a wise man who was called Jesus. And his conduct was good, and [he] was known to be virtuous. And many people from among the Jews and the other nations became his disciples. Pilate condemned him to be crucified and to die. But those who had become his disciples did not abandon his discipleship. They reported that he had appeared to them three days after his crucifixion and that he was alive; accordingly he

was perhaps the Messiah, concerning whom the prophets have recounted wonders.[24]

Apart from references to Jesus by early non-Christian historians, we have many other indications that the Gospels represent reliable accounts. For example, the sources mentioned above also speak of the same Jewish rulers, religious leaders, and Roman overseers that the Gospel writers mention. And a trove of ancient artifacts have been uncovered that corroborate the Gospel accounts, like the *Pilate Stone* (which verifies the governorship of Pilate), the *Pool of Siloam* (the location of Jesus' healing of a blind man), and even the *Ossuary of Alexander* (a burial box used for the bones of a man mentioned in the Gospel of Mark).

Historical Evidence of The Early Church

After the resurrection of Jesus, the New Testament repeats three claims regarding the early church: Its followers grew rapidly in number and the church grew far and wide; Christians were often persecuted; and they often spoke and acted as if Jesus were God. These claims often are corroborated by the same non-Christian sources mentioned above. But because the writings of Pliny the Younger manage to document all three, they are particularly valuable.

Pliny was an early second-century Roman governor of a region in northwest Turkey, and on one occasion he wrote to Emperor Trajan to receive approval for the manner in which he was treating (or, shall I say, mistreating) Christians. In the letter,[25] he describes Christians as coming from "all ages and ranks and of both sexes" and states that Christianity is "not confined only to cities, but has also spread through the villages and rural districts."[26] So great had the movement become that the demand for animals to sacrifice to the Romans gods had dropped substantially. Pliny's response to the movement was to call Christians to trial to recant their beliefs. If they refused, they were executed. Many would not recant and during their trial admitted to "singing in alternate verse a hymn to Christ as to a god, and of binding themselves by a solemn oath, not to wicked deeds, but never to commit any fraud, theft, or adultery, never to falsify their word, nor to deny a pledge when they were called upon to deliver."[27] Although Pliny wrote a few decades after the New Testament narrative was complete, and was certainly not a sympathizer of Christianity, his description is strikingly similar to what the Bible records about the spread of the early church in the Book of Acts, and about their worship and persecution.

The historical nature of the biblical account of the early church can also be confirmed by a detailed search of the people and places recorded by Luke. Luke was an early follower of Jesus who wrote a two-volume history. The first volume we know as the Gospel of Luke and recounts the life of Jesus. The second volume, referred to as Acts, reports on the activities of the early church, particularly the activities centered around its two main leaders, Peter and Paul. Christians had long insisted Acts was written in the first century AD and accurately recorded eyewitness accounts. Sir William Ramsay, who would become the foremost authority on the history of Asia Minor in his day, sought to prove them wrong. In the end, however, he recognized:

> Acts was written by a great historian, a writer who set himself to record the facts as they occurred, a strong partisan, indeed, but raised above partiality by his perfect confidence that he had only to describe the facts as they occurred, in order to make the truth of Christianity and the honour of Paul apparent.[28]

He came to this conclusion after finding not a single error in any of Luke's descriptions of 32 countries, 54 cities, and nine islands and Luke's accurate use of particular titles for various rulers (like *politarch*, *tetrarch*, and *protos*) that only someone familiar with first-century rulers in specific locations could provide.[29]

Of course, all of these corroborative details may not convince you. Perhaps you still find reasons to call the Bible, and particularly the biblical account of Jesus and the early church, an elaborate conspiracy theory. You may surmise, as do others, that the leaders of the early church so enjoyed the limelight they had with Jesus that they sought to keep it going by developing a legendary story line to puff up their cause. This is a possibility, but I question its plausibility on two counts. First, if one takes a look at how the original disciples are portrayed, it often is not very flattering. They are slow to understand Jesus, for which Jesus rebukes them. When Jesus extends mercy, the disciples want to judge people. Jesus told disciples countless times of his ensuing death, but they were nonetheless caught by surprise. On one occasion, the mother of James and John attempts to secure for them a seat next to Jesus in heaven behind the other disciples' back. Peter denies knowing Jesus after saying he would stand with him through thick and thin. Thomas doubts that Jesus rose from the dead even when his friends told him they had seen him alive. In other words, there is as much in the Gospels to make you turn from the disciples as there is to join them. One would think that if the disciples made up the story about Jesus to gain their own following, they would have tweaked the story to make themselves look a whole lot better.

The second reason it is implausible for disciples to fabricate the Jesus story for personal gain is because of the enormous cost associated with maintaining the story. Some of this cost came in the form of persecution that is spoken of in the Bible; some of it, however, is recorded outside of the Bible. And, while this outside record isn't always consistent and sometimes questionable, it's almost never pretty. Speared, beheaded, crucified, exiled is how the record in many cases reads.[30] Undoubtedly, there have been those who have been persecuted for their religion. But in nearly every case where people endure persecution, they do so for what they believe to be true, not for what they know to be false. In the case of the disciples, they would have endured persecution and sometimes even death[31] for what they fabricated and knew to be false. Perhaps it is plausible for one or two of them to endure persecution or death for a lie, but all of them? That seems a bit far-fetched.

THE BIBLE'S AUTHORITY

It's one thing to say the Bible we read today has been copied well and is historically accurate, but it's quite another to say that it is humankind's clearest insight into God himself and that it is a definitive source on how we might enjoy a relationship with God. We don't often read a history book and then begin to worship its main character. And rarely do we alter the way we treat others because of what we read about Marco Polo's travels or the manner in which the pharaohs built the pyramids. So even if the Bible is historically accurate, why should we say that it is the "word of God," and thus more worthy of our attention than any other book?

Self-Testimony
If there is anything I want to avoid in a book like this, it is simply to say

you should believe the Bible because it says so. I say this not because I doubt the Bible is trustworthy but because I know that to trust the Bible just because it says you should sounds like circular reasoning. That said, I still think it's important to see what the Bible has to say about itself. If you bring in a suspect for questioning, along the way you will probably want to ask him if he committed the crime, or at least if he was at the scene of the crime or had a certain motive. Now, of course, he may lie through his teeth, but if he happens to be the perpetrator and freely tells you what he did, your case is pretty much made at that point. The same would be true for the Bible as well. If Scripture said it wasn't God's word to us, or if it pointed us toward some other teaching for direction in life, then we could dismiss the Bible and its divine authority. So what does the Bible have to say about itself?

The Bible frequently claims that its words are indeed from God. For example, the phrase "This Lord says," or something very similar, appears hundreds of times in the Old Testament.[32] While this phrase doesn't preface every statement in the Bible, elsewhere the Bible claims that the prophets who wrote the words of the Old Testament did not write them on their own. Peter, one of Jesus' disciples, was clear on this point when he wrote: "Above all, you must realize that no prophecy in Scripture ever came from the prophet's own understanding, or from human initiative. No, those prophets were moved by the Holy Spirit, and *they spoke from God*" (emphasis added, 2 Peter 1:20-21). Jesus was big on what the Old Testament had to say as well, even declaring that if you "ignore the least commandment and teach others to do the same, you will be called the least in the Kingdom of Heaven" (Matthew 5:19). It's not surprising then that Paul, a big contributor to the New Testament, wrote: "All Scripture is inspired by God and is useful to teach us what is true and to make us realize what is wrong in our lives. It corrects us when we are wrong and teaches us to do what is right" (2 Timothy 3:16). The Scripture Paul spoke of here was probably the Old Testament, but later Peter says that the testimony of the apostles found in the New Testament is of the same authority as what the Old Testament prophets recorded (2 Peter 3:2).

So the Bible clearly declares that it is God's word to humanity and that we ought to heed what it has to say. Again, you might pawn this off as just one more part of a big charade, but given this self-testimony, we can't dismiss the claim that the Bible is God's word as easily as we could if it did not speak of itself in such an authoritative way.

Authenticating Miracles

Suppose each day as you walk to your office, you pass the spot where a local street preacher sets his post. He is not obnoxious, like some you have seen and heard, but nonetheless you often chuckle as you walk by and rarely give him much more than a passing glance. But would you start to pay attention to the preacher if suddenly you saw him perform a miracle or two? If your paraplegic co-worker was healed when he touched her legs or if the blind homeless man, whom you also often walked past, regained his sight at the preacher's command, would you become more interested in what the man had to say? I'm not sure what your answer would be, but I'm guessing the crowd listening to the preacher would quickly swell. And it would swell because anyone can say this or that about God but when he starts doing miracles, it makes one wonder if his words are more than religious ramblings.

The Bible suggests that God understands this dynamic and was willing to use miracles along the way to authenticate the words of those who spoke in his name. For instance, when God tapped Moses on the shoulder to lead the Israelites out of Egypt, Moses protested. One of Moses' concerns was that the people would not believe he had really been selected to be God's spokesman. So God gave Moses a few miracles to perform, like turning a staff into a snake and back again, to verify that the words Moses spoke were from God. Likewise, when Jesus' teaching was doubted, he pointed to his miracles, saying, "Don't believe Me unless I carry out My Father's work. But if I do His work, believe in the evidence of the miraculous works I have done, even if you don't believe Me" (John 10:37-38). You could even argue that the reason the apostles' teaching was taken so seriously after Jesus' resurrection was not just because they could point back to Jesus and his miracles, which they did, but because they too were given the ability to perform miracles. If the miracles in the Bible are historical narrative as they are presented to be, they go a long way in making one believe that those recorded in the Bible were speaking the authoritative word of God.

Fulfilled Prophecy

March Madness and the Super Bowl seem to bring out the gambler in many of us. People who hardly watch a game on television and won't ever spend a dollar on a lottery ticket nonetheless contribute $20 to the office betting pool. In some cases, you only have to pick a winner, but many pools have you bet on a certain score. Unless you have a lot of

participants, hardly anyone ever picks the precise score of the final outcome. There are just too many possibilities to get it dead right. Let's say,
however, that prior to this year's Super Bowl pool, you watch how others
in your office are betting on games throughout the regular season. One
gal's picks really catch your eye. The first week she predicts the outcome
and nails the score precisely. Everyone decries her "lucky" guess, but
the next week, she does just the same, and the week after, and the week
after. In fact, she accurately predicts the precise score of every game on
which she places a bet. At first, you may have ignored her, but when it
comes time for the Super Bowl, you make note of her prediction, skip
the office pool, and place $100,000 with a bookie in Vegas. Before your
betting limit was $20, but now you put at stake what has taken years
to save. Why such behavior? The reason is clear: Consistent, accurate
predictions have given you confidence that the prognosticator is on to
something.

Throughout the Bible, prophets make predictions based on what
they learn from God. They make these predictions not to make a show
of things but so people might gain confidence that what they are saying is from God. Most of the time the prophets spoke about how their
listeners should behave toward God and others, but God knew people
would disregard their words if they were not accompanied by either
miracles or prophecy. On one occasion, God addresses the importance
of authentication when it comes to prophecy. He said,

> But you may wonder, "How will we know whether or not a proph-
> ecy is from the LORD?" If the prophet speaks in the LORD's name
> but his prediction does not happen or come true, you will know
> that the LORD did not give that message. That prophet has spo-
> ken without My authority and need not be feared. (Deuteronomy
> 18:21-22)

When it comes to the predictions the biblical prophets made, quite a
few were fulfilled in the lifetime of the prophet. For example, Isaiah
prophesied the defeat of the armies of Assyria just before that defeat
took place, and Daniel prophesied the defeat of the Babylonians the
night before Persia unleashed a surprise attack. While these prophecies
are noteworthy, some argue that they were added after the event to make
the prophet look like he had some inside track on God. That kind of

argument may have force in some cases, but in other cases (such as when prophecies are made about Jesus), it completely breaks down. Earlier I spoke of the *Dead Sea Scrolls*. These scrolls include prophecies about the Messiah, which Jesus later fulfilled, and were recorded well before the period of time when Jesus lived. Thus, we know they were not added later to puff up the prophet or make Jesus stand out as the Messiah after the fact. Here is a sampling of these prophecies:

SELECTED OLD TESTAMENT PROPHECIES OF JESUS

Prophecy	Prediction	Fulfillment
Descendant of Abraham	Genesis 22:18	Matthew 1:1
Descendant of Judah	Genesis 49:10	Luke 3:23,33
Descendant of David	Isaiah 11:1	Luke 3:23,31
Born in Bethlehem	Micah 5:2	Matthew 2:1
Presented with gifts	Psalm 72:10	Matthew 2:1,11
Preceded by a messenger	Isaiah 40:3	Matthew 3:1
Ministry of miracles	Isaiah 35:5,6	Matthew 9:35
Teacher of parables	Psalm 78:2	Matthew 13:34
Enter Jerusalem on a donkey	Zechariah 9:9	Luke 19:35
Betrayed by a friend	Psalm 41:9	Matthew 10:4
Betrayed for 30 pieces of silver	Zechariah 11:12	Matthew 26:15
Forsaken by his own disciples	Zechariah 13:7	Mark 14:50
Hands and feet pierced	Psalm 22:16	Luke 23:33
Prayed for his persecutors	Isaiah 53:12	Luke 23:34
Killed alongside thieves	Isaiah 53:12	Matthew 27:38
Clothes divided by casting of lots	Psalm 22:18	John 19:23,24
Gall and vinegar offered to him	Psalm 69:21	Matthew 27:34
His side pierced	Zechariah 12:10	John 19:34
Buried in a rich man's tomb	Isaiah 53:9	Matthew 27:57-60
Resurrection	Psalm 16:10	Acts 2:31

In some cases, the prophecies of Jesus may be unremarkable. For example, Abraham had many descendants, so the chance of Jesus being a descendant of Abraham is not that unlikely. But the specificity of other prophecies often does stand out, like that of Jesus' hands and feet being pierced. Roman crucifixion had yet to be invented when King David made the prediction, so the likelihood of the coming Messiah fulfilling that prophecy has to be rather low. Of course, one might argue that Jesus could orchestrate the fulfillment of some of these details, such as riding into Jerusalem on a donkey like a king, but it is hard to imagine Jesus orchestrating his own birth in Bethlehem, his death alongside thieves, the price by which he would be betrayed, and his own resurrection. Just like guessing the score of game after game seems rather implausible without some inside track, so too does the fulfillment of all these prophecies in the life of a single person.

The fulfillment of the prophecies regarding Jesus did not escape the notice of Jews in Jesus' day. The first Gospel in the New Testament was written by Matthew, a Jew who targeted his eyewitness account to Jewish readers. When telling the story of Jesus, Matthew repeatedly referred to passages of Old Testament prophecies that Jesus fulfilled. According to Matthew, Jesus' life and words were worth gold, and that gold was authenticated by the fulfillment of prophecy. Before meeting Jesus, Matthew was all about money, taxing his own Jewish people at the bidding of the occupying Romans. But when he saw Jesus' miracles and recognized the prophecies Jesus consistently fulfilled, he was convinced enough to bet not just $100,000 but his life on following Jesus.

Personal Experience

Some of us are a bit more adventurous than others. Put an unfamiliar menu item in front of us and we dig in; tell us about some new spot to explore and off we go. Others of us, however, are a bit more reluctant to try something new. This is especially so if we find our routines comfortable and reasonably effective. For a number of years after college, I taught tennis. Some of my students were eager to try techniques I suggested, and others were rather skeptical. When, however, a student was willing to give a new grip a try or alter his or her stance a bit, the results often spoke for themselves. At first, my instruction may have seemed unfounded, but when shots started going in with greater force and consistency, I knew I had a believer.

When Jesus was in Jerusalem, he often taught publicly in the temple courts. People found his teachings intriguing, yet they remained skeptical. They wondered, "How can this man claim his message is from God?" Jesus' reply was this: "Anyone who wants to do the will of God will know whether My teaching is from God or is merely My own" (John 7:17).

In other words, Jesus implied that if you want to test that his words are from God, you've got to put them into practice. On the one hand, Jesus' instruction on this matter seems backwards. Wouldn't we want to know his words are from God *before* we put them into practice? But on the other hand, he knew (as I did with my tennis students) that they'd have a hard time believing until they tried it on for size.

There is a chance someone who calls himself a Christian gave you this book. It may be that you've known him before Jesus and the Bible were anywhere on his radar. In fact, maybe the reason you were willing to read these pages is because you've seen a marked change in his life. He is not perfect, for sure, but he is not nearly as angry as he used to be. Furthermore, he is more respectful of others and tends not to get as anxious about events as he did in the past. You may have even seen him navigate a real tragedy with grace, or perhaps he's quit dissing himself for some past failure. If you asked him, my guess is he would say that since he started putting Jesus' words into practice he is more confident than ever that they are from God.

Armand Nicoli served for years as a professor of psychiatry at Harvard University. He also taught a class for more than 35 years called The Question of God, which also became the title of his book. In the class, he had students consider the argument against God as presented by Sigmund Freud and the argument for God as presented by C.S. Lewis. During his tenure at Harvard, Nicoli also completed research on those who became Christians during their time at Harvard. This is what he writes of those who converted to Christianity:

> Before their conversion experience, they referred often to an emptiness and despondency, sometimes calling it existential despair. . . . Yet, after their conversion they spoke of experiencing a sense of forgiveness that apparently helped them become less intolerant of themselves, helped them bridge the gap between what they felt they were and what they thought they ought to be, and provided resources outside themselves that made the future bridging of this gap less hopeless.[33]

For some people, understanding the authenticity of the Bible is important when considering Christianity. For others, recognizing the historical accuracy of the Bible's account is persuasive. For still others, the presence of miracles or fulfilled prophecy is compelling evidence of its authority. But for many, what convinces them that the Bible can be trusted (and is not part of some grand conspiracy theory) is that when they put Jesus' words into practice, their lives took a new course, and for the better. Maybe the same will be true for you.

Key Points

- The Bible can be trusted because it has been copied with great care over the centuries. Its authenticity is supported by:

  › The number of old copies we have available today

  › Copies that date back to near the time of the originals

  › The great similarity between the copies

- The Bible can be trusted because it is historically accurate. This is confirmed by:

  › Archaeological discoveries concerning the people, places, and events of the Old Testament

  › Records kept by non-Christians that speak of the life of Jesus

  › Information that corroborates the biblical record of the early church

  › The implausible claim that the disciples fabricated the biblical account given the inclusion of disparaging personal details and regular persecution

- The Bible's authority as God's word to humanity is supported by:

  › The Bible's self-testimony

  › Miracles by God's spokespeople

  › Fulfilled prophecy, especially that of Christ

  › What we discover when we put Jesus' words into practice

Additional Resources

Can We Trust the Gospels? Peter J. Williams

Cold Case Christianity: A Homicide Detective Investigates the Claims of the Gospels, J. Warner Wallace

Evidence that Demands a Verdict: Life-Changing Truth for a Skeptical World, Josh McDowell & Sean McDowell

The Popular Handbook of Archaeology and the Bible, Joseph M. Holden & Norman Geisler

The Old Testament Documents: Are They Reliable & Relevant? Walter C. Kaiser, Jr.

How Can a Rational Person Accept the Miracle Stories in the Bible?

Barbara's days were numbered. They had been for quite some time. She had been an active teenage girl, but then she began to trip and bump into walls. Gymnastics, her love, became impossible because she could no longer firmly hold on to the rings. The diagnosis was not good: Barbara had progressive multiple sclerosis.

For the next sixteen years, Barbara was in and out of hospitals, sometimes staying months at a time. A diaphragm was paralyzed, making one lung nonfunctional and the other operate at less than 50% capacity. To breathe, she had to be fed oxygen through a tracheostomy tube. She became legally blind, required feeding through a tube in her stomach, and lost complete control of her urination and bowel movements. By the time she found herself in hospice care in 1981, she had not been able to walk for seven years. Her muscles and joints had all become deformed, and her body was twisted into a fetal position. Doctors at the Mayo Clinic knew of no way to stop the cruel disease.

As her clock wound down, someone called into a radio program and urged people to pray for Barbara. Hundreds of people did just that, with about 450 people writing to her church saying that they were praying for her. Not long after the call to prayer, Barbara's aunt and a couple of friends entered her room on June 7, 1981, to read her some of the letters. As they were reading them, Barbara heard a voice that told her to "Get up and walk." At once, she became agitated and a friend plugged the hole in her neck so she could speak. Barbara explained about the voice she heard and asked that her family be called in. But before they arrived, she got out of bed and stood on legs that had not been functional for years. She removed herself from the oxygen. Her lungs, as later confirmed by x-rays, were now completely normal, and her sight returned. Remarkably her musculature regained its form and strength, and her posture was restored. The next day, she went to her doctor, who was aghast. He told Barbara, "This is medically impossible," but he could not refute the fact that she had been totally healed. And healed she was, for even as I write, Barbara Cummiskey is still living a healthy life.[1]

What do we do with stories like these and the hundreds like them?[2] I, for one, find them unsettling. I want to believe, but the skeptic in me still asks, "Could this really have happened?" When I talk to people about miracles, they often say they believe miracles can happen, but when I bring up an example like Barbara's, you can see their mind struggling to make sense of it all. And this is particularly true when it comes to miracles recorded in the Bible. Maybe one can swallow what the Bible says about loving your neighbor, but when Jesus starts making the paralyzed walk or raises the dead, it is easy for doubts to arise. Sure, there might be some historical characters and events recorded in the Bible, as we saw in the last chapter, but shouldn't miracles—especially the resurrection of Jesus—undermine the Bible's credibility in the mind of a rational person?

A Miracle Defined

It's helpful at the beginning of any discussion to define terms. In this case, let's define what is meant by *miracle*. Often we hear someone say something like "I got an A. It's a miracle!" Or perhaps, "The collection office at the hospital told me they cancelled my debt. That's a miracle!" When people use the term *miracle* in this way, they are speaking of something different than what I am addressing here. It might be unusual that we are able to earn an A in a difficult class, and it might have been a moment of compassion that was behind the cancelled debt, but we don't really mean that supernatural causes were responsible for those events.

When we talk of the miracles in the Bible, however, we aren't just talking about events that are unusual. We are talking about events that happened that can not be explained logically by natural causes. If blind people instantaneously gaining sight or deaf people hearing at someone's command are only unusual natural events that happen from time to time, we could pass off the Bible's "miracles" as an interesting cluster of rare yet explainable events. But it's hard to read them that way. The Bible's miracles do not come across as merely unusual occurrences;

they read like "impossible" events. They are events for which there is no known natural explanation. They are also events that do not suggest any future natural explanation. Thus, when I speak of miracles, I speak not of the merely unusual; I speak of *unusual events occurring as the result of a supernatural intervention.* That's why it is fair for you to ask, "Can a rational person accept the miracle stories in the Bible?"

The Possibility of Miracles

Some things are possible, like a major league baseball player hitting four grand slams in a single game, that have never happened. But nothing has ever happened if it wasn't first a possibility. So before we examine more carefully how reasonable it is to believe that miracles have actually happened, it is helpful first to consider the possibility of miracles regardless of whether or not one has ever happened.

If miracles are something that occur because of supernatural intervention, then the supernatural must exist for a miracle to take place. Thus, you cannot believe in miracles as I have defined them unless you also believe in the supernatural. In Chapter 2, we looked at evidence for the existence of God. If God does exist, then miracles move into the realm of possibility. Or, as some have said, "If there is a God who can act, acts of God are possible."[3] But even if you are comfortable with God's existence and recognize the possibility of miracles given a God, you may still have other upfront objections regarding the possibility of miracles. Here are a few that have come up in conversations with others:

Isn't it always more reasonable to believe a reported miracle didn't happen? If you are skeptical of miracles, you probably have David Hume to thank. You may know little to nothing about the 18th-century philosopher, but he may have spawned more doubt in the miraculous than anyone before him. Suppose you hear a story about a woman who has been diagnosed with terminal cancer suddenly coming back with a clean bill of health after her friends began to pray. Are you more likely to believe the original diagnosis and testing were wrong than that a miracle took place? If so, then you are thinking like Hume, who thought the chance of a miracle occurring is always less likely than some other explanation (like lying, or erroneous judgment, or placebo effect). Undoubtedly, a certain level of skepticism is healthy, but if we consistently apply Hume's thinking, we'd have to dismiss a great number of unusual but nonetheless true claims. For instance, suppose your father comes home from a fishing venture and declares that he caught the biggest catch the lake has ever known and that everything in his massive cooler is from a single fish. If you take Hume's approach, you cannot believe your father for the simple reason that the chance he is lying (for good motive or bad) is greater than the chance that he caught a fish that big. In fact, Hume's approach commits you to disbelieving anything that has a lower probability of happening than an alternative event, such as winning the lottery. But this, of course, goes against the fact that we regularly believe that unusual events have taken place as long as the evidence at hand is compelling. So it seems to me that we ought to do the same with miracles. That is, we should not preclude the possibility of miracles just because they are rare, and especially if the evidence of their occurrence is compelling.

I can't understand how miracles happen, so why should I believe in them? When people landed on the moon, there were those who did not believe it took place. Some believed it was a coordinated hoax, but some simply refused to believe what they could not explain. You may take the same position regarding miracles. But just because we struggle with understanding how a miracle actually happens does not necessarily mean we should take them out of the realm of possibility. It may be that understanding the mechanics of a miracle is just beyond our capabilities. A dog's ability to run cannot be understood by a flower (if a flower can understand anything!). And your ability to read an announcement about tomorrow's events is completely inexplicable to your dog. But that does not mean these events cannot happen. It only means that it is beyond the capacity of the flower to understand what a dog does, and beyond the capacity of a dog to understand what a person does. Likewise, if God has abilities that are beyond our own capacity to fully comprehend, we probably shouldn't let our inability to explain a miracle take it out of the realm of possibility. Recently, Barbara Cummiskey's husband of more than thirty years wrote that he and Barbara do not understand the miracle she experienced any more today than they did when it happened.[4] But that certainly has not kept them from believing it took place.

But if miracles happen, wouldn't they break the laws of nature? On the surface, it appears as though miracles break the laws of nature. And since the laws of nature are the most certain thing many of us know, we should be leery of anything that supposedly breaks them. But what if rather than break the laws of nature, miracles simply indicate that another law is in play. If I have set up a series of dominos spaced at a proper distance from one another, I can predict (using the laws of nature) that when the first is pushed the last in line will eventually fall. But what happens if between the pushing of the first domino and the predicted fall of the last a hand is placed between two standing dominos? Of course, the predicted event will not occur. And the prediction will prove false, not because the laws of nature were broken but because a new input was added to the chain of events. Similarly, if I put three quarters in a drawer, and three more on the next day, but find only four quarters on the third day, I do not declare that the laws of mathematics have been broken. Instead, I assume that an unexpected human input has been at play and has run off with two of my quarters![5] Such is the case for miracles. They need not break the laws of nature; they need only to add a supernatural input into the equation. In other words, miracles do not turn 2 + 2 into 5; they add a 1 to the whole calculation. And if that's the case, a rational person can entertain the possibility of miracles without fear that some law of nature has been broken.

While miracles need not break the laws of nature, it is helpful to understand that our ability to recognize them is very much dependent on the laws of nature. That is, if nature acted haphazardly, I am not sure how we would know that a miracle took place and was not just one more random event in the cosmos. As C.S. Lewis noted in his book *Miracles*: "Nothing can seem extraordinary until you have discovered what is ordinary. Belief in miracles, far from depending on an ignorance of the laws of nature, is only possible in so far as those laws are known." Thus, no one who believes in miracles should belittle the laws of nature for a moment. They just might be the backdrop on which God leaves his signature.

My mind is set, so why should I consider the possibility of miracles? When trying to answer a question like this, I find it helps to uncover any presuppositions that might be getting in the way. In my discussions with others, I see those who believe that miracles occur even though they don't have a good reason why, and those who say they wouldn't believe in one even if they saw it. Neither position is very sound. Let's suppose that on life-conducive Planet X, there are little green creatures. No one has ever seen one. One group of people says there are little green creatures on Planet X despite the lack of evidence. The other group says even if they are shown photographs from reliable sources of the little green creatures, they won't believe the creatures exist. From my vantage point, the position of both parties is too settled beforehand. One ought to be open to the possibility or impossibility of little green creatures on Planet X even if one has an initial opinion that goes the other direction. The same should be the case with the miraculous. I see no reason why a rational person should presume that miracles can or cannot happen before looking at any evidence in one direction or the other.

The Actuality of Miracles

Most sporting events can theoretically go on for weeks on end. A basketball game could endlessly tie at the end of every period of extra time. A baseball game could be even at the end of every extra inning. And a football game could have an endless set of penalties, so that one more play is allowed even after the clock reads 0:00. But while it is a possibility that such a game could never end, no one really believes a game has endlessly kept going or will ever do so in the future. And that's because the mere possibility of an event says nothing as to whether that event will actually take place. The same, of course, could be true of miracles. It is one thing to say that miracles are possible if God exists, but quite another to say that a miracle has occurred. To have confidence that miracles actually do happen, we must do more than just support their possibility; we need some way of testing whether one has ever occurred.

I, for one, know of no miracle-testing machine. We may be able to test whether a certain drug has been injected into a body, but we cannot scan for supernatural activity. But this is not entirely problematic in our search for evidence. We do not, for example, have a way to see atoms, but because scientists see their impact, they have long been convinced of their existence. In other words, they are confident of the unseen based on what they can see. Perhaps the same is true of miracles. We may not be able to see the supernatural activity directly, but what we can see may give us confidence that God has been at work. What can we see that could give us such confidence? Consider this criteria:

1. A well-observed "before" condition
2. A well-observed and dramatically improved "after" condition
3. No plausible natural process that can explain the improvement in condition
4. A specific command or prayer spoken with the purpose of supernatural intervention is made just prior to the improved condition

These criteria would not catch all miracles. Certainly, if miracles happen, they could happen with limited or no observers. For example, God could intervene so that a car accident is avoided even though the driver is completely unaware of the actions taken by God. Such an event would prevent the identification of a clear "before" and "after" condition, but the prevention of the accident would nonetheless be miraculous. Also, if miracles do occur, there is no reason to believe that God acts only if there are multiple observers or when someone prays for or commands a miracle to take place. But I employ these narrower criteria, because in doing so, I think they allow us to be even more confident in discerning whether a miracle has happened.

Using these criteria, let's reconsider the case of Barbara Cummiskey. She had a clear "before" condition. Years of progressive MS left her blind and crippled, and she had a partial shutdown of several vital systems. This was all recorded for years by doctors, including those at the well-respected Mayo Clinic. When considering Cummiskey's case, we also have a clear "after" condition that effectively restored Barbara's body, including her sight and ability to eat, breathe, and walk. All of these changes occurred suddenly on a specific day in 1981, and she remains healthy decades later. Furthermore, the changes occurred after a concerted prayer effort on her behalf and immediately after she heard a voice that told her to stand up. No medical explanation, as confirmed by her doctors, is available for this sudden change in her condition after a sixteen-year battle that took her from a healthy teen to counting her last days in hospice. It is possible not to call this a miracle—that some remarkable, natural shift in her body make-up suddenly restored all of her musculature, internal organs, and vision. But I think you would agree that it's hard to blame someone for calling this a miracle.

If Cummiskey's case stood alone, it might be easy to ignore, but it does not. Candy Gunther Brown of Indiana University, along with her colleagues, published research in the *Southern Medical Journal* regarding 22 individuals who received prayer by Christians in the presence of the researchers. The individuals had either severe hearing or visual impairment and were tested prior to receiving up-close and personal prayer on their behalf. What Brown and her colleagues found was that those who received the prayer had significantly improved hearing or vision after the prayer that went well beyond anything that could be explained by a placebo effect.[6] Brown later presented accounts and documentation of many other "miracles" in *Testing Prayer: Science and Healing,* which was published by Harvard University Press. In each case, the criteria I have laid out for miracles were met.

Most recently, the account of a woman whose blindness of 12 years was immediately cured after prayer is chronicled in the medical journal *Explore.* The woman had juvenile macular degeneration, which took her sight in a three-month period at 18 years of age. After prayer, her sight improved to as good as 20/30 vision, and her healing has remained for over 40 years.[7] As in the Cummiskey case, there is a clear and documented "before" condition, a clear and documented "after" condition, no known medical explanation, and an immediate restoration of lost sight after prayer. While these examples may not convince everyone of the existence of supernatural intervention, dismissing the possibility of a miracle out-of-hand is to ignore the evidence. In fact, if you find yourself pushing back on the Cummiskey case or another similar event, it might be helpful to ask yourself if you are doing so because of the evidence or in spite of it.

Evidence & The Miracles of Jesus

The prospect of miracles is an exciting one. As I mentioned earlier, my brother is struggling with cancer as I write, and the thought that miracles can happen gives a glimmer of hope. But my interest in miracles goes beyond "What can you do for my brother today, God?" Much of my interest lies in the potential confidence miracles can provide in the existence of God and the trustworthiness of the Bible. But as I noted in Chapter 8, if the miracles recorded in Scripture really happened, then there is added reason to take notice of the words of those who performed them. This is particularly true of the words of Jesus, who not only is the central figure in the Christian narrative but also performs more miracles than any other person in Scripture.[8] So how do Jesus' miracles match up to the miracle criteria given above? I cannot examine them all, but I will present two that Jesus performed on others and then the miracle of his own resurrection.

Healing of the Blind Mute. In the Gospel of Matthew, Jesus encounters a man who is blind and mute (Matthew 12:22-24). He is said also to be possessed by a demon, but that fact is harder to authenticate than the man's long-standing physical limitations. At Jesus' command, the man is able to see and talk, meaning that the account provides clear "before" and "after" conditions. We also see that the healing takes place immediately after the command of Jesus, and that no natural processes can account for the sudden ability of the man to see and speak. Furthermore, this miracle was recorded by what appears to be an eyewitness and was completed in front of a large crowd of witnesses that included those who hated Jesus because of his growing influence. In other words, all the criteria mentioned above are met. What is particularly telling is that Jesus' detractors did not dispute the miracle but only said that Jesus' power to perform the miracle came from Satan and not from God.

Healing of the Shriveled Hand. On a Sabbath day, early in his ministry, Jesus encountered a man whose hand was shriveled or withered (Mark 3:1-6). This provides us with a clear "before" condition recorded by one who had access to eyewitness reports of the event. At the command of Jesus, the man's hand was completely restored, so that everyone present could see that a miracle had been completed. Jesus' enemies, who were present, were so angry that he performed a miracle on the Sabbath (a day on which they said "work" of nearly any kind was forbidden), they sought to kill Jesus from this point forward. In other words, for this miracle we also have a clear "after" condition witnessed by many people, including Jesus' enemies. As with the miracle of the blind and mute man, the instantaneous change in condition at Jesus' command cannot be explained by natural processes. Again, then, all four criteria for a miracle are met when Jesus healed the man with the shriveled hand.

Of course, you could argue that the accounts of these two miracles were fabricated, but given the evidence for the historical accuracy of the Bible as presented in the previous chapter, any claim of fabrication without supporting evidence is not particularly strong. This is especially so since post-biblical accounts of Jesus by detractors of Christianity consistently confirm the miracle-producing ministry of Jesus (even if they deny they were works of God).[9] In fact, even the majority of modern scholars—skeptical or otherwise—believe it is historically accurate to say that the contemporaries of Jesus experienced him as one who performed miracles.[10]

The Miracle of Jesus' Resurrection

From a biblical standpoint, there is no miracle bigger than Jesus' resurrection. As mentioned previously, the Bible even declares that if the resurrection did not happen as a historical event in actual time and space, then anyone and everyone is free to dismiss the entire Christian narrative (1 Corinthians 15:12-19). So what is the evidence surrounding the resurrection? It includes the following:

- Jesus was crucified by the Romans under the direction of Pontius Pilate and died.
- The tomb in which Jesus was laid after his death was soon found empty, even though leaders who opposed the ministry of Jesus posted guards at the tomb.
- There are records of the resurrected Jesus appearing to a large variety of people over a forty-day period, and in many instances to more than one person at a time. These appearances were in many different settings and showed Jesus eating, talking, and walking with those to whom he appeared.
- After Jesus' resurrection appearances, his disciples were transformed from a scared group of men fearing for their lives to bold proclaimers of Jesus' resurrection. Their proclamations, even in the face of persecution, led to the spread of Christianity throughout the Roman empire.
- Some of those who were against Jesus' ministry, such as Paul of Tarsus or James (the brother of Jesus), began to proclaim that Jesus was the Christ after the resurrected Jesus appeared to them. And they proclaimed this message, despite heavy persecution for making such a claim.

Again, these details are shared in the Bible, but many of them are also reported by ancient writers who were not followers of Jesus or supporters of Christianity, such as Tacitus, Thallus, Josephus, Lucian, Mara bar Serapian, and Phlegon. So how is one supposed to deal with this evidence—evidence that shows clear before and after conditions that are hard to explain? And, in particular, how have skeptics responded to it? Skeptics have generally dealt with it in one of three ways. First, they say that those who originally experienced the events (namely, the disciples) were in some way fooled by what they saw. Second, they charge the disciples and their companions with deliberately creating an elaborate hoax. Or third, they conclude that the resurrection of Jesus is a legend that grew after Jesus' death and has no basis in fact. If the resurrection was some "side show" in the biblical narrative, I'd probably briefly reply to these objections, but given that Jesus' resurrection is the linchpin of

Christianity, I am going to spend a few pages giving my response. So feel free to skip to the particular objection you may have.

Objection #1: The Disciples Were Fooled. If one is unprepared to turn the disciples into grand conspirators, it's possible to say that they were simply mistaken. Some, for example, have suggested that Jesus didn't really die at the time of his crucifixion. Instead, he went unconscious and was later revived. Upon seeing him, the disciples then mistakenly concluded that he had risen from the dead and began to tell others what they saw. But is this explanation plausible?

Apart from the implication that Jesus would have allowed this misconception to continue without correcting it, this theory is questionable given what Jesus would have experienced prior to being placed in the tomb as dead. Not only was Jesus brutally beaten before crucifixion, but he was then nailed to a cross that was designed to suffocate people with 100% efficiency. To ensure his death, Jesus' side was pierced by a Roman guard so that his bodily fluids rushed out from his side while he was on the cross. Furthermore, the same Roman guard specifically reported to Pilate that Jesus was most assuredly dead. Even if somehow Jesus was barely alive, he was then wrapped in burial clothes and placed in a tomb whose entrance was blocked by a massive stone and guarded. Could Jesus really have survived, made his way out of the tomb, and appeared so well that his disciples would triumphantly declare that he had risen from the dead? Common sense says this recharacterization of the resurrection claim is far-fetched. In fact, an article published in the esteemed *Journal of the American Medical Association* examined the likelihood of Jesus surviving the torture and crucifixion he endured and came to the same conclusion:

> Clearly, the weight of historical and medical evidence indicates that Jesus was dead before the wound to his side was inflicted and supports the traditional view that the spear, thrust between his right ribs, probably perforated not only the right lung but also the pericardium and heart and thereby ensured his death. Accordingly, interpretations based on the assumption that Jesus did not die on the cross appear to be at odds with modern medical knowledge.[11]

Given the realities surrounding the crucifixion, others say that the disciples were not fooled by a not-so-dead Jesus but rather by going to the wrong tomb, which happened to be empty. Upon seeing the tomb empty, they errantly concluded that Jesus had resurrected from the dead. This theory is also problematic for a number of reasons. First, Jesus was not buried in an unknown tomb. All four Gospels state that he was buried in a tomb owned by Joseph of Arimathea, who was a member of the Jewish ruling council. There is no reason to doubt this claim since other members of the council would have easily countered the claim if it were not true.[12] Also, if the disciples went to the wrong tomb and then started preaching about Jesus' resurrection, the enemies of Jesus and the disciples would have simply produced the body from the proper tomb. Finally, even if the disciples did go to the wrong tomb, this does not account for the appearances of Jesus after his death.

A third theory held by those who believe the disciples were fooled is that the appearances of a resurrected Jesus were merely hallucinations. That is, the disciples were so distraught by Jesus' death that they imagined they saw him alive again. But while it is true that people hallucinate, there is no modern psychological evidence for the phenomenon of group hallucination. And since the resurrected Jesus often appeared to many people at one time, the hallucination theory is dubious. As Gary Collins, a noted psychologist, has said:

> Hallucinations are individual occurrences. By their very nature only one person can see a given hallucination at a time. They certainly aren't something which can be seen by a group of people. Neither is it possible that one person could somehow induce an hallucination in somebody else. Since an hallucination exists only in this subjective, personal sense, it is obvious that others cannot witness it.[13]

Furthermore, those who saw Jesus did more than see a vision of him. They reported touching Jesus, hearing him speak, and even enjoying a meal with him, even though the record indicates they had no previous hope or expectation of him resurrecting from the dead. Add to this that some who saw the resurrected Jesus did not believe him to be the Messiah prior to his death and it's hard to claim that the sightings were the result of wish fulfillment in the face of loss.

Objection #2: The Disciples Created an Elaborate Hoax. Rather than believe the disciples were fooled, some suggest Jesus' resurrection was a deliberate hoax developed by the disciples and their close companions to gain a personal following after the death of Jesus. This theory also has significant challenges. First, one must still account for the empty tomb. If the disciples made up the story, it would be easy for their detractors to point out that Jesus was still in his tomb. Of course, you could argue that the disciples stole the body to make it look like Jesus left the tomb, but that scenario is not particularly plausible given the vaunted guard posted at the tomb and the fact that the disciples largely fled the scene when Jesus was arrested and crucified.[14]

Second, if the hoax was initiated to build a new movement centered on the disciples, it is hard to explain why there are so many embarrassing details in the Gospel accounts, as discussed in the last chapter.[15] Those who desperately wanted to create a hoax to promote the cause of the disciples would have certainly taken out details about the disciples' own disbelief of Jesus' teaching, their great fear at the time of Jesus' trial and crucifixion, and their reluctance to accept his resurrection. Such details hardly make the disciples venerated heroes of a cause. In addition, the resurrection accounts consistently say that it was women who first discovered Jesus' tomb was empty and met the resurrected Jesus. This, too, is an embarrassing detail. In first-century Jewish thought, the testimony of a woman was of little value,[16] meaning that if the Gospel writers fabricated the resurrection account, they would have undermined their own efforts by making women the first witnesses. If one asks, "Why then all the embarrassing details?" the most reasonable answer is because the followers of Jesus were willing to provide an honest account even if it put them in a bad light.

Third, hoaxes are largely perpetrated because personal gain is somehow expected. Given Jesus' persecution and death, however, the most reasonable assumption of the disciples would have been that they too would experience persecution, and even death, if they sought to further Jesus' claims. Why then would the disciples, who at first responded in great fear at Jesus' arrest and crucifixion, so swiftly create a hoax that had a good chance of leading to their own death? As mentioned in Chapter 7, it is true that throughout history some people have been willing to undergo intense persecution and death for what they believe to be true, but if the resurrection were a hoax, the disciples would have endured persecution and, in some cases, death for something they knew to be false. Think about that for a moment. You might be willing to endure an arduous and life-threatening rescue effort for someone you believed to be in danger (even though your belief later was discovered to be false), but would you do the same if you knew in advance the report of their precarious state was false?

Fourth, suppose the disciples, for some unknown reason, were willing to die for something they knew to be false. Could we really expect all of them to keep up their story when the pressure was on, especially when they were separated and would have had no way of knowing if one of the other disciples had already "given up the game"? Consider if you and a few high school classmates made up a story of seeing a teacher steal a school computer. The school's administrators looked into the matter and then threatened you with severe penalties if you did not recant your story. Even if your story were true, you would be tempted to "confess" the hoax just to avoid discipline. How much more so if you had fabricated the story and if you did not know if the others had already confessed! This illustration is precisely the point made by Charles Colson, who served as Special Counsel under President Nixon. When he and his co-conspirator's involvement in Watergate was discovered, it took them little time, given the pressure of severe penalty, to give up their false alibi. Later when Colson compared the reaction of the Watergate conspirators to the disciples' firm stance on the resurrection, he wrote:

> Here were the 10 most powerful men in the United States. . . . With all that power, and we couldn't contain a lie for two weeks. . . . Take it from one who was involved in conspiracy, who saw the frailty of man firsthand . . . there is no way the 11 apostles, who were with Jesus at the time of the resurrection, could ever have gone around for 40 years proclaiming Jesus' resurrection unless it were true.[17]

Fifth, if the disciples fabricated the resurrection account, one has to wonder to whom they thought the story would appeal. There were two main camps among the Jews regarding the resurrection. One camp did not believe in the bodily resurrection of the dead, period. The other camp believed that *all* the righteous would be resurrected *after* the end of the world. In other words, Jewish audiences had no expectation or belief that an individual could be bodily resurrected in the present age. Given these Jewish expectations regarding the resurrection, a hoax involving a resurrection would have been dead in the water unless there was good evidence at hand.

Some might argue that instead of trying to woo Jews, the disciples sought to appeal to Gentile audiences, and thus drew from pagan myths about resurrection. But, contrary to popular contemporary claims, stories of *bodily* resurrection do not exist in ancient literature. Yes, there are stories of dying and rising gods in pagan mythology, but none of these tales remotely involve a human hero who dies and is bodily resurrected on earth.[18] To this point, noted scholar N.T. Wright declares that in ancient thought bodily resurrection was "something everyone knew could not happen,"[19] meaning that when the ancients read stories about dying and rising gods "nobody in the ancient world took these stories as evidence of *resurrection*"[20] in a bodily sense. Furthermore, it is interesting to note that many of the non-Christian stories about dying and rising suddenly began to appear *after* the death and resurrection of Jesus,[21] suggesting that it was not Christianity that borrowed from ancient mythological sources but the other way around.[22] So, as with the Jews, the resurrection account of the disciples could not have hoped to generate much interest among the Gentiles unless there was solid evidence the bodily resurrection of Jesus had occurred.

Finally, even if the disciples had something to gain from propagating the resurrection story, it is hard to see what someone like Paul of Tarsus would have had to gain. He was advancing well up the ranks of Judaism in part because of his willingness to search out and persecute Christians. Unless Paul saw the resurrected Jesus as he claims, one must question why he would go from persecuting Christians to boldly proclaiming a resurrected Christ and enduring severe persecution himself. The same is true of Jesus' brother, James, who was a skeptic until after the appearance of the resurrected Jesus.[23]

Objection #3: Jesus' Resurrection Is a Legend. If the theory that Jesus' disciples were fooled is not well founded, and if the idea that the disciples created a hoax is equally problematic, could it be possible that the evidence provided by Jesus' resurrection is not the product of reliable eyewitness accounts but a later embellishment? In other words, could it be that after Jesus' demise a legend grew up about his resurrection, and that these legendary accounts have been mistaken as historical facts? These are valid questions given that legends have certainly arisen around historical characters that do not accurately represent history. (Just think George Washington and the legend of chopping down a cherry tree.) Had the stories of the resurrection not come about until many years after the death of the disciples and other witnesses of the resurrection, it would have been easy to claim the resurrection account as legendary embellishments. But New Testament scholars (both supporters and critics of Christianity) almost unanimously agree that the four Gospels accounts were written in the 70 years after Jesus, and three of the four within 40 years. In addition, scholars date a number of the other New Testament books that also speak of Jesus' resurrection to within 20 to 40 years of Jesus' death. One particular portion of 1 Corinthians contains a creed about the resurrection that many, including skeptics, date back to within ten years of Jesus' death.[24] All in all, then, there was little time for a legend to grow without encountering opposition from those who would have been well aware of the actual details concerning Jesus' death and who would have had motive to disprove the disciples' account.

This said, it is still possible for a legend to have grown up even in a short time span, as it did for Alexander the Great soon after his death or for George Washington. (The legendary story of him chopping down a cherry tree was first printed only seven years after his death.) But if one claims that the resurrection of Jesus was an early legend, we face many of the same problems associated with the hoax theory. For example, how does the legendary development account for the empty tomb or for the conversion of Paul and James, all of which are historical facts affirmed by the vast majority of New Testament scholars, skeptic or otherwise?[25] And why would the disciples endure persecution even to death if the resurrection was just myth. Also, if the resurrection were an early legend, why would the church grow so rapidly even in Jerusalem, where people would have known the facts about Jesus' death and entombment, and at a time when persecution was expected for those who followed Christ?

The Best-Fit Explanation of the Evidence. Theories, whether they have to do with the makeup of the cosmos, historical events, or a crime scene, try to make the best sense of the available evidence. Suppose, for example, that a man is found lying dead on the ground. Four main theories are possible: He died of natural causes, as a result of an accident, by suicide, or at the hands of a murderer. If, however, he is found with multiple knife wounds in his back, that evidence better supports the theory that he was murdered.[26] Is it possible that one of the other three explanations is true? Yes, it is possible, but without substantial evidence pointing in some other direction, the theory that he was murdered is the most plausible.

When it comes to the resurrection, theories that suggest the disciples were fooled, developed an elaborate hoax, or were simply figures in a legendary account, have considerable weaknesses when considering the evidence. But what happens if we consider the possibility that the resurrection was a historical event—which the disciples and others really experienced, and they interacted with a resurrected Jesus within days of his crucifixion? In this case, we can account for the empty tomb and the early records of Jesus' resurrection by multiple witnesses. In addition, if it is a truthful story, not concerned with embellishment, the inclusion of women in the resurrection account and the embarrassing details concerning the disciples' initial lack of belief in the resurrection make sense. A historical resurrection also accounts for the disciples' willingness to boldly speak of Jesus' resurrection even in the face of great persecution, and the willingness of skeptics like James and Paul to start doing the same. Finally, given that there was no social power or privilege afforded by following the teaching of the disciples, the historical resurrection of Jesus provides an explanation as to why the church grew far and wide within years of the event.

When looking at the evidence, is it possible to arrive at a conclusion other than a bodily resurrection? Of course, it is. But the more important question is: Does an alternative conclusion better fit the evidence? I don't think so. The historical resurrection of Jesus is the most plausible explanation of the evidence. It accounts for *all* of the evidence, something that no other explanation can adequately do.[27] As resurrection expert Dr. Gary Habermas has said, "Sometimes people just grasp at straws trying to account for the appearances [of the resurrected Jesus after his death]. But nothing fits all the evidence better than the explanation that Jesus was alive."[28]

The resurrection of Jesus is a miracle, but as with the other biblical miracles, there is a clear "before" condition (he was dead), a clear "after" condition (he was alive), and no known natural process that could have caused the change in condition. In addition, Jesus claimed in advance that his resurrection would take place. This means that all four criteria for a miracle have been met—good reason to believe that the bodily resurrection of Jesus actually took place.

Returning to the Original Question

Can a rational person believe the miracle stories in the Bible? That's the question this chapter asks, and perhaps it is a question you have asked as well. When you were younger you may have told a friend with utter confidence that Santa Claus was real. Maybe you even got in an argument about it. Later, you realized your friend was right. What you were convinced was true was nothing but a fairy tale. I think people have that same fear when it comes to the Bible. They recognize it has some good things to say, but they don't want to get caught standing up for something littered with fanciful stories that have little basis in fact. I understand this fear. I, too, have stood up for things I later found to be false. But I don't have that fear when it comes to the miracles of the Bible. Oh sure, they are remarkable events—that's why we call them miracles—but unlike the story of Santa Claus, there is good reason for a rational person to believe they took place. And, if they took place, they lend a lot of credence to all the other stuff the Bible says, stuff about love and forgiveness and eternal life. They even lend credence to the words Jesus spoke just before his death and resurrection:

> Don't let your hearts be troubled. Trust in God, and trust also in Me. There is more than enough room in My Father's home. If this were not so, would I have told you that I am going to prepare a place for you? When everything is ready, I will come and get you, so that you will always be with Me where I am. (John 14:1-3)

Key Points

- Miracles are not just uncommon events. They are events in which natural events are altered by supernatural intervention.

- Miracles are only a possibility if the supernatural exists.

- Miracles do not break the laws of nature; they simply involve an additional input into the normal chain of events.

- Whether or not miracles happen should be a question of evidence.

- Evidence clearly points to the miraculous if we see these four elements:

  › A well-observed before condition

  › A well-observed and dramatically improved after condition

  › No plausible natural process that can explain the improvement in condition

  › A specific command or prayer spoken with the purpose of supernatural intervention is made just prior to the improved condition

- Jesus performed miracles that had these four elements.

- Evidence that supports Jesus' resurrection includes:

  › His certain death by crucifixion

  › The empty tomb

  › Multiple appearances of the resurrected Jesus

  › The bold proclamation of the resurrection by the disciples in the face of persecution

  › The bold proclamation of the resurrection by former skeptics, like Paul and James, also in the face of persecution

- There are substantial weaknesses to the arguments that:

  › The disciples were fooled into thinking Jesus was resurrected

  › The disciples created an elaborate hoax around the fabricated story of the resurrection

  › Jesus' resurrection is a legend

- The evidence surrounding the resurrection accounts provides ample reason to believe the resurrection was a historical event. This is why a majority of scholars support the historical nature of the resurrection.

- Given the evidence for the miracles of the Bible, we have additional reason to trust the Bible's teaching, including Jesus' words about the possibility of eternal life.

Additional Resources

The Case for Miracles: A Journalist Investigates Evidence for the Supernatural, Lee Strobel

Miracles, C.S. Lewis

The Miracles Answer Book, Lee Strobel & Mark Mittelberg

The Case for the Resurrection of Jesus, Gary R. Habermas & Michael R. Licona

The Case for Easter: A Journalist Investigates Evidence for the Resurrection, Lee Strobel

Isn't the Bible Out of Step with the Times?

Don't you hate it when it happens? You show up to an event under the impression that casual attire is appropriate, and everyone is dressed in their finest. The opposite is nearly just as bad. I mean, who likes to arrive for a party in coat and tie or an evening dress to find everyone else in jeans? For some reason, it seems that as I've gotten older, I make the wrong fashion call more often than in the past. And when I do, I feel like walking out the side door and making a quick change. It's just no fun to be out of step with the times, even if "the times" is a three-hour evening event.

But matters can get much worse than picking the wrong clothes for a party. In grad school, I took a course on the sociology of sports. As part of the class, we had a discussion on sports as a sort of religion. The conversation was fascinating, but comments in the class made it clear that no one was particularly keen on traditional religion, and Christianity in particular. I didn't feel compelled to show my true colors, but somehow a question came directly my way that gave me no way out. Either I had to speak up on where I stood or I had to fit in with the rest of my classmates. With a racing heart, I chose to confirm my Christian faith and the class went silent. And though I made every effort to be friendly and congenial in my comments, on that day I stood alone as one clearly out of step with the times.

No one wants to be in the awkward place I found myself in during that class. So, it's no surprise when people are concerned that the Bible often finds itself at odds with some prevailing thought or practice, sometimes even with the consensus position on the most pressing issues of the day. In fact, maybe you've found yourself saying, "There may have been a time when the Bible made sense to people, but haven't times changed? Don't we know better now?"

Have the Times Always Gotten It Right?

People of every generation think that they've figured it out—that they know better how to answer the questions of life than those before them. In some cases, this might be true. For instance, I am confident we know more about DNA and cancer than people did 70 years ago. On other issues or ideas, however, I am not so sure we have any better answers than did those in ages past. People have always struggled with keeping their marriages together, for example, and I don't see much evidence that we've gotten a whole lot better at that. And when it comes to civility, I think plenty of evidence, at least in the United States, shows that we've taken a step back. Nonetheless, there is an ever-growing consensus that the present-day take on issues from sexuality to the environment and from racial justice to economic reform must trump where we've been in the past. At times, it even feels like ideas of the past are being dismissed for no reason other than that they are old. As one author poetically stated:

> the newer is the truer,
> only what is recent is decent,
> every shift of ground is a step forward,
> and every latest word must be hailed as the last word on
> its subject.[1]

Such a perspective, however, welcomes significant critique. If we are quick to dismiss voices just because they are old or don't meet the standards of today, what will the people of tomorrow do? Will they not dismiss the positions we are claiming today and say that our take on issues is unworthy of consideration—and perhaps even worthy of disdain—because our stance is out of step with their times? And if they do, it won't be just the Bible that is out of step with the times but the purveyors of today's moral standards as well. To this point, British author and producer Barry Cooper writes:

> Many social, cultural and sexual views which seem self-evidently right to most people currently living in London or Manhattan

did not seem right to Londoners and Manhattanites 200 years ago. And they don't seem right to most people currently living in Nairobi or Jakarta. Presumably, we'll believe something else in 200 years' time. If we dismiss biblical teaching as being a product of its time and place, we have to be honest and recognise that we ourselves—the ones offering the criticism—are just as much a product of ours.[2]

In the early 1900s, you likely would have found yourself out of step with the cultural tide if you did not embrace eugenics. Eugenics was quite the fad at the time and called for proper human breeding to keep "undesirables" in society from propagating. The movement led to more than half the states enacting forced sterilization laws that were carried out against not only the disabled but anyone considered "feebleminded," a label that could be attained through simple poverty or being the victim of rape. These laws earned the approval of even the Supreme Court. So intrigued was Hitler by what he saw in the States that he soon modeled the Nazi sterilization program after what he saw taking place in America.[3] One hundred years ago, eugenics was what the times were calling for, and had you stood against it, you likely would have been told your beliefs were antiquated, backward, or perhaps even dangerous.

Of course, it's not just eugenics that enjoyed popular consent in the past. Throughout history, cultures and their governing bodies have supported all kinds of repressive actions against women, various racial groups, the uneducated, religious communities, the poor, the disabled, and the list could go on and on. Clearly, then, just because the times are in support of a current course of action, we should not close ourselves off from hearing from voices that speak against whatever practice might currently be celebrated. Maybe they are the voices that will free us from something like eugenics. Certainly, this does not mean that a counter-culture voice is always right, but it should make us cautious to dismiss the Bible out of hand simply because its teaching may not fit with what is currently popular.

Is Progress Always Really Progress?

I doubt there has ever been a time, at least in the United States, when people have been freer to be who they want to be and do what they want to do. In saying that I am not suggesting that there aren't still societal ills that keep people unduly stuck. I am only saying that it's probably more acceptable now to pursue any profession you like, wear any clothes you want, and sleep with anyone of your choosing. So who would want to turn back the clock? I think this is the fear for many people when it comes to the Bible. They fear that using it as the measure of morality would hamper all the progress we have made. But just how are we to measure progress? Oh sure, I am as glad as the next person that progress now allows us to flick a switch to enjoy light or even lets Siri do it for us, but I am not so sure that everything we call progress is really progress.

I mentioned at the start of this chapter that while society has certainly made progress in understanding DNA and cancer, can we really say we've made progress in many of the deeper issues of life? I, for one, doubt that people are much better at being kind to one another, or forgiving each other, or giving others a helping hand than a generation or two ago. And if we look beyond individuals to nations, there still seems to be plenty of territorialism, imperialism, and terrorism to go around. Mortimer Adler, the late chairman of the *Encyclopædia Britannica* Board of Editors, agreed:

> And the most serious doubts about man's moral progress come from the fact that in the twentieth century human beings seem to be just as inhumane toward other human beings as they were twenty-five centuries ago. Not only in two great world wars, but in concentration camps and enforced labor camps and in a variety of ways, one seems to see man's inhumanity toward man unchanged. This is disheartening, and it seems to argue that there is no progress in man's moral character, that as he improves his institutions, as he improves his command over nature, he does not improve in his heart and soul, that man is as much the beast and brute today, only with more power than he had twenty-five hundred years ago or five thousand years ago. These are the most serious reasons for doubt that progress happens always and in all spheres of human activity.[4]

So maybe the progress we've made isn't as impressive as we are quick to claim. Perhaps all the efforts to cast off the "constraints" of religion in general, and Christianity in particular, aren't in our best interest. In fact, maybe the way forward to a better world is not by continually setting new standards of personal freedom but by looking back at the wisdom passed down through the 1,400 years the Bible was written. I like C.S. Lewis' words to this effect:

> We all want progress. But progress means getting nearer to the place you want to be and if you have taken a wrong turning, then to go forward does not get you any nearer. If you are on the wrong road, progress means doing an about-turn and walking back to the right road; and in that case, the man who turns back soonest is the most progressive man.[5]

This, of course, does not mean that progress can't be made by leaving old thinking behind. Sometimes it can. I'm only suggesting that progress and present-day popularity are not necessarily equivalent, and we should not pretend that they are. In some cases, the road we are on, such as eugenics, is just plain wrong. And when that is the case, going back to an old way of thinking might well be "the quickest way on."[6]

The Bible as a Valuable Plumb Line

The Old Testament is largely a story of God's interaction with the people of Israel, and one of God's chief means of communicating with them was through his prophets. One such prophet was named Amos. He was not a prominent figure in his day. In fact, the only biographical information we have on him is that he was a shepherd and a sycamore tree farmer. Nonetheless, God saw Amos fit to speak to the nobles of his time.

When Amos came on the scene, Israel was enjoying a significant period of prosperity, but like in many economic upturns the wealth largely stayed with those at the top while those at the bottom were considered little more than pawns for the rich. So God gave Amos a vision of a plumb line—a long string with a weight on the bottom used to make sure that building structures were constructed straight up and down and did not lean to the right or to the left. This vision was God's way of telling Amos that Israel's behavior was about to be judged not by the standards of the day but by the plumb line of God's own character (Amos 7:7-8). As you might imagine, this plumb line revealed Israel to be leaning significantly off center.

My guess is that when Israel's leaders were confronted by Amos, they offered all kinds of "sensible" justifications. Perhaps their thinking went something like this: "We deserve all we have. We work hard." "Sharing a woman with my son is like sharing a good drink." "The judgment we dished out might not have been fair, but they needed to be put in their place." As far as the Israelites were concerned, the standards of justice laid out by Amos, which were consistent with what God had said in generations past, were no longer relevant. The people knew better now, or so they thought. Within just a few decades, Israel would be overrun by the Assyrian army just as God had warned.[7]

It doesn't take marauding armies, however, for us to feel the effects of not measuring up to the biblical plumb line. Over the years I have met many men who have not been faithful to their wives. By the time they come to me, their world often has fallen apart. In the moment or season of unfaithfulness, they felt justified, and no doubt they found others who condoned their actions. But given the very real consequences of their choices, they are having serious second thoughts about the wisdom of their ways. It's at this point that they often are willing to admit that what the Bible says about their sexual forays may not be so outdated after all.

The Bible offers itself as God's plumb line, the measure outside of ourselves that can help us know how to build our lives without them falling over. It does not do so with the aim of holding us back from experiencing life to the fullest, but instead living with the sense that God's plumb line can help us find the good life without first having to run into a ditch.

The Advantages of a Timeless Plumb Line

I played a lot of sports when I was a kid, baseball and soccer in particular. I enjoyed them both, but one thing about them I didn't like too much: I didn't like that I was not in control. If practice was on Tuesday and Thursday, then that's when I had to show up. And if I played outstandingly well but my teammates faltered, I'd have to swallow the loss. Then I was introduced to tennis, and soon the other sports were left behind. I played when I wanted (which became all the time), and the results were all on my shoulders. But even when it came to tennis, I was not in control of something—the rules of the game. And come to think of it, that never really bothered me. I can't imagine if at the start of every match I had to negotiate the rules with my opponent. As much as I liked how tennis let me be in control of how I trained and the trophies that came as a result, I recognize the real advantage of not having to be the one who made up the rules of the sport or having to adjust to new rules in every season of play.

Similarly, having a consistent plumb line like the Bible can really work in our favor. In other words, we have some real advantages to not having to write up a rule book about life on our own or constantly having to adjust our viewpoints to fit in with the times. Here are a few of those advantages:

Having a consistent plumb line like the Bible can keep you from the exhaustion of calling your own shots. Suppose you have an uninformed and unsuspecting customer. Fudging a few facts about your product would hardly get noticed, but just how much do you try to get away with? A bigger lie could lead to a bigger sale. In the end, you make the call and even walk away with a nice profit. But then the next customer arrives and you have to begin the whole process of assessing what you can get away with all over again. You may see it all as a game of sorts, but that does not mean it will not take its toll. That's a toll that the sales-person who consistently values honesty does not experience.

You and I have the freedom to love or hate people as we please. We may not be able to act out against everyone as we desire, but we can harbor anything we want in our hearts. The Bible says we are wise not to exercise that freedom. The plumb line God sets is love and not hate. I had a neighbor who wasn't interested in this plumb line. He hated one of my other neighbors for years and told me about it nearly every time we spoke. He even left the neighborhood for three years, and upon his return the first words out of his mouth spoke of how much he hated his neighbor. His neighbor hadn't said or done anything in three years, but his hate would not go away. Oh sure, my neighbor is free to decide whom he will love and whom he will hate, and thus forgo the plumb line of the Bible, but holding on to that kind of freedom can be exhausting. Yes, the biblical call to love others consistently (or to be an honest salesperson) can be difficult at times, but I still find it to be the lighter load.

Having a consistent plumb line like the Bible can give you direction and confidence in the midst of competing voices. We still have much to do to eliminate racial discrimination today, but undoubtedly Martin Luther King, Jr. did a great deal to improve the situation. When I read of Dr. King and his supporters, I am amazed at their fortitude. The threats, the beatings, the lynchings, and the imprisonments would have kept many quiet. However, Dr. King would not stay silent, but neither would he start a violent uprising. Many white church leaders told him to tone it down, while some Black leaders encouraged a more aggressive approach. What gave him direction and confidence in the midst of competing voices? It was the biblical plumb line. In a 1957 article published in the *Christian Century*, MLK wrote:

> At the center of nonviolence stands the principle of love.... Along the way of life, someone must have sense enough and morality enough to cut off the chain of hate. This can be done only by projecting the ethics of love to the center of our lives....
>
> In speaking of love at this point, we are not referring to some sentimental emotion. It would be nonsense to urge men to love their oppressors in an affectionate sense. There are three words for love in the Greek New Testament.... When we speak of loving those who oppose us ... we speak of a love which is expressed in the Greek word *agape*. *Agape* means nothing sentimental or basically affectionate; it means understanding, redeeming good will for all men, an overflowing love which seeks nothing in return. It is the love of God working in the lives of men. When we love on the *agape* level we love men not because we like them, not because their attitudes and ways appeal to us, but because God loves them. Here we rise to the position of loving the person who does the evil deed while hating the deed he does.[8]

Having the plumb line of the Bible was indispensable to Dr. King's remarkable influence. It's what kept him from refusing to be silent when some told him to be quiet, and it is what kept him from turning the movement into a retaliatory blood bath. In other words, the Bible helped him be confident of his position in the midst of competing voices. Did it come with a cost because of the cultural climate of his day? Absolutely, it cost MLK his life. But, as almost anyone would recognize today, it was a cost borne in honor not shame.

Having a consistent plumb line like the Bible can keep you from using power to hurt other people. Power has a remarkable effect on us, as a number of studies have brought to light. For example, in one study of 27,000 working adults in 27 different countries, participants were asked how often it's okay to: (1) claim government benefits to which you are not entitled; (2) avoid paying a fare on public transportation; (3) cheat on taxes; and (4) accept a bribe. Their responses were then correlated with the wealth of those surveyed, or shall we say their economic power. Sadly, those with more economic power were more likely to say it's okay to act in the ways described.[9] Or consider "the cookie monster" study that brought together numerous groups of three undergraduates. Through a random process, one person in each group of three was named the supervisor and was given the task of leading the trio in re-writing an aspect of university policy. After 30 minutes, a plate of five cookies was brought to each group. It was assumed that virtually no one would take the last cookie, due to the "law of politeness." The question was who would take the fourth cookie after each in the group already had one. Interestingly, the randomly selected supervisor of the group was nearly twice as likely to be the one to take the fourth cookie. These same supervisors were also more likely to eat with their mouths open, smack their lips, and spill crumbles.[10] What just 30 minutes of power can do!

Given this tendency of power to corrupt, how valuable it is for those with power to have a consistent plumb line that reminds them not to use their power for themselves but for the good of others. Maybe that's why the mother of an ancient biblical king gave him this advice:

> O my son, O son of my womb,
> O son of my vows,
> do not waste your strength on women,
> on those who ruin kings.
> It is not for kings, O Lemuel, to guzzle wine.
> Rulers should not crave alcohol.
> For if they drink, they may forget the law
> and not give justice to the oppressed. . . .
> Speak up for those who cannot speak for themselves;
> ensure justice for those being crushed.
> Yes, speak up for the poor and helpless,
> and see that they get justice. (Proverbs 31:2-5, 8-9)

Having a consistent plumb line like the Bible can give you dignity when others think little of you. I am sure everyone has experienced the feeling of rejection at one time or another. You may have felt it because of the shape of your nose, the accent of your voice, the slowness of your mind, the limp in your step, the number of X chromosomes you possess, or the color of your skin. And if you've ever been belittled because of characteristics like these, it is easy for the voices to be internalized—to go from hearing "You are a loser" to believing "I am a loser." This is precisely the time when having a plumb line like the Bible can be immensely valuable. Rather than thinking of you as a loser, it consistently declares your dignity whether or not you are in sync with the crowd. Personally, I have found the Bible to be gloriously out of step with the times when it reminds me that God "knit me together in my mother's womb" (Psalm 139:13) or that despite what others say of me, "nothing can ever separate us from God's love" (Romans 8:38).

Sarah Shin, an Asian American and graduate of MIT, beautifully imagines the impact of rooting our dignity in what the plumb line of the Bible says regardless of how others may label us because of our ethnic background. She writes:

> [Jesus] renames us and calls us to what he is inviting us to become. He flips the lie of what we have been called or called ourselves on its head.
>
> Instead of "slave" and "less than," Jesus calls black men and women to be prophets, leaders, queens, and kings in his name.
>
> Instead of "unwanted foreigner" or "stranger," Jesus renames Latinas and Latinos as those who teach us the *familia* embrace of God so that all may know his name.
>
> Instead of being defined by family scars and expectations, Jesus calls Asian and Asian American men and women to be restorers and repairers of our families and beyond.
>
> Instead of "heathen" and "savage," Jesus honors Native women and men as the holy priestesses and priests of the living God.
>
> Instead of "unwanted" or "terrorist," Jesus invites Middle Eastern men and women to be honored guests at the table.
>
> Instead of "broken halves" of "incomplete wholes," Jesus tells multiracial women and men that they are fully white and fully Latino, fully Asian and fully black, fully Haitian and fully white. And they know better than anyone else how to navigate the complexity of multiple cultures. . . .
>
> Instead of "oppressor" and "enslaver," Jesus calls white men and women to be freedom fighters, advocates, and allies: sisters and brothers in arms who use their power and position to work alongside others to help restore the *imago Dei* [image of God] in all.[11]

Having a consistent plumb line like the Bible can help us find our true identity. My wife was a three-time All-American tennis player in college. Although still an amateur, she played enough pro tournaments in college to be ranked inside the top 200 players in the world. Nearly everyone who knew her knew her for one reason—she was a good tennis player. That was her identity. When she finished college, however, she chose not to turn pro and travel the circuit as she had always imagined. For a variety of reasons, the decision itself was not too difficult, but in the aftermath of the decision, she quickly began to wonder who she was. Before, she was Ann the tennis player, but who was she now? It was at a time like this that looking to the Bible became extremely valuable. For the first time, she came to understand that her true identity was not as a tennis player but as a child of the God spoken of in Scripture.

From a biblical perspective, who we are in relation to God is the foundation of our authentic self. It is true that some of us are tennis players and others are gifted artists; some are teachers and others are doctors. But when the hands and legs no longer work well and the mind is no longer sharp, or when people start screaming that "our type" is no longer welcome, we need not lose our identity or go searching for it in something that will one day be out of date. Instead, if we trust in the words of Scripture, we need not wonder "Who am I?" This is yet another advantage of having a biblical plumb line.

Does Dismissing the Bible Really Free Us from Its Constraints?

When people say the Bible is outdated, what they often mean is that they no longer want to be subject to constraints. At best, they see the Bible as cramping their style; at worst it is spreading dangerous ideas. I wonder, however, if in leaving the Bible behind we really free ourselves from constraints. Suppose, for example, that you read a time-tested book on health and fitness. It tells you that if you want to live longer, have more energy, and engage in more robust activity for decades to come, you need to exercise regularly and watch what you eat. You try it for a while but soon find it too restrictive. Who wants to get up at 5 a.m. for a morning jog or eat chicken and broccoli when a meat lover's pizza is just a phone call away? So, you get rid of the book. "Who needs it?" you say. But, of course, getting rid of the book will not really make you free from constraints. Yes, you may no longer have to set your alarm an hour earlier or eat vegetables at every meal, but there is a good chance you will soon find your friends leaving you behind when they head for a climb or having to decline your grandkids' offer to play ball. You see, you can get rid of the book and call it passe, but you can't really rid yourself of constraints no matter how much you have "evolved" in your thinking. Bad eating and no exercise will constrain you whether you like it or not.

The Bible gives quite a description of love that often shows up in weddings. It says:

> Love is patient and kind. Love is not jealous or boastful or proud or rude. It does not demand its own way. It is not irritable, and it keeps no record of being wronged. It does not rejoice about injustice but rejoices whenever the truth wins out. Love never gives up, never loses faith, is always hopeful, and endures through every circumstance. (1 Corinthians 13:4-7)

You can ignore these biblical words and try to find "love" by avoiding anything the Bible has to say on the matter, but I doubt it will work out too well for you. Undoubtedly, being patient and kind and not demanding your way are "constraints," but they are constraints you can't really avoid. If you want to know a sweet, intimate, and fulfilling relationship with another, you will probably find that these are constraints you must ultimately embrace.

And it's not just love that has constraints—so does forgiveness. You are free to harbor hate and resentment toward another, but in doing so you simply allow the one who offended you to keep doing so over and over again to your detriment.[12] Or how about contentment? You can seek it in stacking up millions in the bank, but you can't get away from the fact that money won't bring you as much satisfaction as deep personal relationships. Modern research has just begun to tell us that,[13] but the Bible could have told you that long before you worked 60-hour weeks for 30 years straight and began to wonder if there's more to life than a nice house, a country club membership, and a few nice vacations.[14] Yes, the current times give us lots of freedom to live without constraints, but that does not mean we are free to find peace in relationships and contentment in life any way we want. Like it or not, "human beings thrive in certain environments and break down in others."[15] From the Christian standpoint, when the Bible offers instructions on how to live life, it has in mind our thriving. And if that is the case, we do well to heed what it says even if our current place and time gives us the freedom to do otherwise.

Maybe the Bible Will Get Smarter

Sexism, racism, ageism, economic equality, same-sex marriage, transgenderism, abortion, doctor-assisted suicide, the opioid crisis, immigration, human trafficking, and pornography. The list of social issues that currently have emotions running high could go on and on. Even during your lifetime, you may have changed your stance on a number of these issues—perhaps because you really did your homework, or perhaps you just followed what everyone else seems to think is right these days. And now you might find yourself at odds with what you've heard the Bible has to say. You say that you are fine with that, though, and see no relevance to what the "old book" has to say.

I wonder, however, how many teenagers have said something similar to their parents. Mom and dad were so "out of it" and simply did not understand how things are done today. And then life moved along, and as the years rolled by, the once self-assured teenagers began to see that their parents weren't so dumb after all. The admonition and instruction and perspective the parents gave a decade or two ago keeps getting smarter and smarter as the years go by. The teenagers could not see their parents' wisdom when they were 16 and were quick to say, "Why can't I do that! Everyone else is doing it!" But now, they see things differently. Of course, the advice of mom and dad hasn't gotten any smarter; it's just that their once aghast teenagers have found the parents' advice to have much more value than they ever dreamed.

I wonder if the same is true of the Bible. Maybe today you think it is hopelessly out of date. But maybe one day, as the years roll by, it will get smarter and smarter. Not because its words have changed but because life will bring you to a place where you find it to have more value than you ever imagined. If so, you will no longer see the Bible as being full of bygone constraints but rather filled with life-giving words that lead to a better way. That seems to be what the ancient prophet Jeremiah was trying to get across when he wrote:

Stop at the crossroads and look around.
    Ask for the old, godly way, and walk in it.
Travel its path, and you will find rest for your souls.

(Jeremiah 6:16)

Key Points

- Every generation tends to look back on previous generations as being deficient in understanding how we ought to live. This means that what is held as a moral imperative today may be passe tomorrow.

- Popular opinion is always changing. Thus, it is difficult to rely on current consensus to discern what is right or good. We need a standard outside present-day social norms.

- Progress in life, either individually or as a society, doesn't always mean adopting new ideas. Sometimes it means going back to time-tested ideas.

- The Bible offers itself as a consistent plumb line that helps us discern what is right and good.

- There are several advantages to having a timeless biblical plumb line:

  › It can keep us from the exhaustion of calling our own shots.

  › It can give us direction and confidence in the midst of competing voices.

  › It can keep us from using power to hurt other people.

  › It can give us dignity when others think little of us.

  › It can help us find our true identity.

- Dismissing the Bible doesn't free us from constraints. We can choose not to do what it says, but we aren't necessarily free from the consequences of those choices.

- Just because we don't see the value of the Bible today doesn't mean it won't become "smarter" over time.

Additional Resources

The following resources are examples of how Christians have sought to apply the biblical plumb line to current social issues.

Culture Shock: A Biblical Response to Today's Most Divisive Issues, Chip Ingram

The Secular Creed: Engaging Five Contemporary Claims, Rebecca McLaughlin

Generous Justice: How God's Grace Makes Us Just, Timothy Keller

Oneness Embraced: Reconciliation, the Kingdom, and How We Are Stronger Together, Tony Evans

Gay Girl, Good God, Jackie Hill Perry

PART FOUR: CHRISTIAN CLAIMS

10

If God Is Real, Why Is There So Much Evil and Suffering?

I hardly ever watch news on TV. The main reason is I just can't stomach much of it. Maybe I am guilty of sheltering myself, but right or wrong the endless stream of evil and suffering gets to me. One needs to sit through the news for only a few minutes to hear about:

- a gruesome murder
- a deadly wildfire
- a new strand of a killer virus
- a child killed in an automobile accident
- the latest victim of an evil drug cartel
- racism rearing its ugly head
- a tornado devastating a community

Even as I write, I received news of a young woman who lost her mother three months ago and now her own child died just moments after birth. And earlier today, I read of a man who broke into a home and murdered a stranger, mistaking him for someone he really wanted to kill. Evil and suffering are out there everywhere, dressed up in every kind of uniform. And while we each have experienced the pain of it to different degrees, no one has been untouched. But how are we to explain an evil- and pain-filled world if God is both loving and all-powerful? Being loving, wouldn't he want to stop the carnage, and being all-powerful, wouldn't he be able to do so?

I suppose we could say the existence of evil and suffering are proofs that an all-powerful and loving God does not exist. Or, I suppose we could say that the co-existence of God, evil, and suffering is a mystery we must accept without explanation. But I am not inclined to take either of those approaches. Not because I have all the answers but because the more I've looked, the more I have found at least partial answers to these questions—answers that are better than throwing our hands up in defeat or pulling out the mystery card. Before exploring them, however, let me offer a few disclaimers up front.

First, when the question of evil and suffering comes up in conversations, I find that frequently it is not as much an intellectual inquiry as it is an expression of personal pain. People feel like God has abandoned them or been unfair to them. I get that, and so do many writers in the Bible who voiced similar feelings. Look, for example, at the words of King David when he found himself surrounded by enemies: "My God, my God, why have you abandoned me? Why are you so far away when I groan for help? Every day I call to you, my God, but you do not answer. Every night I lift my voice, but I find no relief" (Psalm 22:1-2). And when people are at a place like David, when they have lost a loved one or seen circumstances crumble around them, a listening ear is often far better than a list of reasons of why God would do this or that. So please know that if you sit in a place of pain and suffering, especially if your circumstances came about by the evil intentions of another, I'd rather be hearing your story face to face than rattling off any of what you will read below.

Second, while I've endured some dents and dings along the way, there is a good chance that the hurt and pain you have endured is beyond anything I have experienced. So while I hope that at least some of what I share will make sense to you and perhaps even provide some helpful insight, I am not so naïve to think that it will suddenly take away the hurt and pain you may be experiencing today. It may settle down some of your questions and give you a bit more peace, but I do not anticipate the sting of cancer treatments or the painful loss of a child to magically dissipate because of any newly discovered reasons for why a loving and all-powerful God would allow evil and suffering.

Third, I don't believe there is a one-size-fits-all reason for why God would allow evil and suffering in your life or the lives of others. Sometimes people say the reason a disaster came upon a community or even upon a family is because God's judgment has been levied against their sin. I, for one, don't know how we can make that judgment unless God writes something in the sky. Certainly, if Jesus endured a gruesome death and he was without sin as the Bible says, we cannot say that our pain and suffering is always a result of cheating on our taxes, storming out of a room in anger, or holding a grudge toward our spouse. And if this is the case, then I suspect that God might have different reasons for allowing pain and suffering in different circumstances and that not every reason and perspective I give here will explain the evil and suffering that has come your way.

INITIAL PERSPECTIVES

When we look deeply at evil and suffering, we long for answers. And if we don't find them right away, it becomes increasingly easy to push God aside or dismiss him all together. That's where these initial perspectives might prove helpful. Although they are not reasons why God would allow evil and suffering, they may help in understanding how God, evil, and suffering can exist at the same time.

Maybe God Has Overriding Reasons for Pain & Suffering

There are lots of things I didn't enjoy doing as a parent of young children. I didn't relish changing diapers or cleaning up food off the floor. I didn't like having to go through the hassle of getting kids in and out of a car seat, and I wasn't much for being awakened in the middle of the night. But perhaps my least favorite part of parenting (and I admit this was mostly a task my wife bore) was taking the toddlers to the doctor when I knew they were going to receive a shot. They'd enter the doctor's office unsuspecting and happy, and why shouldn't they? They were with their dad, and all seemed good in the world. Then in an act of seeming betrayal I handed them off to the doctor to be vaccinated. The look on their faces as they received the shot was awful, and they reached out their arms with screams of terror. They could not believe I let a strange man or woman stick a big needle into their bottom or thigh, and no explanation on my part could comfort their little minds.

What is instructive about this scenario is that, as a parent, I loved my children and had no interest in seeing them undergo pain and suffering. I also had the power to stop the procedure or to avoid the doctor's office altogether. But despite my love and power, I still chose to have my children vaccinated. In fact, it was because of my love and with my power that I made sure that it all happened. Why? Because I had overriding reasons that were more important than preventing the suffering they would experience that day.

You probably can see where I am going with this illustration. I am suggesting that maybe God has good overriding reasons for allowing pain and suffering. Of course, you might rightfully respond, "But what kind of overriding reason would God have for taking my wife or seeing my business fail?" That's a fair question, and one that may not be answered to your satisfaction. But for now, what I want you to consider is that a loving and all-powerful God is not necessarily inconsistent with the occurrence of evil and suffering if overriding reasons do exist.

Suffering Needs God To Be Unjust

Most people don't have a problem with suffering; they have a problem with *unjust* suffering. If someone, in a fit of anger, punches his hand through a wall and as a result breaks a few knuckles, our sympathy is limited. The poor guy is suffering, for sure, but most would say his suffering is deserved. This is wholly different from the reaction we have when someone is killed by a drunk driver or a friend's house is engulfed in flames.

A few years back I was walking down my sidewalk when I witnessed a rather violent scene. An army of ants (and in this case "army" is the perfect term) was attacking a hairy spider that was many times larger than any of the ants, and yet, in a matter of minutes, the ants made dinner of the spider. But as deadly as this event was, it's curious that I never thought to myself, "That is so unjust. That is so wrong." I figured it was just the way of the wild, and you probably would have thought that too. But why don't we say it's the way of the wild when a group of young men gang up and attack a woman or when a greedy executive bilks millions out of investors? Why do we say that evil has been done when people are involved and that the suffering caused is unjust? Why don't we just say some people find themselves in the wrong place at the wrong time, like the spider on my sidewalk, and leave it at that? In other words, where do we get the idea of evil and unjust suffering in the first place?

It seems to me that the only way we can call something evil or unjust is if there is someone outside the wild world in which we live who sets the bar and declares, "That's wrong!" This is the same conclusion that Andrea Dilley came to. She grew up as a child of medical missionaries in Kenya, and early in life she came face to face with extreme poverty and injustice. Often, she visited patients with her father one day only to see them die the next. Eventually she could not square a loving and all-powerful God with such things, and she left her faith behind. But as the years rolled by, she was disturbed deeply by the idea that if there is no God, nothing could really be called evil or unjust. Here is how she describes coming to this place of understanding:

> When people ask me what drove me out the doors of the church and then what brought me back, my answer to both questions is the same. I left the church in part because I was mad at God about human suffering and injustice. And I came back to church because of that same struggle. I realized that I couldn't even talk about justice without standing inside of a theistic framework. In a naturalistic worldview, a parentless orphan in the slums of Nairobi can only be explained in terms of survival of the fittest. We're all just animals slumming it in a godless world, fighting for space and resources. The idea of justice doesn't really mean anything. To talk about justice, you have to talk about objective morality, and to talk about objective morality, you have to talk about God.[1]

Dilley's epiphany was not all that different than that of C.S. Lewis. As an atheist, he too struggled with how a good God could exist given all the evil in the world. He wrote: "My argument against God was that the universe seemed so cruel and unjust. But how had I got this idea of *just* and *unjust*? A man does not call a line crooked unless he has some idea of a straight line."[2] In time, the straight line, for Lewis, became the goodness of God, without which we are not in a place to call anything evil or unjust.

Another way to put all this is to say that evil cannot exist on its own. It is the corruption of something that already exists. Rust on a car, for example, cannot exist if there isn't a car, and rot can exist only as long as the tree exists.[3] Likewise, when we call something evil, what we are really saying is that something good has been adulterated or is missing. That's why we use the prefix "un-" so very often. We say something is *un*kind, because there is something good called kindness. We say something is *un*sportsmanlike, because there is good sportsmanship. And we say something is *un*healthy, because there is that which is healthy. So while it might seem that evil counts against the existence of a good God, there is a strong case to be made that it actually does the opposite.

God Is Probably Different Than We Think

Not too long ago I sat in a living room with a 14-year-old named Chris and his father. He was wrestling with whether he should believe in God because of all the evil and suffering he saw in the world. That might seem like a heady issue for a fellow his age, but in my experience, people start asking questions like this at a much younger age than adults think they do. My young friend put his take like this: "If God is the kind of God that allows the evil and suffering we see in the world, then I don't want to believe in him." I told Chris that I agreed that some of what we see in the world is hard to swallow if God's involved. But I also told him that when we discover something about God we are uncomfortable with or even dislike, it does not necessarily follow that God does not exist.

"What is your least favorite color?" I asked Chris. He took the question seriously and pondered it. Finally, he decided on puke green. (Not a bad selection; I'm not much for puke green either.) I asked Chris, "What would happen if God showed up right now and lo and behold he was puke green in color?" He looked surprised and said, "What do you mean, what would happen?" To which I replied, "Well, if God showed up and he was puke green in color, would that make you believe he didn't exist?" He said no, which is probably a good answer. When we discover something about people we don't like or are uncomfortable with, we don't then conclude they do not exist. It just doesn't work that way. In fact, we may believe in them more than ever after our discovery; we just believe in them in a different way because we know more about them. I tend to think that the reason some people stop believing in God when life throws them a serious curveball is because their understanding of God is that he throws only fastballs belt-high and right over the middle of the plate. But maybe disbelieving in God is the wrong response. Maybe the right response is to change one's view of God as one who on occasion might show up looking different than we first pictured.

God or No God, We Still Must Face Evil & Suffering

If there is one big question that has bewildered humanity longer than any other, it is the question of evil and suffering. It is not a question that is reserved for academia or for the poor and oppressed or for a certain ethnic group in a certain time period. Throughout the ages, regardless of one's belief in the Christian God or other gods, evil and suffering refuse to be ignored. Yes, I know that my friends of Buddhist or Hindu backgrounds may say that evil and suffering are an illusion that can be transcended through some form of enlightenment, but I still see them weep and wail at the loss of a loved one or wince when jamming their finger in a door. And I certainly would be hesitant to say that someone who has endured great suffering, like that of an Auschwitz imprisonment or an ISIS gang rape, was just not enlightened enough to recognize their suffering wasn't real. If anything, pain and suffering rank among the most real things you and I will ever experience in this life.

I say all this because if you conclude that evil and suffering prove that God does not exist, you do not get to rid yourself of evil and suffering as well. In other words, evil and suffering don't go away just because you do away with God. Rather, as I've already suggested above, you are simply stuck with a cosmos that randomly dishes evil and suffering out without discrimination. With God you might have the hope of redeeming purposes and perhaps even an explanation for suffering's origin, but without God you are stuck with little explanation of evil and pain. This line of reasoning does not mean that God exists, but given the curious kind of creatures that we are, the universal experience of evil and suffering ought to incentivize the search for some sort of explanation beyond "it is what it is."

A FEW REASONS GOD MIGHT ALLOW EVIL & SUFFERING

The initial perspectives I offer might help you see that an all-loving, all-powerful God is not necessarily inconsistent with the existence of evil and suffering, but they do not provide reasons why he would allow evil and suffering to abound. My hunch is many more reasons exist than I cite here, but these are at least a start.

Evil Is the Risk of Real Relationship
I owned two dolls as a kid. One was G. I. Joe, and the other was Stretch Armstrong. If you've ever seen the latter, you know the reason for the name. The poor guy could be stretched and put into just about any pretzel configuration. I am not sure what happened to either, but I suppose somewhere along the way I decided I was too old for dolls. That changed a couple of years ago, however, when I was introduced to the Mr. Wonderful Doll. He's a lumberjack-looking guy with a pasted-on smile, perfect hair, and big brown boots. But the most outstanding thing about the Mr. Wonderful Doll is what he says when you press his left hand. Here are

just a few of the lines he speaks that apparently make him Mr. Wonderful:

> "No, you don't look at all fat in that dress. How could anything make you look fat?"
>
> "Ah, can't your mother stay another week?"
>
> "Did you have a hard day, honey? Why don't you sit down and let me rub your feet?"
>
> "You're going shopping by yourself? Why don't I tag along and carry your bags?"
>
> "The ball game isn't really all that important. I'd rather spend more time with you."

I know not every woman is the same, but I am guessing that there are more than a few who would fall out of their chair if their man said any of this! But as wonderful as it might be to hear these words, I doubt there are many women who would be satisfied with a Mr. Wonderful Doll. The real Mr. Wonderful isn't the one who is programmed to spit out certain responses; the real Mr. Wonderful is the one who freely offers up words like these for the one he loves. In fact, it is safe to say that for love to be real, it must be freely given.[4]

The biblical story says that God made people so that he might enjoy relationship with them. He could have made them like Mr. and Ms. Wonderful Dolls and preprogrammed them so they always did and said just what God wanted. But if he did that, God would not enjoy real relationship with them, because love has to be freely given and not coerced. So instead of creating robots, God took a risk. He made man and woman with the capacity either to love and obey him of their own accord or to do the opposite if they so wished. He knew the latter would lead to hardship and suffering, and he even told them so in advance (Genesis 2:16). But it was a risk he was willing to take to enjoy a loving relationship. It's possible to point the finger at God and blame him for putting us in a world with so much evil and suffering. It's also possible to thank him for giving us the chance to love him fully—to be more than preprogrammed dolls, even if we do make a mess of things sometimes.

Pain & Suffering Act as a Warning

I have had the chance to travel to some rather impoverished places in the world, and I have seen not only hunger but also great physical deformity and untreated illness. I've yet, however, to see someone with leprosy. For that I am glad, because for thousands of years it was a disease that not only took countless lives but also required that those affected be permanently quarantined away from family and friends. The most visible symptom of leprosy is skin sores, but below the surface, damage occurs to the nerves. If not treated in ample time, the nerve damage can lead to a dangerous loss of feeling, and soon victims cannot sense when a hand or leg or foot is cut or burned. This can result in wounds and infections that eventually require amputation of limbs and appendages.

These details about leprosy provide a helpful illustration when applied to the question of evil and suffering. We can probably agree that it would be good for people who have contracted leprosy to regain the ability to feel. And it would be good because, while this ability would cause them to feel pain when they stub their toe or when they inadvertently touch a hot stove, it would also alert them to the fact that something has gone wrong and should be addressed.

The Bible tells us that God has our best interests at heart, and he recognizes we have been infected by something life-threatening. Lurking just below the surface of our lives is selfishness, anger, pride, apathy, and so much more. At times, we are able to keep these destructive forces packed away neatly where no one can see, but sooner or later they come spilling out in spiteful words, underhanded business practices, broken relationships, and disregard for the great needs around us. Of course, all of this contributes even more to the pain and suffering in the world— both ours and others. We could protest that we must endure the pain this world offers, but what would we be asking for? Wouldn't we be like the one who has leprosy, yet does not want to regain the ability to feel? Maybe the reason God allows us to feel pain and suffering in the world is to alert us to the fact that something has gone awry inside each of us. If so, God is not uncaring by allowing it but instead after what is best for each and every one of us.

Pain & Suffering Can Build Character

You should have seen our son's face. In the morning, he was put under the command of the U.S. Coast Guard Academy. He knew what was coming, but that still did not prepare him for the onslaught. Over the next eight hours, he would be yelled at, corrected, punished, and belittled more than he had been his entire life. By the time his mother saw him during the 15-minute good-bye period, he looked like he had been stunned by a Taser gun. And that was just the first day; the seven weeks of "Swab Summer" and the first year as a cadet were often hellish. But as he looks back on it, there is little he would change. Even though he didn't like what he experienced in the moment, he soon understood that if he was going to learn respect and teamwork and endurance, he had no other road to take.

Paul of Tarsus, one of the early church leaders, provides an even better example of how God uses pain and suffering to build our character. Paul was once on the side of the Christian-haters, so it's no surprise that he endured a great deal of persecution and suffering when he decided that Christians had it right after all. In one letter, he writes that over the years he had been imprisoned multiple times, flogged and left for dead, beaten with rods, stoned, shipwrecked in the open seas, and subject to hunger, thirst, and nakedness (2 Corinthians 11:23-27). Nonetheless, he embraced the hardship that came his way for following Christ, writing: "We can rejoice, too, when we run into problems and trials, for we know that they help us develop endurance. And endurance develops strength of character, and character strengthens our confident hope of salvation" (Romans 5:3-4).

I've seen a fair share of people who have endured life-threatening cancer, disease, and heart failure. And I am always amazed at how many of them on the backside are grateful for what they learned from the experience. It's not that they would choose to go through it again, but it was those very circumstances that helped put life and loved ones in a very different light. In many instances, a significant shift in their mindset occurs, and time and energy get redirected from that point forward. Again, you might object, and say, "Okay, I admit some pain and suffering can prove helpful in our development, but when a tsunami washes away thousands, how can they learn from those circumstances when they are dead?" Your point is a valid one, and that is why I said in the beginning that not every one of my reasons fits for every instance of evil and suffering that comes our way. Though character building can't explain why God would allow every painful or evil situation, it does provide a reason for it in some circumstances.

Suffering that Leads to Death May Be an Upgrade
David Benatar is a smart guy. A philosophy professor at the University

of Cape Town, he is also director of the school's Bioethics Centre. He has written a number of books that have been published by none other than Oxford University Press. So, it might surprise you when he argues that it would be better for all of us if we had never been born.[5] His argument goes like this: If this life is all there is, and we undergo pain and suffering, it would be better if we weren't born. We wouldn't miss being alive, and we would avoid the hard stuff. His logic isn't all that bad, but it makes a big assumption: that this life is all there is. But, as far as I see, if this life is not all there is, his whole argument begins to crumble.

Suppose there is the possibility of a beautiful life after this one, just as Jesus claimed there is (John 14:1-3), and that entrance into this grand afterlife requires that at the very least we've lived this life first. Could we say then that it is better that none of us have lived? I don't think so, especially if the next life is so much better than this one. Consider the person who does not experience a "character-building" type of pain and suffering but instead loses her very life to a massive stroke or stray bullet. What if that person leaves this world and enters into a much better life? No doubt those left behind will feel a big loss. But, according to the Bible, if she is one who trusted in Christ, not only does she get an upgraded home, but she avoids future pain as well. I think this is what the ancient prophet Isaiah was getting at when he wrote: "Good people pass away; the godly often die before their time. . . . *No one seems to understand that God is protecting them from the evil to come* (Isaiah 57:1, emphasis added).

God Is Being Patient with Our Own Evil

There might be a few who have fallen fully onto the Dark Side and embrace evil at every turn, but most people would probably vote to do away with evil if they could. I mean, who really wants to be mocked or raped or pillaged—or see others experience the same? So if God is as good as people say he is, wouldn't he want to get rid of evil too? That certainly sounds like a reasonable expectation of God, but I wonder if the ramifications of ridding the world of evil are more far-reaching than most people have considered. Suppose that on this very day God chose to remove every source of evil from the world. In that case, what would happen to you?

You may think of yourself as being above average on the goodness scale, but isn't it true that you are the source of at least some of the evil in this world? You might say, "Yeah, but I only tell a few white lies here and there and only cut people off in traffic when I'm really in a hurry." But what about the time when you made a joke at the expense of another in grade school? What if it was that joke that sent someone down a certain bad road, one that has resulted in a lot of evil and suffering? Like it or not, we have all been contributors to evil in this world, and if God were to rid the earth of all the sources of evil, he'd have to get rid of us too.

Jesus told a great number of parables, and one in particular helps explain why evil still exists in the world (Matthew 13:24-30). The parable involves a wheat field that weeds have invaded. The farmer's hired hands asked if they should pull out the weeds, and this was the farmer's response: "No, you'll uproot the wheat if you do. Let both grow together until the harvest. Then I will tell the harvesters to sort out the weeds, tie them into bundles, and burn them, and to put the wheat in the barn." In sharing this parable, Jesus teaches us that there will be a time when the weeds and the wheat will be separated, but he also says that if that happens prematurely a lot of potential good stuff won't come to fruition. Later in the Bible, we are told that God is being patient for our sake, because "he does not want anyone to be destroyed, but wants everyone to repent" (2 Peter 3:9). If God were to get rid of all evil in the world (the weeds of which Jesus speaks), he would undoubtedly get rid of many people too—including you and me. But according to what Jesus said, he is being patient. He wants to give people time to turn back to God so that instead of being like weeds to be burned and destroyed, we become like wheat that is worthy to be gathered.

We Aren't So Good After All

I doubt anyone would argue that the American legal system is perfect. And it seems most imperfect when someone is put in prison for 20 or 30 years, only for evidence to show up later that completely exonerates the convicted. I cannot imagine the mental anguish such a prisoner endures or the unrecoverable loss of so much life experience. It seems that part of the prisoner's life was stolen from him for something he did not do. To varying degrees, we feel the same way when "innocent" people we know are minding their own business and then due to misfortune endure some form of terrible pain or loss.

But what if we change the scenario just a bit? Suppose rather than calamity falling on an "innocent" person, it falls on someone who has made lots of bad choices along the way that even contribute to the suffering currently experienced. In that case, there is a good chance that we would feel some sort of cosmic justice has been served. Yet this is precisely where the rub comes in. I know that you and I often compare ourselves to others and think we are good people, but comparison has never been the best of measures. I may have murdered only one person while you murdered five, but that does not make me a good person just because I'm comparatively better than you. If you or I are to know whether we are good, and thus have been treated fairly or unfairly by God, we need to have a standard that goes beyond mere comparison with other people.

In the opening pages of the Bible, we are introduced to Adam and Eve. Everything was going quite well for the two of them, and daily walks with God seemed to be the norm. As far as the story goes, they were as innocent as two people can be and there was utterly nothing in their life of which to be even remotely ashamed. Then came the fruit-eating episode. God said not to eat from one particular tree, but thinking God was holding back on them, they ate the fruit anyway. Now, take a step back and consider what Adam and Eve did. They didn't kill anyone. They didn't burn down the garden. They didn't get in a big fight over who gets what treehouse to live in. All they did was eat fruit. And with that simple indiscretion came the curse of God, a curse that unleashed on the world pain and suffering and ushered in the consequence of death. If this story were new to me, I know what question I would ask: How is that fair? One piece of fruit and a lifetime and beyond of suffering—that seems completely out of line. And it is, unless something deeper has taken place.

There is a simple rule of justice that seems to apply in every culture. That rule is that consequences are commensurate with the stature of the offended. If my son hits my daughter, I might send him to his room for a couple hours or have him do some extra chores. If, however, the next day he hits his teacher at school, the consequences most surely escalate. They escalate not because of any difference in behavior but because the stature of the person offended is greater. Let's extend the illustration out a couple of years to when my son is driving. Suppose he is pulled over by the police and hits the officer. What kind of consequences will he receive then? I am guessing they will be even greater, again because of the stature of the one offended. Finally, let's say that a few years later at a presidential rally he hits the President of the United States. Now, he is really in for it—not because his behavior escalated, but because the stature of the person offended increased.[6]

So let's take this line of reasoning back to the garden. Adam and Eve were told not to eat of the tree. If you or I had been the one who told them not to eat, a scolding might be all that is in order given our similar human stature. But it was God who told them not to eat of it, and it was God who told them in advance of the consequences. To disobey and distrust God is to offend not a sister or a teacher or a police officer or a President but the eternal, omniscient Creator of all. God's stature is impossible to top, making even what we would call the smallest grievance an incalculable offense.

When I first understood this, it took my breath away and not in a good way. It kind of made my stomach sick. Comparing myself with other people had me thinking I was doing just fine; in fact, it seemed God probably owed me a thing or two. But once I saw that throughout my life, I had done something way worse than hit a teacher or police officer, I found it harder to call God unjust for any pain and suffering that came my way. Tragedy seems unfair if encountered by a good person, not so much for the evil one. And the more I looked at the big picture, the more I realized I belonged in the latter category even if all I ate was a piece of forbidden fruit.

"Natural" Evil Acts as a System-Wide Alarm

There have been a lot of natural disasters, but the one that sticks out in my mind most is the earthquake and resulting tsunamis that hit Southeast Asia in 2004. Watching videos of it still gives me the shakes. I cannot imagine staring down a 100-foot wave, watching cars and buildings rush down what used to be streets, and hearing the screams of people hanging from treetops for dear life. But disasters from the outside are just part of the scary things this world has to offer. Some of the biggest threats are from things we cannot see with the naked eye, such as a fast-spreading coronavirus.

We might be able to understand why God would allow us to suffer the direct consequences of our own misbehavior or that of those around us. They are consequences that reasonably fall out when God gave us free will. But even if we can swallow that part of the story, one still has reason to ask, "What about natural disasters and disease? No one's choices caused those." The question is a good one, but perhaps our choices are linked with natural disasters or disease in a way we've never considered.

Previously I discussed the idea that God wants to alert us to the fact that something has gone awry in our lives. Our behavior and choices have pushed God to the periphery and put us in great peril, and because this is so, God put in place a system-wide alarm to wake us up. This alarm is in the form of natural disasters and diseases, and sometimes it is in the form of common, personal pain like that at childbirth or that which arises from a tough day's work. At other times, this alarm is sounding off in the distance, and we know of it only from our news feed. But whatever the case, it acts as God's "megaphone to rouse a deaf world."[7]

To this point, Jesus once spoke of a tower that collapsed and killed eighteen people. His admonition to those who heard of the disaster was to get right with God because danger was lurking for all (Luke 13:4-5). On another occasion Jesus healed a lame man but soon after tells him to "stop sinning or something even worse may happen to you" (John 5:14). And at yet another time, Jesus harkened back to the flood of Noah's day to explain the suddenness with which the final judgment will come (Matthew 24:36-39). In other words, in all three cases, we see Jesus urge people to listen to the "alarms" going off around them and get back to God.

Now, to some, this might seem overboard on God's part. Tsunamis and pandemics are way too jolting an alarm. But what if we are in greater peril than we realize and this is the only way God can get our attention? In that case, it may be more justified than we first think. Suppose your son is playing in the street. You see a car heading quickly toward where he is playing. You call out to him, but he does not heed your call. So you run toward him, and just before the car would make impact, you yank on your son's arm, pull him to the ground, and drag him away from certain death. As a result of your efforts, your son has his shoulder dislocated and bruises on one whole side of his body. But most importantly, he is alive. Had you caused such pain and suffering to come upon your child because he sneezed, you likely would have been arrested and your son would have been taken from you. But under these circumstances, you are lauded for your efforts as a hero. The pain and suffering were called for in order to save your child. Yes, if he had heeded your calls, it would not have been necessary, but because he didn't, your actions are justified. No doubt, when we experience the alarm of natural disasters and disease, it can cause quite some damage. But if grave eternal danger is lurking, not just for us but for those around us, is not God justified in designing a system that yanks our arm and pulls us to the ground even if in the form of tsunamis and pandemics?

SOME FINAL PERSPECTIVES

I hope you found a few of the reasons I suggest for why God allows suffering to make some sense of our common landscape of evil and pain, but I imagine you may be thinking, "I still don't understand why God would…" or "I don't care if God has his reasons; I don't like what's happening anyway." Or perhaps, "I don't see how any of this helps me deal with what I am going through now." I can assure you that at times those very words have crossed through my mind as well. It's then that these final perspectives have proved helpful.

God as the Grandmaster

I used to play chess with a friend named Isaku back when I was in elementary school. I don't think I was ever any good, but I liked to think I was. Now I play a game or two on my phone when I am somewhere with nothing important to do. I don't know who's behind the chess app, but I am lucky to achieve a draw even on the easiest level. I am guessing that if I sat down with a grandmaster, she would begin with a couple moves that make no sense to me and yet with just a move or two more, she would declare checkmate.

I like to think of God as a grandmaster. I mean, if he made the whole world, he's got to know how to move things around on the board of life a lot better than I do. If that's the case, then I have to believe there are going to be times when his moves make no sense to me. But, of course, that does not mean there isn't a very good reason behind them. This is a very important point when I am scratching my head to figure out why God would allow such and such to happen. I can still ask him "Why?" but I also can assume there will be times when I just won't be able to understand the good behind the moves he is making.

Not Made To Understand

I've talked a good bit about Adam and Eve in this chapter. You may have a hard time believing they existed, but I point to them anyway because they help us understand much of what the Bible has to tell us about evil and suffering. This first couple was placed in a pristine world, beyond our comprehension in majesty and wonder. Eye-popping fruit hung from tree after tree and was delicious to eat. Springs and rivers sparkled without a hint of pollution. Animals abounded and had no fear of humanity. And the man and woman romped around the garden as naked as can be, totally enamored with one another.

Clearly, God gave Adam & Eve minds to think. The animal-naming game gives us a clue there (Genesis 2:19-20), and it's evident they understood God's command concerning the forbidden fruit. It's also apparent that he made them able to grasp things that were good, like enjoying "trees that were beautiful and that produced delicious fruit" (Genesis 2:9). There is no indication, however, that their minds were crafted to fully comprehend evil. That doesn't mean they couldn't take the road of evil, and even know when they did, but it does mean they couldn't fully comprehend the evil that would unfold in the lives of others. And I don't think we can either. That's why we continue to shake our heads in utter bewilderment when we read of the evil exploits of Hitler or Stalin or listen to a news report of a man who for years has held sex slaves captive. Heck, I couldn't even understand why my seven-year-old boy wouldn't stop pestering his sister for no good reason. And I can't understand it, because like Adam and Eve, my mind was made for a perfect garden, and not so much for the imperfect world in which we all live.

A God Who Knows Our Pain & Does Something About It

An angry god is not hard to find in the myriad of religions that have been embraced by humanity over the millennia. Neither is it hard to find a god in other religions who fiddles with our worldly affairs. But if we conclude that Christianity is just an offshoot of ancient mythologies by presenting a God who is angered from afar, we have not properly understood Christianity. In fact, we have not even understood why it is called Christianity in the first place.

Christianity rests on the shoulders of Christ (a Greek term meaning *messiah* or *promised deliverer*), who was given the name Jesus at birth. Here is some of what we are told about Jesus:

- He was misunderstood by his parents. (Luke 2:41-50)
- He experienced hunger and thirst. (Luke 4:2; John 4:7)
- He became weary and tired. (John 4:6)

- He was deeply distressed. (Mark 3:5)
- His heart ached for people. (Matthew 9:36; 23:37)
- He cried for his friends. (John 11:35)
- He prayed "with a loud cry and tears." (Hebrews 5:7)
- His family thought he was crazy. (Mark 3:20-21)
- His hometown rejected him. (Matthew 13:53-57)
- His kind acts were often met with disdain. (Matthew 12:22-24)
- He was betrayed and abandoned by his best friends. (Matthew 26:56, 69-75)
- He was put on trial with a rigged jury. (Matthew 26:59-60)
- He was mocked, beaten, scourged, and crucified. (Matthew 27:26-56)
- His life was traded for that of a murderer. (Mark 15:6-15)
- He was ridiculed while he was dying. (Mark 15:31-32)

To put it rather simply, Jesus was not one who stood far away from the suffering of this world. He came down into it. As one writer puts it, "The God on whom we rely knows what suffering is all about, not merely in the way that God knows everything, but by *experience*."[8] And if that's the case, Jesus is one who can sympathize with the very pain and evil we are experiencing, and even welcomes us crying out to him. He is the one who can give us reassurance in our pain, even if he does not give us an explanation for our pain.

But if Jesus were only a shoulder to cry on, God would still fall short in addressing the hurt that fills our world. It is one thing to have a partner in suffering, and something completely different to rescue us from it. Jesus made it clear that this life would be full of evil and suffering, but as will be discussed even more later, he said that his own suffering became the gateway to a future life in which "he will wipe every tear from their eyes, and there will be no more death or sorrow or crying or pain" (Revelation 21:4). Some say God must take a certain pleasure from our pain, but that is not what the Bible has to say. It reads, "As surely as I live, says the Sovereign Lord, I take no pleasure in the death of wicked people." (Ezekiel 33:11). If God simply held our hand while we suffered and did nothing to bring it to an end, he'd get style points at best. But if Christ is right, he has done more than that. He promises to all who trust in him a pathway forward—a pathway to a place that is free of evil and suffering.

When I started this chapter, I explained that while I hope that what I write helps you make better sense of God and suffering, I do not expect that this chapter will necessarily make you feel better if you are experiencing some suffering of your own. I stand by those words. There are ways to see how God and suffering are not inconsistent with one another. There are also reasons why God might allow evil and suffering, and there are perspectives that can help us accept the fact that evil and suffering are often beyond our comprehension. But none of these reasons or perspectives necessarily make the pain or loss we feel suddenly go away. Instead, it seems that if we are to find comfort and strength in times of personal suffering it is to be found in friends who understand what we are going through, stand with us when we ride the roller coaster of grief and anger, and gently lead us to a place where the sun can shine again. The enduring friend, and even Savior, that Christianity offers is the risen Jesus.

Key Points

- Upfront Disclaimers When Talking of God and Evil and Suffering

  › Evil and suffering are personal, and in most cases a listening ear and kind support are more important than providing answers as to why God would allow evil and suffering.

  › Knowing why God would allow something wouldn't necessarily make us feel better.

  › Not every reason why God allows evil and suffering applies to every circumstance.

- Some Initial Perspectives on God, Evil, and Suffering

  › God and suffering are not as incompatible as they might seem. Good people who have the power to stop suffering sometimes have overriding reasons not to do so. Perhaps it is the same for God.

  › Without God, we have no basis for calling things evil or any suffering unjust, so maybe our sense of evil and suffering confirms the existence of God.

  › The God who allows evil and suffering might look different than we originally pictured, but that does not mean he doesn't exist.

  › Everyone must deal with the problem of evil and suffering. If we get rid of God, we don't get rid of evil and suffering; we just have no hope-filled way of explaining it.

- Possible Reasons Why God Allows Evil & Suffering

  › It's part of the risk of real relationship.

  › Suffering alerts us to the fact that something isn't right.

  › God is more interested in building our character than in our momentary comfort.

  › God may want to give us an upgrade.

  › God is patiently putting up with our own evil to give us time to repent.

› We aren't as innocent as we think we are. Our choice to disobey and distrust God is an incalculable offense.

› Natural disaster and disease are necessary, system-wide alarms to wake us up to the grave dangers that are lurking.

• A Few More Perspectives on God, Evil, and Suffering

› Not knowing good reasons for some event doesn't mean there is not one.

› We were not made to fully understand evil and suffering.

› God knows the pain of evil and suffering. He has set in motion a plan to vanquish it, and in the meantime welcomes us crying out to him.

Additional Resources

The Problem of Pain, C.S. Lewis

Why Does God Allow Evil? Compelling Answers for Life's Toughest Questions, Clay Jones

Walking with God through Pain & Suffering, Timothy Keller

The Goodness of God: Assurance of Purpose in the Midst of Suffering and Evil, Randy Alcorn

With So Many Religions, Why Say Christianity Is the Only Way?

Some of the nicest people I have ever met are Muslims. When spending three months in Central Asia, I could not enter a home without being fed like a king and treated with utmost respect. Over my years in Houston, Texas, I have found Muslims to be people of great hospitality and kindness. And the same can be said of Hindus or Jews or Buddhists I have met around the world. Kindness and care have come from every spot along the religious spectrum. In fact, for me, one of the great advantages to living in a multiethnic city like Houston is the incredible diversity of backgrounds and beliefs. So if good and gracious people come from every religion, why should we say that any one religion is better than another? And why should Christians, like me, ever suggest that Jesus is the only way to God?

I believe questions like these reveal a soft heart toward humanity, a desire to leave no one out. If you have asked these questions, you have probably done so with friends in mind—friends you love and respect. How could you or I ever say that our respected, admired, and loved friends are not on the right path in life simply because they hold a different religious view than you or I? Many have grown up in a Christian family and heard that belief in Jesus is the only way to be right with God and enjoy eternal life, but after developing great friendships with people of different faiths, they have arrived at the conclusion that the Christian stance is unfair, intolerant, and arrogant. Perhaps this is your experience.

Exclusivity, Intolerance, and Narrow-Mindedness

We don't like the word "only." A club that says "men only" has probably been picketed, if not brought before the courts. Our stomach turns when remembering restrooms or drinking fountains that were labeled "whites only." And we likely feel no better when learning we've been left off a guest list because only people of a certain net worth are to be invited. "Only" reeks of exclusion, and we don't like it for good reason. No one wants to be left out. But while exclusivity is objectionable in many instances, we must admit there are other times when exclusivity is what we demand.

I grew up a few hours from Disneyland, and once a year or so, my family would make a trip to the Magic Kingdom. As it is for so many today, going to Disneyland was one of childhood's greatest thrills. In my day, we had fewer roller coasters than are there now, but we did have the Matterhorn, the big white mountain in the center of the park with screaming riders weaving in and out of its "caves." I was enough of a thrill seeker as a child that I could not wait to ride it. Yet wait is just what I had to do. In those early years, I just wasn't tall enough to meet the standards. Only people 48 inches and taller were allowed to ride. As a five-year-old I thought that seemed very exclusionary. I wanted on that ride, and I knew I could handle it as well as anyone else. My protests, however, went unheeded, and I wasn't allowed on board. This, of course, was for good reason: The ride was not built for people my size. The exclusionary policy was not there to say that other people were better than me, or because taller people were arrogant and narrow-minded. The policy was there for my safety.

I know that not all "only" statements are there for our good, but it doesn't take long to see that many are. *Only* licensed drivers are allowed to drive. *Only* medical providers who have received extensive training and passed state exams are allowed to practice medicine. *Only* unleaded gasoline is allowed in most cars. And *only* you are allowed to access the funds in your bank account. Simply put, there are many instances when we think that exclusionary boundaries or restrictions are best for everyone involved. This should make us slow to dismiss an exclusionary claim or policy simply because it is exclusionary. Sometimes, it may be that a rule or standard has been put in place only as a means to unjustly favor one group of people over another, but at other times there may be something true and real and valuable behind the restrictions that justifies their existence. If this is the case for laws about jumping off tall bridges or about drinking and driving, maybe it is also the case for certain religious claims.

One reason we decry exclusivity is because it can reek of intolerance. Intolerance might say, "You think differently than I do, therefore you are worthy of disdain or disrespect or perhaps something worse." Intolerance, of course, can be a terrible thing. But we must recognize that there is a difference between intolerance toward people and intolerance toward ideas or behaviors. I, for one, don't want to vilify my neighbor just because she votes for a different candidate than I do, but that does not mean that I need to be tolerant of her putting campaign signs in my yard.

Recently I came upon a manufacturing company named In Tolerance. It specializes in manufacturing aluminum, stainless steel, and plastic parts for the aerospace market and making them according to tight quality control specifications. In other words, its clients don't have much tolerance for parts that are just a little off in size or suffer from inferior stress capacity. And for that I am grateful. I certainly don't want to fly in a plane where just any part will do. In this case, and in many others, a large dose of intolerance is a very good thing.

I am not sure anyone wants to be labeled narrow-minded, and perhaps that is your concern when the discussion of religions comes up. But just as with inclusion or tolerance, open-mindedness isn't always the best alternative. For a long time, I have said that my goal is not to be open-minded or narrow-minded but to be right-minded—not just in matters of religion but in all of life. If I will use only a certain highway to flee a wildfire when there are multiple, even safer, ways to exit, my narrow-mindedness might cost me my life. If, however, only the highway will take me to safety, then it is narrow-mindedness that will save my skin, and not the idea that any old road will do. This is all to say, there is simply no virtue in being open-minded or narrow-minded, but there is virtue in landing on a right-minded solution, whether that solution allows for ten roads to be taken or only one. This holds true for rescue routes from wildfires, and I see no reason it should not hold true for religion as well. If all religions are equally true and I say only one is true, I am not being right-minded in my exclusive thinking. However, if only one way is true and I claim that all religious roads are equally valid, I am not only errantly open-minded but heading down a path that has no good end.

Sincerity Is Not Enough

I have personally seen hundreds line up to offer incense at a beautiful Buddhist temple in British Columbia and even more kneel for prayer in the Blue Mosque of Istanbul. I have known of Catholics who never miss Mass, Jews who faithfully observe every sacred holiday, and Mormons who give away millions to their church. When my Muslim friend observes Ramadan, gives gifts to the poor, and spends years saving for a trip to Mecca, I cannot doubt his sincerity. Neither can I doubt the sincerity of the Jehovah's Witness women who regularly leave literature at my door. Each earnestly believes that their actions give them a better shot in the afterlife, and their sincere devotion provides more than lip service to their religious beliefs. If sincerity is the measuring stick, many people from every religion will find reward in the life to come.

But what if sincerity is not the most important element of finding ourselves in good stead with God in this life and the life to come? I am not suggesting that sincerity is not valuable, but sincerity in and of itself does not always prove helpful. Consider Jim Marshall, who played defensive end for the Minnesota Vikings. Jim was great enough to compete in more games as a defensive player than anyone else in the NFL, but in a game against the San Francisco 49ers in October 1964, he picked up a fumble and ran the wrong way. With all sincerity he raced to his own end zone and in celebration threw the ball toward the stands. Unfortunately, despite his sincerity, it was the 49ers and not the Vikings who were awarded points for his efforts.

Of course, misplaced sincerity can do more than affect the score of a game; it can have deadly consequences as well. Caretakers at Carriage-by-the-Lake nursing home in Bellbrook, Ohio, administered what they thought was oxygen to ten different patients on December 7, 2000. Tragically, bungled labeling on the tanks meant maintenance workers at the nursing home errantly connected nitrogen to the patient delivery systems. Before the mistake was found, four patients died, while six others became ill. The caretakers were undoubtedly sincere in their care of the residents, but sincerity was not what was most important—oxygen was.[1]

Ultimately, sincerity may be a venerable trait, but it does not ensure truth or a good outcome. Successful entrepreneur and motivational speaker Jim Rohn recognized this fact before his death. He wrote: "Sincerity is not a test of truth. We must not make this mistake: He must be right; he's so sincere. Because, it is possible to be sincerely wrong. We can only judge truth by truth and sincerity by sincerity."[2] If this is the case when it comes to football, oxygen tanks, and business, it's safe to say that's the case when it comes to God and the life to come.

One Way or Many Ways?

My wife and I enjoy inviting people into our home. Usually, that involves a meal. Neither of us is a great cook, but we know this: Ending an evening with a good dessert can more than make up for a mediocre main course. That does not mean we serve only one kind of dessert, because while it's true that dessert can leave people with a good taste in their mouths, we know we could make dozens of different kinds of desserts that would get the job done. One wonders if the same is true for the world's religions. Maybe it does not matter which one people choose; they all can leave people in a good place when all is said and done. Before coming to this conclusion, however, it's probably wise to see what some of the major religions have to say about this. I'll begin with Christianity.

The Exclusive Claims of Jesus

Jesus and his disciples were emphatic that there is only one way of enjoying life after death with God. That way is trusting that Jesus is the only one who can forgive your sins and make you right with God. Jesus and his disciples made this point so central to their message that before Jesus' followers were called Christians, they were called followers of *The* Way, not *A* Way.[3] Consider their words, with my emphasis added:

> Jesus continued, "You are from below; I am from above. You belong to this world; I do not. That is why I said that you will die in your sins; for *unless you believe that I AM who I claim to be, you will die in your sins.*" (John 8:23-24)

> Jesus told him, "I am the way, the truth, and the life. No one can come to the Father except through me." (John 14:6)

> Then Peter, filled with the Holy Spirit, said to them, "Rulers and elders of our people . . . *There is salvation in no one else! God has given no other name under heaven by which we must be saved.*" (Acts 4:8, 12)

> Then he [the jailer] brought them [Paul and Silas] out and asked, "Sirs, what must I do to be saved?"
> They replied, "*Believe in the Lord Jesus and you will be saved,*

along with everyone in your household." (Acts 16:30-31)

Why would Jesus say he is the only way to God and his disciples say the same? They said so based on the claim that Jesus is God himself.

> [Jesus said], "The Father and I are one."
>
> Once again the people picked up stones to kill him. Jesus said, "At my Father's direction I have done many good works. For which one are you going to stone me?"
>
> They replied, "We're stoning you not for any good work, but for blasphemy! *You, a mere man, claim to be God.*"(John 10:30-33)

> Jesus answered . . . "*Anyone who has seen Me has seen the Father!* So why are you asking Me to show Him to you?" (John 14:9)

> And now we live in fellowship with the true God because we live in fellowship with his Son, Jesus Christ. *He is the only true God, and he is eternal life.* (1 John 5:20)

Now, as you might guess, claiming that you are God and that the only way to enjoy God forever is by trusting in you is rather audacious. For many in Jesus' day, this claim was utter blasphemy and remains so even today. In fact, the only charge that was sustained against Jesus before his death was that he claimed to be God himself. He was not sentenced to death because of an act of sedition or because he was taking money from under the table; rather, Jesus was sentenced to death because he said that if you are looking for God, look no further than to him.[4]

Over the centuries people from many different religious backgrounds have recognized Jesus as a good moral teacher, but they fall short of calling him God and the way to eternal life. Jesus' teaching, however, does not afford us the option of merely calling him a good moral teacher. Jesus presented himself as God and said that our only way to eternal life is to trust in his sole authority to forgive our sins. If Jesus was wrong about this, then he was not a good moral teacher. Either he knowingly lied about himself, or he was severely deluded as to his own identity and led his followers astray. C.S. Lewis bluntly said the same in his best-selling book *Mere Christianity*:

I am trying here to prevent anyone saying the really foolish thing that people often say about Him: "I'm ready to accept Jesus as a great moral teacher, but I don't accept his claim to be God." That is the one thing we must not say. A man who was merely a man and said the sort of things Jesus said would not be a great moral teacher. He would either be a lunatic—on a level with the man who says he is a poached egg—or else he would be the Devil of Hell. You must make your choice. Either this man was, and is, the Son of God: or else a madman or something worse. You can shut Him up for a fool, you can spit at Him and kill Him as a demon; or you can fall at His feet and call Him Lord and God. But let us not come with any patronizing nonsense about His being a great human teacher. He has not left that open to us. He did not intend to.[5]

If we are to form our view of Christianity from the words of Jesus and his early followers, we must come to the conclusion that Jesus was God himself, and it was his life and death and resurrection that paved the way for all who trust in him to be made right with God now and throughout eternity. We must also conclude that this claim was exclusive in nature. That is, Jesus did not say, "I am *a* way to God, but there are others as well." Instead he said that he was the only way. Undoubtedly, Jesus' claim was exclusive in its day, and it remains exclusive today. The only question is whether such exclusivity is warranted.

The Exclusive Claims of Other Religions

Jesus made exclusive claims about himself and about the way to God. That, in and of itself, might make you wince. But making exclusive claims is not unusual among religions. A quick review of major religions indicates that exclusive claims are par for the course.

Islam. Next to Christianity, Islam has more adherents than any religion in the world. Like Christianity, Islam makes exclusive claims. For example, Islam is strictly monotheistic and renounces any form of polytheism, pantheism, or monism common to Eastern religions. It holds that we have one life to live and rejects the idea of reincarnation. Furthermore, Islam says that the path to Allah is through adhering to these Five Pillars of Faith:

- Sincerely reciting the Muslim profession of faith: "There is no God but Allah, and Muhammad is his messenger."
- Performing ritual prayers in the proper way five times each day
- Giving alms equal to 2.5% of one's wealth (not income) each year for the benefit of the poor
- Fasting during the daylight hours of the month of Ramadan
- Completing a pilgrimage to Mecca

Those who do not live up to these pillars, particularly the first pillar, are not likely to fare well before Allah. In other words, Islam says there is a pathway to Allah—and Christianity, Hinduism, and Buddhism are most definitely not it. The Qur'an even makes sure to point out that those who believe Jesus is God and Savior are forbidden from Paradise and will find themselves in "the Fire."[6] If you are looking for inclusivity, you won't find it in Islam any more than Christianity.

Judaism and Christianity share common roots and a similar respect for the Old Testament Scriptures. Judaism, however, rejects the claim of Jesus' Messiahship and the idea that God consists of three persons (Father, Son, and Holy Spirit). In fact, many Jews today do not believe that a personal Messiah will ever come. For Jews, a Messiah who sacrifices his life for humanity's sin is unnecessary, since sacrifices, penitence, and good deeds are enough to earn God's favor. Of course, in saying this, Judaism makes claims that are in direct contradiction to Christianity. But Judaism does not just distance itself from Christianity; it contradicts other religions as well. For example, Judaism holds that its Scriptures have been properly preserved, and rejects the Muslim claim that they have been corrupted and are in error. Or consider Judaism's embrace of strict monotheism. It is not only at odds with Christianity's trinitarian beliefs but also in contradiction with pantheism or monism[7] as taught by Eastern religions. Again, like it or not, Judaism makes exclusive claims.

Hinduism. Many recognize that the great monotheistic religions like Christianity, Islam, and Judaism make exclusive claims but suggest that Eastern religions like Hinduism are properly inclusive. A closer look indicates otherwise. Consider some of what Hinduism teaches:

- God is one and more than one at the same time.
- God, or Brahman, has no personality.
- Brahman can be evil as well as good, so there is no divine will that

sets the standard for what is right and wrong.

- Brahman didn't create the world; he just dreamed it, so what we see and experience is just an illusion, including our own individuality.
- Brahman dreamed up the world for play, so there is no purpose to it.
- Life is fatalistic. What you are experiencing today is karma for your past, and there is no way around it.
- After death we reincarnate, until we ultimately become enlightened.
- Part of becoming enlightened is understanding that we are all part of one really big soul. We are all Brahman.

You can see that these claims of Hinduism are rather exclusive. They rule out the possibility that the world is real, that we have free will that is subject to divine moral standards, or that there is a day of reckoning before a personal God, all of which are common elements of the great monotheistic religions. And while Hindus might say you can worship Mohammad or Christ within Hinduism, they do so only because they believe both figures will lose their individuality and ultimately be absorbed into Brahman. Thus, while Hinduism is often cast as an inclusive religion, Hindus are just as likely as Christians, Muslims, or Jews to exclude the claims of other religions, even to the point of persecuting Christians or Muslims in their midst.[8]

Buddhism seems to be the hippest of religions in recent years, but it is no less exclusive than other religions. It even sets itself apart from Hinduism, from which it finds its roots. For instance, it rejects Hinduism's caste system and questions the authority of the Hindu *Vedas*, or scriptures. By not recognizing an almighty God and by believing there is no such thing as sin, Buddhism also finds itself excluding the three great monotheistic beliefs of Christianity, Islam, and Judaism. This is brought home to me regularly by a Buddhist friend who likes to counter nearly any Christian claim I might make. If you are looking for a religion that does not make exclusive claims, Buddhism is not the place to turn.

Of course, there are more religions than the ones that I have quickly reviewed here, but I think you can see the trend. Religions all across the board are good at making exclusive claims. Regularly, I hear from others that all religions basically teach the same thing, but those who say this have probably not taken the time to study the different religions. While it may be true that many religions tell you to be kind to your neighbor, there are fundamental differences in how different religions view God, humanity, reality, the way to God, and the afterlife. Of course, claiming that all religions are the same sounds inclusive and even tolerant, but such a claim does not accurately represent what the followers of different religions declare about their own religion. Imagine telling the average Muslim that what he believes is really no different from what a Jew believes or suggesting to a Mormon that their beliefs are really the same as those held by Jehovah's Witnesses. I am guessing you will get a lot of pushback, and you will get pushback because they do not believe the same thing. They make claims that are exclusive of one another.

Don is one of my colleagues in southern California. Some years back he held a forum that allowed attendees to hear from various religious leaders. Among Don's panelists were local Hindu, Buddhist, Baha'i, and Christian leaders who were each given a chance to share the main tenets of their faith. Once they made their presentations, Don posed the following question to the crowd, "Do you think, after what you've just heard, that the world agrees about God?" To his surprise, the crowd almost unanimously said yes. But it was not just Don who was surprised; the guest panelists were stunned and even disturbed. Their response was "They are not listening to us. We do not believe the same things." The religious leaders had made exclusive claims—claims that were opposed to one another—and to suggest that their beliefs were one and the same was just plain wrong.

If we are to be honest about the various religions of the world, including Christianity, we must admit that they make claims that are exclusive of one another. And when claims are exclusive of one another, it may be that all are wrong, but they cannot all be right. Either we must reject all religions as lacking the whole truth, or we can recognize one of the religions as having gotten it right. We are not left with an option of believing them all to be true in all they proclaim without bumping into some severe contradictions.[9]

One Reason We Incorrectly Lump All Religions Together

It is not uncommon for people such as those in the crowd at Don's event in southern California to believe that all religions are the same. Some of this has to do with a lack of knowledge about what the various religions teach. At other times, however, it has to do with confusion over the use of similar terms. Two religions, for example, may use the term *God* but define God in very different ways.

Suppose in a conversation I mention a friend named Christy. I begin to describe her, and you say, "I know Christy." You make that claim because the things I have shared about Christy match the Christy you know. For instance, if we were to list out the characteristics I shared about Christy early in the conversation, it might look like this:

My friend Christy	Your friend Christy
Tall	Tall
Dark Hair	Dark Hair
Ran on Track Team	Ran on Track Team

Since what I say of Christy matches up with what you know of Christy, you have reason to believe that the Christy we each know is one and the same. But what if I go on and give more details that are no longer consistent with what you know to be true of your friend Christy?

My friend Christy	Your friend Christy
Father was a doctor	Father was a lawyer
Was in bad car accident	Was not in bad car accident
Graduated from OSU	Graduated from USC

Given these new details, it is best to say we no longer are speaking of the same person. Our friends may share the same name, but they are not the same person.

The same dynamic exists with the teachings of various religions. At times, we errantly believe different religions are saying the same thing because of common terms, but a closer examination reveals different religions to be making very different and even exclusive claims. Ask leaders of each religion to describe what God is like, his interaction with humanity, and his demands on humanity and you are bound to find great disparity. Thus, while most religious roads lead to a god of some sort, they are not leading to the same God, for the simple reason that they are not speaking about the same God.

It's Hard Not To Be Exclusive

At this point, you may recognize that all religions do not say the same thing. You may also be willing to admit that they make exclusive and contradictory claims that keep all of them from being completely right. At the same time, you might believe that none of them have it right; that they are all wrong. Of course, this is a possibility. When two exclusive claims are made, such as 2 + 2 = 5 and 2 + 2 = 3, it is not possible for them both to be right, but they could both be wrong as we see for both of these equations. Could this be the case for the various religions as well? Could they all be wrong? Could the truth be found outside any of the present religions of the world? Again, this is a possibility, but if you come to that conclusion, you ought to recognize you are still opting for an exclusive claim. You are saying that new option X is correct and old options A, B, C, and D, are not. Even if you try to remove yourself from having to choose a religion by saying something like, "I don't believe it is possible for anyone to know which religion is correct," you are still making an exclusive claim. You are saying it can't be known which religion is correct, and those who say otherwise are wrong.

Consider the well-used tale of the blind men and the elephant. In this story, several blind men feel a different part of an elephant. One touches the side of the elephant and says it is a wall. Another touches the trunk and says it is a snake. A third touches the tusk and says it is a spear. The trend continues as several other blind men touch different parts of the elephant. As an argument ensues among the blind men as to the nature of the elephant, a wise ruler is awakened by the commotion. Upon hearing the complaints of the blind men, the ruler tells them that none of them properly understands the whole of the elephant. Each has only one part of the story right.

The elephant metaphor long has been used to say that every religion provides some portion of the God story, and we get the whole story only if we put them all together. At first blush, this approach appears to be a rather inclusive way to view the religions since each religion is able to contribute to the whole. But a closer examination reveals that the story falls short of its aim. Rather than the ruler telling the blind men that it does not matter what each man believes because whatever they believe is essentially the same and leads to the same end, he instead tells them that each of their viewpoints is lacking and that there is a single and proper way to view the elephant as whole. Furthermore, he does not say that the elephant is the same as a lion or a bear. In doing so, the ruler declares that there is an accurate, even exclusive way to describe an elephant, and other ways of describing it are shamefully incomplete or just plain wrong. This means that the blind men, if they are going to embrace truth, must discard their old conception of the elephant and replace it with something completely new. So, instead of the elephant metaphor supporting inclusivity, it supports an exclusive view of truth and once again shows us that it's hard not to be exclusive when it comes to religion.

Why Christianity? The Answer is Jesus

So far I've tried to explain that there is nothing inherently wrong with suggesting that one religion represents the truth while others do not. I've also attempted to show that every religion makes exclusive claims and would frankly have a difficult time doing otherwise. What I have not done, however, is directly address the question: Why Christianity? Why do I believe Christianity is the only religion that properly represents what we can know about God and our relationship with him? I could approach this question in more than one way, but there's great value in focusing the answer on the person of Jesus. It's not to say that other characters in the Bible don't also speak to the truth of Christianity, but since the story of Christianity is centered so squarely on Jesus, its truth rests largely on him. That said, let me share with you several reasons why Jesus gives me reason to embrace the claims of Christianity instead of the other world religions.

Jesus was a real person. I hope by now you've come to see that the historical evidence for the life of Jesus is really quite remarkable for someone who lived 2,000 years ago. Especially when you consider that Jesus didn't lead armies, build an impressive earthly kingdom, offer the world a new invention, or have the wealth of Jeff Bezos. Many religions do not speak of historical figures showing up in distinct cities or confronting specific rulers; they speak only of mystical gods or teachings of the wise. This puts them at a decided disadvantage. How can we have any confidence that they are telling us the truth if they are not tied into at least some historical evidence that we can examine? In Jesus, though, we have a flesh-and-blood person that can be fact-checked. If what we find in the annals of history matches up with what Christianity says about Jesus, then a deeper look into Christianity is worth checking out.

Having historical evidence about Jesus is particularly handy when other religions mention Jesus too. Take, for example, the Muslim claim about Jesus' crucifixion. According to the Qur'an Jesus was not crucified by Pilate. But since we have eyewitness accounts of the crucifixion as recorded in the Gospels, as well as five non-Christian accounts of the event written within 100 years of Jesus death,[10] it is difficult to trust the writings of Mohammad that were authored some 600 years after the event. Or consider the Mormon claim that after his death and resurrection, Jesus came to North America to spend time with a group of Jews who somehow made their way across the Atlantic to the Americas. You won't find historical evidence to support the Mormon narrative, but the evidence does support the biblical record of Jesus. This gives Christianity a decided credibility edge, and once again highlights the value of Jesus being a real person that can be historically evaluated.

The unique claims of Jesus. Earlier I presented the claims of Jesus. He said that he is equal to God and that by trusting in him a person can enjoy life with God, now and forever. Of course, just because someone says something like that doesn't make it true. But as I outlined earlier, given the documented historical nature of these claims we are left with three options: We can label Jesus a liar, dismiss him as a lunatic, or take him at his word. The liar option seems rather hard to swallow, given that Jesus' adversaries had a hard time pinning any kind of wrongdoing on him. (More on that later.) The lunatic option also seems far-fetched when we consider Jesus' great compassion toward others, his verbal acuity when dealing with critics, and his avoidance of crowd adulation.[11] At least in my experience, that's not the behavior of a madman. But if Jesus is not a liar or a lunatic, that only leaves open the option of his claim to be Lord.

Jesus authenticated his claims. If Jesus is really God and the one we ought to follow, I want something that gives weight to Jesus' claims. I want something beyond words that has the fingerprints of God all over it. When we look at Jesus, that's what we get. Take, for example, Jesus' meeting with a paralytic.

Soon the house where [Jesus] was staying was so packed with visitors that there was no more room, even outside the door. While he was preaching God's word to them, four men arrived carrying a paralyzed man on a mat. They couldn't bring him to Jesus because of the crowd, so they dug a hole through the roof above his head. Then they lowered the man on his mat, right down in front of Jesus. Seeing their faith, Jesus said to the paralyzed man, "My child, your sins are forgiven."

But some of the teachers of religious law who were sitting there thought to themselves, "What is he saying? This is blasphemy! Only God can forgive sins!"

Jesus knew immediately what they were thinking, so he asked them, "Why do you question this in your hearts? Is it easier to say to the paralyzed man 'Your sins are forgiven,' or 'Stand up, pick up your mat, and walk'? So I will prove to you that the Son of Man[a] has the authority on earth to forgive sins." Then Jesus turned to the paralyzed man and said, "Stand up, pick up your mat, and go home!"

And the man jumped up, grabbed his mat, and walked out through the stunned onlookers. They were all amazed and praised God, exclaiming, "We've never seen anything like this before!" (Mark 2:2-12)

I am not sure the paralyzed man was looking to be forgiven on the day he was carried to Jesus, yet that was what Jesus initially offered him. But how could Jesus forgive his sins? It's not as if the man said something stupid to Jesus the week prior, and Jesus was telling him to forget about it. No, Jesus had never met the man before, which means that when he offered to forgive the man's sins, he was including all those deep dark things the man thought he'd done in secret but God knew all about. Who could forgive sin like that except God alone? That is exactly why the religious leaders sent up a red flag. This was blasphemy of the first degree.

But Jesus didn't leave it there. He didn't just say, "You've got to take my word for it." He knew very well that forgiveness was an invisible transaction and that anyone could say something similar. So to verify that forgiveness had taken place and that he, as God, had the authority to grant such forgiveness, he healed the man in front of their eyes. This is what I mean when I say Jesus authenticated his claims by doing the supernatural. If Jesus had done this only once, he would demand some attention, but he did it repeatedly.[12] That's what makes me think there is substance to his claims.

Not long before Jesus' death, he was approached by a woman named

Martha whose brother Lazarus had died. She had great respect for Jesus, and says, "Lord, if only You had been here, my brother would not have died." Jesus tells her that her brother will rise again. She figures that Jesus is speaking about some future resurrection. Instead Jesus tells her, "I am the resurrection and the life. Anyone who believes in me will live, even after dying. Everyone who lives in me and believes in me will never ever die" (John 11:25-26). That's a nice claim, but why should she believe Jesus? Why should she believe that Jesus has power over life and death for all eternity? So Jesus authenticates his claim by raising her brother to life after Lazarus had been lying dead for four days. Undoubtedly, this miracle emboldened Martha to trust in Jesus, but would it be enough to sustain her hope if Jesus could not conquer death for himself?

I know I already shared a great deal about Jesus' resurrection back in Chapter 8, but I really did not share a great deal about its significance. So, let me do so now. Jesus claims to be the way to eternal life with God. He said that if we ask him to forgive our sins and trust him for our future that we can enjoy life with God forever. But why should we trust him on this? Again, anyone can make such a claim, and we usually steer far away from those who do. That's what makes Jesus' resurrection so important. He demonstrated that he really does hold the keys to life and death. Look up any other religious leader and you will find that they died, end of story. They may have said they knew the way to life after death, but how can you trust them? Only in Jesus do we find one who authenticates his power over death.

The way Jesus treated others. Jesus did not just make great claims and turn heads with well-timed miracles; he treated people with remarkable compassion and care. This means he not only noticed society's throwaways but pursued them, sometimes even ministering to people others would not even touch. Take, for example, a leper, whose disease required him by law to keep his distance from all but other lepers. If people inadvertently came near, the leper would have to call them off so that they kept their distance. Employment was impossible, family relations were lost, and death was imminent. Nonetheless, we read that in a fit of desperation, a leper comes kneeling at Jesus' feet. Jesus had every right to call him off, but instead Jesus reaches out and *touches* the man. In doing so, Jesus not only healed the man but also embraced those whom others deemed to be "untouchable."[13]

Or consider Jesus' interaction with Zacchaeus, a tax collector. You and I might not be fans of the IRS, but we do not think that all who work for it should be frowned upon. In Jesus' day, however, no self-respecting Jew would have a good word to say about a tax collector. Tax collectors where Jesus lived and traveled were Jews hired by the occupying Romans. Their job was to collect taxes from the Jews to support the very ones that were oppressing the Jews. In other words, tax collectors were traitors. Add to this the fact that tax collectors would often pad their own pockets with extra surcharges and it is easy to see why they were despised. But Jesus didn't despise them at all. One day he sees a tax collector named Zacchaeus taking particular interest in Jesus' teaching, so Jesus invites himself to Zacchaeus' house. This is no small gesture. Culturally, that would have been like saying, "Zacchaeus, I like you, so let's hang out." What were the results? By the end of Jesus' stay Zacchaeus becomes a different man, giving half his possessions to the poor and returning the money he had stolen through the years.[14]

Finally, there is Jesus' conversation with a woman at a local watering hole. Because she was a woman, Jesus would have done well by society's standards to keep her at a distance. Perhaps he could be forgiven if she was the sweet grandmotherly type, but the woman had been married five times and was now living with a sixth man—hardly the kind of woman with whom a rabbi would initiate conversation. But that's not all. She was also a Samaritan, which meant she was of a people who mixed a little Judaism with a little worship of other gods. A good Jew would literally add miles to their journey just to avoid even the best of Samaritans. And yet we see Jesus purposely travel to where she lived and begin a conversation that in a matter of hours sets her free from every poor choice and disadvantage that had burdened her for so long.[15] Throughout his ministry, Jesus was accused of being a friend to tax collectors and sinners,[16] like Zacchaeus and the woman at the well. He would treat them no other way. For that reason alone, Jesus' life seems to point to the truth.

The sinless life of Jesus. Religions aren't big on declaring their leaders sinless or without fault. Muhammad recognized his own need for forgiveness.[17] Buddha tried asceticism for six years before realizing that was not on the proper road. Moses murdered a man and was prevented from going into the promised land for losing his temper. But Jesus is presented as one who never chose a wrong path, or succumbed to temptation, or lined his own pockets, or made unwarranted judgments of others, or did in private what he forbade in public. There is hardly anything that irritated his enemies more than this fact. Repeatedly, they tried to trap him in his words or find him doing something wrong.[18] And yet after every attempt, they'd leave more befuddled and angrier than before. In the end, they had to hire false witnesses to make up lies about Jesus, but even these did not stick. The only charge they could ultimately make against Jesus is that of blasphemy for claiming to be God.[19] Today, we fear following leaders, especially religious ones. We've been burned too many times before. Those we thought were worthy of honor had serious skeletons in their closets. Not so with Jesus.

The sacrificial offer of Jesus. If Jesus came to earth to show off that he was God but then left without saying how I might be made right with him now and forever, there wouldn't be much in Christianity for me. Likewise, if he came and offered a detailed self-help plan with all kinds of prayers and practices and rituals that could never be perfectly upheld, he would have done little more than what other religious leaders did before and after him. Instead, Jesus did something wholly different. He basically said, "I love you, but you know as well as I do that your best efforts will never meet God's standards. So here is what I am going to do. Even though you deserve judgment for the ways you have fallen short of the glory of God, I will take the brunt of that judgment for you. I will offer my life as a sacrificial payment for all you have not done, cannot do, and will never do in the future. All I ask in return is that you humbly recognize the error of your ways and willingly receive the gift of salvation that I offer."

Years ago, I sat at an old friend's hospital bedside. His name was Cliff, and his last days were upon him. We had talked of God over the years, but I was still unsure of where he stood. So as he lay in bed, I told him a parable of Jesus. It reads like this:

> Two men went to the Temple to pray. One was a Pharisee, and the other was a despised tax collector. The Pharisee stood by himself and prayed this prayer: "I thank you, God, that I am not like other people—cheaters, sinners, adulterers. I'm certainly not like that tax collector! I fast twice a week, and I give you a tenth of my income."
>
> But the tax collector stood at a distance and dared not even lift his eyes to heaven as he prayed. Instead, he beat his chest in sor-

row, saying, "O God, be merciful to me, for I am a sinner." I [Jesus] tell you, this sinner, not the Pharisee, returned home justified before God. For those who exalt themselves will be humbled, and those who humble themselves will be exalted. (Luke 18:10-14)

After sharing these words, I said, "Cliff, just cry out to Jesus like the tax collector, and Jesus will take you home to be with him." Cliff was in no place to do anything more than what I asked. Cliff was not in a place to make a big donation to charity. It was too late to reverse his years of alcoholism. And he was in no condition to visit the nearest house of worship and recite certain prayers. But, based on what Jesus said, none of that was necessary. Cliff simply had to turn his heart heavenward and recognize he needed Jesus—the one who offers mercy, not a report card.

About two weeks later, I gathered in a room with a couple hundred others. They all came in remembrance of Cliff. The gathering was not at a church or a funeral home but at a private club where food and wine was provided in abundance. Through a surprising set of events, I was asked to speak. I spoke of fun things I remembered about Cliff, like the fact that he would give a dollar to each of my children on every one of their birthdays. But then I told the crowd what I shared with Cliff at his bedside. I spoke of the parable, and let them know that after sharing it with Cliff, I said, "Cliff, just cry out to Jesus and he will take you home to be with him." And as I looked across the room, filled with people who were little more religious than Cliff, I could hardly find a dry eye. Why was that? Why did the tears flow? I believe it is because the sacrificial offer of Jesus is like no other. It is there for the best and the worst of us. It is an offer that remains to our last dying breath.

Why do I think Christianity is the only way among the world's religions? It has largely to do with Jesus. He simply is like no other. Nearly every religion wants a piece of Jesus. Muslims call him a great prophet. Buddhists consider him an enlightened one. Hindus see him as a venerable avatar. Mormons, Jehovah's Witnesses, Christian Scientists, and many others look to Jesus as a great example. So why not go with the one religion that puts Jesus front and center, the one religion that is supported by the historical record? It's the one religion that deeply recognizes our own failings and yet offers God's mercy, no strings attached. And it's the one religion that offers not just principles and rules but a person—

Jesus Christ—to worship and follow. There is a reason Jesus said, "I am *the* way, *the* truth, and *the* life. No one can come to the Father except through me" (John 14:6, emphasis added).

Sundar Singh (1889-1929) was born into a wealthy Sikh family in what is now northern India. His mother raised him to be a Sadhu, an ascetic yogi concerned solely with the spiritual life, and he was deeply educated in Hindu thought. He angrily fought the attempts of Westerners to bring Christianity to his region and burned any Bibles that came into his hands. Singh's religious pursuits, however, left him empty, and by age 16, he was prepared to take his life. But an encounter with Jesus changed him overnight.

His family was stunned and pleaded that he return to his ancestral faith, later chasing him out of his home. Persecution, including an attempted poisoning, nearly ended his life, but Singh survived and traveled far and wide to tell others of Jesus. In addition to venturing to Nepal and Tibet, he traveled east to Burma, China, and Japan. Later he headed to Australia, Hawaii, North America, and throughout Western Europe. Though he sought no fame, crowds made up of not only commoners but curious intellectuals often greeted him. Among these was a professor of comparative religions at the University of Cambridge. The professor asked Singh, "What have you found in Christianity that you have not found in your old religion?" Singh replied, "Professor, I have found the dear Lord Jesus." Not fully grasping Singh's reply, the professor pressed on: "Oh, yes, I quite understand, but what principle or doctrine? Tell me, what new philosophy have you found in Christianity?" Again, Singh simply replied, "Professor, I have found the dear Lord Jesus."[20]

I know that saying biblical Christianity is the right or only way may sound exclusive or intolerant or narrow-minded. And in one sense it is. But if Christianity is true, if Jesus is who he said he is, it is none of these things in a pejorative sense. As discussed earlier, we are exclusive or intolerant or narrow-minded about plenty of things, and rightfully so. We don't want any quack providing any dose of any kind of pill. We want what makes us well, even if there is only one prescription to get us there. Christianity makes a robust claim that Jesus is the only prescription for our souls. Christianity does not declare this out of arrogance but makes this claim because Jesus himself said he is the only way and has supported his case well. But note this: When it comes to Christianity, the prescription is not only for a few, nor is it out of people's reach. It is something Jesus offers free of charge to people of every race and every gender and every background regardless of their rap sheet. It is something that is available to those who grow up in the Christian tradition of the West or the Sikh tradition of the East. So even with all of Jesus' exclusive claims, it's hard to be more inclusive than that.

Key Points

- A position on any matter can be exclusive and wrong, or it can be exclusive and right.

- It is good to be tolerant of people, but this does not mean we should be tolerant of all ideas or behaviors.

- Sincerity is a valuable trait, but it does not validate someone's efforts or beliefs. A person can be sincere about something (including a religious viewpoint) and yet be completely in error.

- Jesus made exclusive claims. He said he was God and that trusting in him is the only way to enjoy forgiveness and eternal life.

- All religions make exclusive claims. Even religions that seem to be inclusive of other religions say that their position is correct and that others are wrong.

- It is impossible not to be exclusive. When people say that all religions are the same, or all religions are wrong, or that it cannot be known which religion is right, they are still making claims that exclude other viewpoints.

- Reasons to believe that Christianity is the only way center on the person of Jesus. His historical nature, his unique claims, the authentication of those claims, his treatment of others, his sinless life, and his sacrificial offer all point to the fact that Christianity is true.

- Jesus gave his life so that he can offer the free gift of eternal life to people of every race, gender, and background. This is very inclusive.

Additional Resources

God Among Sages: Why Jesus Is Not Just Another Religious Leader, Kenneth Richard Samples

Choosing Your Faith: In a World of Spiritual Options, Mark Mittelberg

Neighboring Faiths: A Christian Introduction to World Religions, Winfried Corduan

Between One Faith and Another: Engaging Conversations on the World's Great Religions, Peter Kreeft

Putting Jesus in His Place: The Case for the Deity of Christ, Robert M. Bowman, Jr. and J. Ed Komoszewski

I'm a Good Person—
Isn't That Enough?

Heart trouble will get your attention. It certainly did for Dave. He had not been feeling well, and scans showed he needed a couple of well-placed stents to open two arteries. Doctors casually call this kind of surgery an everyday procedure, but it doesn't seem so commonplace if you are the one needing the operation! I asked Dave if he had any concerns about dying. He said the thought had crossed his mind, but judging by the look on his face, the thought was more the size of an 18-wheeler than a mini-scooter. As we talked further, I asked, "Dave, if you were to die, do you think you would be good with God? Do you think you'd make it to heaven?" Dave didn't answer immediately but gave it some thought. Eventually, he said, "I think so. The way I look at it, life is like a scale, and if you put more good things on one side of the scale than bad things on the other, you'll probably be okay." Dave's answer is not unusual. In fact, it is the most common answer I get when I talk with others about how to get it into heaven. If there is a way through the pearly gates of eternal bliss, most people say a positive balance of good works is the answer.

Why the Good Works Model Makes Sense

When people think of heaven, they usually imagine something good. They describe heaven as filled with fishing or golf, seaside walks or espressos at a favorite coffee shop. That's why if you are the type of person who enjoyed long hikes before you breathed your last, someone will probably say something sentimental at your funeral like, "Jane is probably enjoying a 'heavenly' hike in the mountains right now and looking down with a smile on us all." Heaven, if it is heavenly, is filled with the good stuff. But for most people, heaven isn't just where the good stuff is; it's also where the good people are. At least, I don't think most people's picture of heaven has Stalin, Hitler, and Kim Jong-un of North Korea sitting at a table planning out how they are going to one-up tyrants of old like Atilla the Hun and Genghis Kahn in the next round of rape, pillage, and murder. No, if heaven is a good place, it must be full of good people doing good things.

This is why the "good works" model for getting into heaven makes so much sense to Dave and many others. If heaven is as grand as we hope it to be, then only good people must be allowed. And if we want in, we better be more nice than naughty. We must have a resume filled with plenty of good deeds.

Why the Good Works Model *Doesn't* Make Sense

If I created a "Good People Club," it makes sense that I would require people to show proof of goodness before I admitted them. So, I understand why people look to the scales of their life as they ponder their own qualifications for heaven. But over the years, I have noticed a number of shortcomings when it comes to the good works model. You may have noticed the first of these shortcomings. It has to do with who sets the standard. In other words, if it's good works that gets you into heaven, who decides what is good?

My wife is reading a story right now of a man who killed his wife's ex-husband because the ex was doing things he shouldn't have with her daughters. It may be a little hard keeping all those characters straight, but all you need to know is that the revengeful husband who killed the ex is now spending life in prison without parole. As far as our justice system is concerned, he is a bad guy and deserves to spend his life behind bars. Not too infrequently, however, I read of honor killings in places like the Middle East. Someone violates some young girls, and in a manner of days the offender is killed by the young girls' family and with plenty of community support. In other words, in some places murderous revenge is not only acceptable but also even lauded.

The variation in what is considered good and bad occurs not just across cultures but within cultures as well. Consider some of the property damage and looting that may transpire in the aftermath of a police shooting. Business owners whose stores are damaged may look at such action as bad, but some protestors may feel such actions are important and good in order to see societal change. So which is it? In situations like this, who is good and who is bad? And who decides? If we can't get these questions answered, I'm not sure anyone can be too confident they are headed to heaven.

The second problem I see with the good works model is that even if we knew what counted as good works, we are still left guessing as to whether we have done enough. In other words, can we really answer the question: How good is good enough? I, for one, have not been good at keeping an accounting along the way. And even if I did, how would I know if the ledger counts in my favor or not? I don't know anyone who thinks they are perfect, which means that if we have a hope of getting into heaven by way of our good works, we must be under the impression that we do not need a perfect score. But what score do we need? Do we need to have completed 90% of all the good deeds we could have done, 75%, 51%? And what if all our deeds, good or bad, came with different scores? The recent sitcom *The Good Place* assigned +2.09 points for stepping carefully over a flowerbed and +295.98 points for supplying pure water to a small village. At the same time, you receive a score of -90.90 for ruining an opera with boorish behavior and a whopping -433,115.25 for committing genocide.[1] You might laugh at this, but based on the people I've talked to, there's a good chance you think along these lines.

Undoubtedly, the whole scoring business complicates things, but it gets downright messy when we consider whether it is outcomes or intentions that matter when it comes to good works. Imagine taking your friend to the emergency room because she has not been feeling well, and in your hurry to get there you cause an accident that results in serious neck and back injuries for your friend. Your intentions toward your friend were good, but the outcome was not. So does this count for or against you? Or suppose you've always been a bit insecure when it comes to your siblings. You want to prove that you are smarter than all of them and put them in their place. Your hard work and ingenuity pan out. Wealth and success come your way, and all are impressed. Furthermore, to get your family's attention, you make a big donation to a local hospital that ends up helping thousands of kids. Most would argue that the outcome of your efforts was good, but do you get credit in God's system given your rather self-centered intentions?

This all brings me to one more problem with the good works model for getting into heaven. With all this confusion about what counts as a good work and how many good works are necessary to make it into heaven, it seems like we could lay some blame on God. In fact, if the good works model really is our way in, then God turns out to be a rather unattractive character—one we can hardly consider just or loving. That might seem like a stretch, but let me explain. My guess is that at some time in your academic pursuits you ran across a teacher or two who were fuzzy on what constituted success in their class. Instead of providing you with a detailed syllabus with timelines and objectives or telling you what to expect on upcoming exams, they simply said, "If you study hard, you will do just fine." When you heard that, I am guessing you weren't too thrilled. And if you ended up doing poorly in the class, or even failing despite an earnest effort, you were probably downright angry. What kind of teacher keeps the standards so vague? Certainly not a fair or caring one. Well, if that's the case for a teacher who is fuzzy on what is necessary to succeed in a class, wouldn't that also be the case for God if he is similarly unclear in letting us know how we make it into heaven? What keeps us from thinking of God as a tyrant if he refuses to tell us just what we are to do, how often we must be successful, and what our current score is? Imagine getting to the gates of heaven, and God saying, "Sorry, but you are one good deed short." That's hardly a God you'd want to spend eternity with! So maybe the good works model for getting to heaven isn't all it is made out to be.

We Aren't Good Enough

You may have never thought about the shortcomings of the good works model. Most people haven't. But there is something else you may have never considered. You might even be quite surprised by it. Although it is commonplace among the world's religions to say, "Do this or that and do it lots of times so that all goes well for you in the life to come," Christianity boldly says forget about good works when it comes to getting into heaven. Don't get me wrong, the Bible encourages us all along to do things that God likes (like being generous with others or not cheating on your wife), but it is emphatic that no matter how many good things we do, it will never be enough to earn our way to heaven. That might be hard to swallow if you've always thought that good people like Mother Teresa or Mahatma Gandhi or your dear sweet aunt who made you cookies every Sunday were shoe-ins given their track record. But it might be a bit easier to understand if you examine the bar God sets to get in and how short any of us come to reaching it.

First, let's take a look at the Ten Commandments.[2] Lots of people think they are a pretty good measuring stick for how we are doing with God. Take a glance at the list and you might be quick to say you've never worshipped an idol or murdered someone, so all is well and good. But can you really say you've never stolen anything? Didn't you at least take something from your brother when he wasn't looking or conveniently forget to return something you knew wasn't yours? And how about the commandment about not taking the Lord's name in vain? Yes, that includes blurting out "Jesus Christ!" with perhaps a few other choice words when your team gives up a touchdown. How are you doing on that one? Or consider the last of the commandments; it has to do with not coveting your neighbor's wife or property. Maybe you were never interested in his bride, but what about the F-250 Platinum truck equipped with an off-road package that is parked in his garage? Clearly, if living up to the Ten Commandments is the standard for getting into heaven, things aren't looking too good.

But our situation gets worse when we get to Jesus. He brings up these same commandments but says that even having thoughts that lean toward violating a commandment lands us short. For example, Jesus mentioned the commandment "Do not murder" and then said that anyone who has a hateful thought toward another is just as worthy of judgment as a murderer (Matthew 5:21-22). That might seem like overkill, but maybe we are not seeing sin in the right way. Imagine someone hands you a glass of water. Just before you drink it, your friend tells you that it has a drop of cyanide in it. Of course, you put down the glass immediately and ask her what on earth she was thinking when giving it to you. And if she said, "Well, I only put a drop in it. It's not like I poured a whole bottle in," you would probably be aghast and reply, "But a drop is enough to kill me!" And you'd be right—a drop would be enough to kill you. Similarly, a drop of sin is enough to kill our chances at heaven, because God has no intention of letting heaven be tainted by even a hint of sin and its destructive forces. We might do lots of good things and be labeled as a good person by those who know us, but we all still carry with us at least a drop of sin. And that's the last thing God wants to let into heaven.

A few years ago, I sat with an older man named Ted who told me he had recently started reading the Bible. Ted said the one thing he did not like about the Bible is that it says we are all sinners. He emphatically disagreed. Ted told me all the good things he had done and declared himself not a sinner. I then brought up Jesus' words. In fact, I told Ted about the time when Jesus said, "You have heard the commandment that says, 'You must not commit adultery.' But I say, anyone who even looks at a woman with lust has already committed adultery with her in his heart" (Matthew 5:27-28). That's right, Jesus said that it doesn't take a sultry hookup with someone to break God's commandment about adultery; you can do it in your mind! You should have seen Ted's eyes when I told him this. They were as wide as saucers, and as we parted that day, Ted told me, "You have given me much to think about." And I think that was Jesus' point. Jesus wanted to give us much to think about. He wanted us to recognize that try as we might we always fall short of what God's standard is for us—a standard that is equal to the perfect character of God. James, Jesus' brother, wrote: "For the person who keeps all of the laws except one is as guilty as a person who has broken all of God's law" (James 2:10). Given that perspective, no wonder that Jesus and his followers conclude that "No one is righteous—not even one" (Romans 3:10), and that all have earned God's judgment.

This really hit home for me some years back. I was watching a film that had a man standing in front of a large white wall. On the wall were all kinds of words like selfishness, lust, rage, gluttony, arrogance, and bitterness. There were also words that mentioned good things left undone, like the time you could have helped some people but purposely ignored them. The presenter in front of the wall said that if all his thoughts and deeds of the last month were publicly displayed on a wall like the one he was standing in front of, he would be utterly ashamed. He would leave town, change his name, and make sure no one ever connected him to that wall of shame. When he shared this, I knew exactly how he felt. I knew that if all the things I didn't do that I should have done, and all the things I did do that I shouldn't have, along with every thought that ran through my head, were made public, I would be disgraced and would run for the hills. Even before my family and friends I would be utterly ashamed. But if I couldn't show my face to them, what makes me think I would be in a good place with God? What makes me think God would consider me good enough to get into heaven? When I considered the wall of my life, it became clearer than ever: No one can be good in God's book by good works, because no one is all that good. I think that's what the Bible is getting at it when it says, "For no one can ever be made right with God by doing what the law commands" (Romans 3:20).

The Standard Is Perfection

My wife teaches tennis at a beautiful club. It is as nice as any I have visited around the country. It has a wonderful clubhouse that can easily hold lavish events for hundreds of people. There are patio seating options shaded by towering pines, and two wonderful pools that are kept sparkling clean. The 34 courts are always well kept, and the grounds make you feel like you've left the city whenever you play. Membership into the club is pricey, and monthly dues are substantial. To get in, you must go through an interview process and be recommended by existing members. One qualification that does not exist for getting into the club, however, is that you play perfect tennis. You can mishit every other ball you swing at, forget the score of every game, and hold the racquet like you're gripping a frying pan and they'll still let you in, as long as you meet enough of the other standards, and, of course, dish out the necessary funds.

If you tend toward believing that heaven exists, there is a good chance that you think that enjoying its streets of gold is probably like becoming a member of my wife's club. You've got to give a little of yourself to others from month to month, pass a basic interview, and maybe have a couple friends vouch for you. You don't anticipate, however, that anyone will check out whether you have a background of being perfect. You figure that just as the tennis club admits people who are far less than perfect players, so God must be good with anyone who at least has a little interest in doing good. As much sense as this makes, Jesus had a very different take.

Among the most pious of the Jewish people were a group of men known as Pharisees. They were well schooled in the laws that God handed down through Moses, and they were sticklers at maintaining these laws. In fact, they added a number of rules and regulations beyond what God declared, just to make sure they'd be good with God in this life and the next. If anyone was going to qualify for heaven, these men were convinced they were the best candidates. That's what makes Jesus' words about them so very startling. While others were impressed with the Pharisees, Jesus was most certainly not. He warned everyone who was willing to listen, "Unless your righteousness is better than the righteousness of the teachers of religious law and the Pharisees, you will never enter the Kingdom of Heaven" (Matthew 5:20). This, in and of itself, must have been enormously discouraging to all who heard Jesus speak. Most were weary of keeping up with half of what the Pharisees taught, and now Jesus was saying that you've got to score even better than the Pharisees to get into heaven. Then to make matters worse, Jesus says in the very same speech, "But you are to be perfect, even as your Father in heaven is perfect" (Matthew 5:48). Perfect?! What in the world is Jesus thinking? How in the world can he ask that we be morally perfect in every thought and action all the time? How can he set that as the standard for heaven?

There are a lot of really great people in the world. Many that put me to shame in the ways they sacrifice their own time and energy and resources for others. There are also many people who are much kinder and forgiving and gracious than I will ever be. But if we measured everyone up against God's standard of perfection, there is not a soul who would come even close. I like to picture it in this way. Imagine an endurance swim race that starts on the shores of Los Angeles and ends in Honolulu. In addition to its absurd distance, it also requires participants to be fully committed. That is, once you hit the water, it's literally do or die. There is no turning back. On the beach are Olympic greats like Michael Phelps and Katie Ledecky as well as your neighbor next door who walks with a cane. The gun goes off and everyone enters the water. Some make it just a few feet, others like Phelps and Ledecky endure for miles, and a few little-known endurance athletes make it 100 miles before petering out. But as you might guess, no one makes it to Hawaii. Not even close.

I think this is the way it is for us when we look at God's standard of perfection. You can line up representatives of humanity throughout the ages and they all fall short. People like Billy Graham, Nelson Mandela, or Gandhi, or even the woman who has run the local halfway house for 30 years might be well ahead of people like you or me when it comes to good deeds. We, in turn, might be a good bit out in front of dictators like Hitler, sexual predators like Jeffrey Epstein, or the woman who drowns her own babies. But none of us come even close to being perfect in every thought and deed. If there is an ocean between paradise and us, most of us will die with the shore we left still in sight. That's why the Bible is so blunt in declaring, "It's your sins that have cut you off from God" (Isaiah 59:2).

But What About the Love of God?

At this point, I'd love to know what is running through your head. I'm guessing that you might be a tad uncomfortable with what I've written thus far about good works, getting into heaven, and Jesus' standard of perfection. In fact, you might just flat out disagree. And if you disagree, you might do so for a very good reason. You may have long believed that if there is a God out there, he is a God of love. And if he is a God of love, it simply does not add up to think that God would disqualify all of us from heaven because we are not perfect. You and I certainly don't permanently dismiss people who are less than perfect, so you might ask how I could possibly hold onto the belief that God is loving when he disqualifies everyone from heaven. That's a fair question, because if all I've said about God's unbending standard of perfection somehow diminishes God's love, maybe I have it wrong. The Bible is quite adamant about God's love,[3] and I for one find that trait enormously attractive. But what if love does not call for God to lower his standard? In fact, what if love actually demands that he maintains it?

I have a son who is an officer in the U.S. Coast Guard. He is 6'1" and 200 pounds. His body fat is about five percent, and he has muscles popping out in places I did not know muscles existed. Most people would collapse in exhaustion during one of his training regimens, and that's while he is still warming up! Of course, the "machine" that I call his body doesn't come cheaply. The amount of food he eats is frankly insane. Besides my son, I also have a daughter. She is 5'4". As you might guess, she does not eat very much in comparison to my son. Imagine, then, the scene at my dinner table: my son salivating at everything that is digestible and my daughter just doing her best to secure a minor share. If my son lacked manners, there is no chance my daughter would get more than a crumb. Suppose, in fact, that every time we sat down for dinner, our son filled himself up nicely while our daughter came away with little to nothing. What should be our response as loving parents when our daughter cries for justice? What if we said, "Sweetheart, I know you are hungry, but we love your brother and have no intention of penalizing his behavior, especially when he is good in so many ways. You're just going to have to get over it." Of course, at this point our daughter would not think us to be very loving at all. And she would not think that, because love at times calls for justice or it is not love at all.

I find it very helpful at this point to remember that sin is not just an infraction against God's standard. Sin also has a human cost. This is easy to see in the case of murder. While murder clearly breaks God's commands, it also has a very human cost, not just to the one who was killed but also to family and friends and to all those who could have been positively impacted by the one who was murdered. But less violent thoughts and behaviors also have their impact. A man whose thoughts are filled with material gain may not pay much attention to his own wife and children. As a result, his kids may never witness a good family dynamic, and later their own families fall apart. Recently, my beloved Houston Astros were caught in a cheating scandal. Members of other teams may have been deprived of a championship, bonus pay, and future contract bargaining power as a result of the Astros' conduct. So the question is: Would it be loving of God to overlook the anger we spill out in our homes, the abuse we bring upon the innocent, or the suffering and injustice we conveniently ignore[4] when such actions have such far-reaching consequences? Would it be loving of God to disregard the victims of our sin and give us a free pass? I don't think so. As far as I see it, God's love needs to walk hand in hand with God's justice or it just isn't a very admirable love.

If No One Measures Up, Then What?

So far in this chapter, I have put two big thoughts on the table. The first is that Christianity does not endorse the good works model for getting into heaven. Secondly, I made the point that Christianity is not too impressed with any of our purported goodness. We might be good relative to others, but we all fall woefully short of God's perfect standard. Both of these ideas may have come as a surprise to you, but I hope you see they create a window of opportunity. On the one hand, none of us is good enough to earn our way to heaven, but on the other hand Christianity clearly states that our goodness is not what gets us in anyway. That means that if there is some other way to get right with God and get into heaven, maybe we still have a chance.

At some point, you may have heard Christians talk about "good news." You may have thought that was a modern term for what Christianity proposes to offer, but actually it's a term that goes back to the earliest days of Christianity. If you do a search, you will find the term "good news" sprinkled throughout the New Testament. Of course, many translations use the word "gospel" for "good news," but they mean one and the same thing. The obvious question is this: What is the good news about which Christians speak? If you think about it, the term "good news" has its greatest weight when it's put in the context of some looming bad news. For example, if you go to the hospital with chest pain, but the doctor says your heart is fine, that is very good news relative to the bad news he could have told you. Or, suppose your teenage daughter has gone missing. She was to visit her grandmother outside of town, but she never arrived, and you can't reach her on the phone. It's getting rather late, and all kinds of terrible possibilities run through your head. Just then you get a call. It is from the police, and your heart sinks. In a matter of seconds, however, they tell you the good news. Your daughter's car had broken down, her cell phone quit working, and she had spent the last several hours walking back into town. You see, good news is almost always recognized as particularly good in the context of potential bad news.

When we consider God's standard of perfection and our inability to meet it, I think it's pretty clear what the bad news is. Our sin has broken our relationship with God and disqualified us from heaven. We must face the judgment of God for all that stuff written on the wall of our life. I know that sounds harsh, but the Bible is clear on this.[5] If we had to bear the weight of God's judgment by ourselves, we'd be in trouble. This, however, is precisely where the good news comes in, and why it is so good. Repeatedly, the Bible tells of another route to heaven, another route to life with God. It is not one that has to do with our own good works; it is one that has to do with Jesus. Take a look at the following verses and see if you can discover it for yourself:

> For this is how God loved the world: He gave his one and only Son, so that everyone who believes in him will not perish but have eternal life. God sent his Son into the world not to judge the world, but to save the world through him.
>
> There is no judgment against anyone who believes in him. But anyone who does not believe in him has already been judged for not believing in God's one and only Son. (John 3:16-18)

> And anyone who believes in God's Son has eternal life. Anyone who doesn't obey the Son will never experience eternal life but remains under God's angry judgment. (John 3:36)

> I tell you the truth, those who listen to my message and believe in God who sent me have eternal life. They will never be condemned

for their sins, but they have already passed from death into life. (John 5:24)

They replied, "We want to perform God's works, too. What should we do?"

Jesus told them, "This is the only work God wants from you: Believe in the one he has sent." (John 6:28-29)

For it is my Father's will that all who see his Son and believe in him should have eternal life. I will raise them up at the last day. (John 6:40)

I admit not everything in the Bible is black and white, but when it comes to how we can be made right with God and enjoy life with him forever, the Bible is straightforward. It says the way we get into heaven is not through good works but by believing in God's Son, Jesus Christ. This might be a bit baffling and could leave you with a thought like this: "You mean to say that the only way we measure up with God is by believing in Jesus?" Yes, that is what Jesus said and that is what Christians have called good news for 2,000 years. But maybe I can help you make a bit more sense of it.

Our Sin and Jesus' Sacrificial Death

When a crime is committed, it is just and right for a penalty to be paid for the infraction, and for that penalty to be commensurate with the crime. If I throw litter out my car, a fine of $250 might be appropriate, but if I steal money from my clients' retirement accounts, a much greater penalty ought to be paid. In some cases, the penalty associated with a crime is the same irrespective of who was harmed by my actions. In other words, if I steal from a small neighborhood market, the penalty may be no different than if I steal from a giant grocery store conglomerate. In other cases, however, the stature of the offended party impacts the penalty substantially. I spoke about this in Chapter 10 when I suggested that the penalty due my son would likely be significantly different if he hit his sister versus hitting his teacher, a policeman, or the President of the United States. And it would be different not because his behavior was different but because the stature of the person offended is different. Understanding this principle of justice helps us understand the magnitude or our own sin. We like to diminish our own sin, as though it's nothing more than hitting a sibling when our parents aren't looking, when we ought to be thinking of it as hitting a person of great stature and renown. And this isn't just true if our sin is murder; it is true when we disregard any of God's commands, even his commands regarding our thought life.

If it is true that even the smallest of sins against the God of the universe rightfully calls for the greatest of penalties because of the infinite stature of the one offended, then there is little hope that you and I on our own can ever right the ship. It should come as no surprise then when we read the verses above that our default state is that of condemnation, and eternal separation from God. How then do we get out of this default position? It seems our only hope is if the condemnation we have earned can somehow be borne by someone else. But this someone has to be rather special; he must not need to bear the consequences of his own sin. In other words, if my sin is worthy of death, and your sin is worthy of death, you cannot die to cover the penalty for my sins, since you must first pay the price for your own sins. So, if someone is going to carry our guilt before God, we need someone who has not sinned to do that for us. We need someone whose life is as pure and great and righteous as God himself. We need someone whose sacrifice is certified as satisfactory to God by his very resurrection from the dead. I know of no one who fills this bill other than Jesus.

Jesus lived a perfect, sinless life.
Jesus died for our sins.
Jesus paid the penalty that we could never pay.
Jesus made it possible for us to be made right with God.

This is not something that Christians made up over the centuries. The ancient prophet Isaiah, whose words are not only in modern Bibles but also in the Dead Sea Scrolls, spoke this in anticipation of Christ coming to Earth: "But he was pierced for our rebellion, crushed for our sins. He was beaten so we could be whole. He was whipped so we could be healed" (Isaiah 53:5). Peter, the head of the church in Jerusalem after Jesus' death, echoed Isaiah, saying, "He personally carried our sins in his body on the cross so that we can be dead to sin and live for what is right. By his wounds you are healed" (1 Peter 2:24). Paul, who took

Jesus' teaching to the Gentiles, wrote that Jesus "was handed over to die because of our sins" (Romans 4:25) and "For God made Christ, who never sinned, to be the offering for our sin, so that we could be made right with God through Christ" (2 Corinthians 5:21). And John, perhaps Jesus' closest friend, wrote of Jesus: "He Himself is the sacrifice that atones for our sins—and not only our sins but the sins of all the world" (1 John 2:2).

For some the death of Jesus is outrageous. If Jesus was the sinless Son of God, how could God allow him to be put to death? Indeed, Jesus' death was outrageous. It was enormously unfair on two counts. First, Jesus did nothing to deserve death. And secondly, we did nothing to deserve him dying for us. If we demand fairness, then Jesus shouldn't have died and we should die. But Jesus wasn't after that kind of fairness. He was after a love that does not wink at sin but that still offers mercy to all who will receive his free gift of reconciliation. Think of Jesus as a judge, one who presides over a court. Because he is a just judge, he cannot simply dismiss your sin and pretend like nothing happened. So, he hands down a sentence in keeping with the stature of the one offended. That sentence is death. But instead of watching you pay that penalty, he walks down from the bench and offers to pay it himself so you can be made right with God. This is the good news that Christians talk about. This is the good news that reveals both the love and justice of God.

The Choice Is Yours

On August 5, 2010, a cave-in at the San José copper–gold mine, located in northern Chile, trapped 33 men 2,300 feet underground. The extent of the cave-in made it impossible for the men to escape. They had food and supplies that if properly rationed would allow them to survive for several weeks, but if they did not receive help from the outside, their death was certain. Above the surface rescue efforts were coordinated from around the world. Three separate drilling rig teams, numerous corporations, nearly every arm of the Chilean government, and even NASA provided ingenuity, support, and resources. After a number of failed attempts to locate the men, the miners were found and finally lifted one by one out of the cave on October 13, a full 69 days after they became trapped.

The rescue attempt was viewed on television around the world, and it was difficult not to shed a tear as the men were brought to safety. Had it not been for the rescue efforts, the men would have died. But even with the rescue efforts, the men still could have met their death. They could have refused to get into the little capsule that would take them to the surface. In an act of defiance or with a sense of self-reliance, they could have remained in the cave.

Earlier I shared that Christianity is rather clear on the idea that good works are insufficient to get us to heaven. Our sin has separated us from God like the Chilean miners were separated from their loved ones outside the mine. And just as any effort of the miners would have been insufficient to free them from their predicament, so is our effort to make things right with God through our good works. We need to be rescued by someone who can do what we cannot do. We need Jesus. But even if Jesus' death is enough to pay the debt we owe to God for our sins, there is still something we must do. We must be willing to receive the gift that Jesus offers us. As I noted, the miners in Chile were saved by the efforts of others, but if they did not exercise trust in the rescue efforts and allow themselves to be lifted to safety, they would have died. And the Bible says the same is true for us. To be made right with God, we must recognize our desperate state apart from Christ's work on our behalf and must cling to Jesus as our only hope of rescue. As you can see, this means more than just believing a few facts about Jesus, like that he lived a long time ago or even that he died on a cross. It means believing in Jesus like you would a rescuer who reaches out a hand before you take your last breath. It means believing enough to get in a boat when you realize you cannot swim to Hawaii. It means believing that because "God loved the world: He gave his one and only Son, so that everyone who believes in him will not perish but have eternal life" (John 3:16).

Yes, Christianity says good works won't get you to heaven. But it has better news than that. It says Jesus has done what is necessary for you to be made right with God now and forever. You can jump on board with the good news of what Jesus has done for you, or you can keep swimming on your own by relying on your own good works. The choice is yours. And according to Jesus, it's the choice between heaven and hell.

Key Points

- If heaven is where good people go, it makes sense that good works would get us into heaven. But the good works model for getting into heaven has several shortcomings:

  › We don't know whose standard we are to use when deciding what is good and what is bad.

  › We don't know what percentage of our actions must be good.

  › We don't know if our different deeds (good or bad) are weighted differently when calculating just how good we have been.

  › We don't know if we will be judged by the outcomes of our actions or our intentions.

  › If God does not provide us clarity on how we measure up, he certainly doesn't seem just or loving.

- In contrast to the good works model, the Bible teaches that:

  › We are accountable for both our actions and our thoughts, and it says that on both counts no one lives up to God's commands.

  › God's standard for getting into heaven is equal to his own character, which is perfection. It is a standard no one meets.

  › It may seem unloving of God to punish our inability to live up to his demands, but dismissing our sin without penalty would make God unjust. Love does not dismiss justice.

  › Our sins are not small grievances because of the unmatched stature of God. Justice, therefore, demands that we be separated from God and denied heaven.

  › Because Jesus is sinless, he is the only one able to bear the consequences of our sins for us.

  › Out of love for us, Jesus willingly gave his life for our sake to rescue us from judgment and restore our relationship with God.

  › Although Jesus has made it possible for us to be made right with God through his sacrificial death, we still must accept his offer to rescue us from condemnation. We must believe that Christ makes possible what our good works can never do and have faith in the salvation only he can offer.

Additional Resources

How Good Is Good Enough, Andy Stanley

What Is the Gospel?, Bryan Chapell

"What about Good Works?" in *I'm Glad You Asked*, Ken Boa & Larry Moody

13

If God Is Loving, Why Would He Send Anyone to Hell?

I haven't met too many people who are very fond of hell. Oh sure, in a moment of rage, they may wish that someone finds his or her way to the fiery pit in a hurry. But I am guessing that when many people say, "Go to hell!" they don't really mean it beyond their moment of anger. Hell, as most people imagine it, is not something you'd wish on anyone beyond perhaps serial killers, wicked tyrants, or someone who sexually assaults a young child. We don't haphazardly wish hell upon people, because hell, well, it's hell.

In fact, of all the things that Christians believe, hell might be the belief that is the hardest to swallow. You might not find the possibility that a God exists too distasteful. If you struggle to believe in miracles, you may still admit it would be pretty cool to witness one. The stuff about Jesus and his death and resurrection may seem mythological, but if it makes people feel better about life after death, you may not forcefully reject the idea. But then there is hell—that horrid place Christians say people go if they do not believe in Jesus. For many, this is where Christianity has gone too far. How, it is asked, can a loving God possibly send people to hell for eternity?

For some, hell seems like a marketing scare tactic. You've probably seen a scary commercial for bathroom cleaner, or some other product. The narrator speaks of all the dangerous mold and mildew that is lurking in every corner of your shower and will most certainly make you deadly sick if you don't buy Super Cleaner X for $19.99, plus shipping and handling. In other words, your bathroom is bordering on hell and you better buy your way out fast. It's not hard to imagine, then, that if Christians wanted to sell their beliefs, they'd add in some marketing scare tactics over the centuries to get people on board. And what could be a bigger scare than being sent to a place of eternal pain and suffering? If this theory about a marketing scare tactic is correct, then maybe we can silence the whole hell idea Christians are peddling by going to the Bible and showing that hell is either absent from its pages or not as bad as reported.

What the Bible Says About Hell

The Bible is made up of two parts. The Old Testament was written before the time of Christ, and the New Testament was written after Jesus lived. The Old Testament does not say a great deal about hell (or heaven, for that matter). It speaks of *Sheol*, or the place of the dead, but the descriptions of *Sheol* are often ambiguous and don't let us know if we are headed there because we've been good or bad.[1] Apart from mentioning *Sheol*, however, the Old Testament repeatedly mentions a coming day of judgment when God will express his anger toward sin.[2] For example, the prophet Isaiah declares: "For the Lord of Heaven's Armies has a day of reckoning. He will punish the proud and mighty and bring down everything that is exalted" (Isaiah 2:12). Another prophet, named Daniel, tells us that this same judgment is not temporary but enduring. Daniel writes: "Many of those whose bodies lie dead and buried will rise up, some to *everlasting* life and some to shame and *everlasting* disgrace" (Daniel 12:2, emphasis added). So while the Old Testament doesn't give us a lot to go on, it certainly doesn't let us off the hook when it comes to hell.

Perhaps talk about God's judgment in the Old Testament is what you expect. For many, God seems particularly wrathful in that part of the Bible, so maybe it's Jesus and the New Testament that softens the blow when it comes to hell.

I meet with lots of people who aren't very familiar with the Bible. If they are willing to meet with me regularly, I like to read through one of the New Testament Gospels with them. Most people have heard a thing or two about Jesus, but they've never really seen what is said about him in the Bible. Often, my reading companions are surprised by what they read. In particular, they are surprised by Jesus' willingness to discuss issues others tend to avoid. This includes the topic of hell and judgment. In fact, you won't find any character in the Bible who speaks more about hell than Jesus did. Sometimes he spoke of hell rather directly, like when he said, "And if your eye causes you to sin, gouge it out. It's better to enter the Kingdom of God with only one eye than to have two eyes and be thrown into hell, 'where the maggots never die and the fire never goes out'" (Mark 9:47-48). At other times, Jesus developed stories with the very moral being the judgment of hell. For instance, he taught:

> The Kingdom of Heaven is like a fishing net that was thrown into the water and caught fish of every kind. When the net was full, they dragged it up onto the shore, sat down, and sorted the good fish into crates, but threw the bad ones away. That is the way it will be at the end of the world. The angels will come and separate the wicked people from the righteous, throwing the wicked into the fiery furnace, where there will be weeping and gnashing of teeth. (Matthew 13:47-50)

Furthermore, Jesus' teaching on hell was not reserved for pagan outsiders. He said that fellow Jews were just as in danger of hell as any other people, sometimes suggesting that Jews were in greater danger of eternal doom than Gentiles:

> And I tell you this, that many Gentiles will come from all over the world—from east and west—and sit down with Abraham, Isaac, and Jacob at the feast in the Kingdom of Heaven. But many Israelites—those for whom the Kingdom was prepared—will be thrown into outer darkness, where there will be weeping and gnashing of teeth. (Matthew 8:11-12)

Words like these weren't just for the wayward Jew. Even revered Jewish spiritual leaders could not escape Jesus' harsh words of the danger of hell. To some of the religious elite he said: "Snakes! Sons of vipers! How will you escape the judgment of hell?" (Matthew 23:33). As you can see, Jesus wasn't afraid to speak of hell to anyone's face.

All of this talk of hell and damnation might seem rather startling coming from the mouth of Jesus. But if you take a good look at all Jesus said, you might notice that he never wished hell upon people. Instead, he spoke of hell as a warning. Like one speaks of an impending storm, Jesus tells his listeners to make preparations now to avoid danger later. This comes across rather forcefully in Jesus' teaching near the end of the Gospel of Matthew:

> A faithful, sensible servant is one to whom the master can give the responsibility of managing his other household servants and feeding them. If the master returns and finds that the servant has done a good job, there will be a reward. I tell you the truth, the master will put that servant in charge of all he owns. But what if the servant is evil and thinks, 'My master won't be back for a while,' and he begins beating the other servants, partying, and getting drunk? The master will return unannounced and unexpected, and he will cut the servant to pieces and assign him a place with the hypocrites. In that place there will be weeping and gnashing of teeth. (Matthew 24:45-51)

And if a warning like this wasn't clear enough, Jesus ended what he had to say about hell in Matthew by declaring that those who do not follow his teaching "will go away into eternal punishment," while "the righteous will go into eternal life" (Matthew 25:46). Now, that's what I call making the stakes clear!

Based on what the New Testament Gospels say, Jesus believed hell was real, final, terrible, and eternal. We probably shouldn't be surprised, then, when every New Testament writer outside the Gospels, including Paul, James, Peter, John, Jude, and the author of Hebrews, mention hell in terms similar to what Jesus used.[3] All of this means that if you hope to dismiss the idea of hell by looking to Jesus and the New Testament, you have a hard case to make.[4] What is hinted at in the Old Testament about hell is spoken of clearly in the New Testament. Rather than hell being a marketing scare tactic developed by Christians over the centuries, it is what early Christians, and more importantly Jesus, discussed as a real place we should want to avoid.

Properly Painting a Picture of Hell

Medieval paintings of hell are rather gruesome. Often, they include images of demons capturing, torturing, dismembering and eating humans. If you sat in church in the 15th century and your child was unruly, I am sure it was tempting to point in the direction of one of these paintings as a way of encouraging your child to behave. As detailed and sobering as some of these paintings remain, I am not sure our image of hell should be fully informed by such works of art. The real thing may be no less scary, but if we limit our view of hell to what the Bible tells us, ghastly torture chambers probably get left out.[5]

When we look at what Jesus and others say of hell, the images include a lake of fire, a lake of burning sulfur, a fiery furnace, weeping and gnashing of teeth, undying worms, darkness, people tied up and thrown outside or trampled as in a winepress, a man in agony in a fire, servants beaten and cut into pieces, and exclusion from a long-awaited wedding.[6] Considering that it is hard to conceive of a place being filled with both fire and darkness at the same time or a place where people are cut into pieces and yet somehow are still weeping or gnashing their teeth, those who study the Bible have almost uniformly considered the biblical images of hell to be metaphors and not necessarily literal depictions of what hell is like. But as with all metaphors, they are still meant to help us better grasp something that is real. So, just what is the Bible trying to tell us about hell when using these images? More than anything, the images of hell point toward two broad ideas: conscious punishment and eternal banishment from the goodness of God.

These two broad ideas are on full display in a story Jesus tells of an unnamed rich man and a poor man named Lazarus:

> Jesus said, "There was a certain rich man who was splendidly clothed in purple and fine linen and who lived each day in luxury. At his gate lay a poor man named Lazarus who was covered with sores. As Lazarus lay there longing for scraps from the rich man's table, the dogs would come and lick his open sores.
>
> "Finally, the poor man died and was carried by the angels to sit beside Abraham at the heavenly banquet. The rich man also died and was buried, and he went to the place of the dead. There, in torment, he saw Abraham in the far distance with Lazarus at his side.
>
> "The rich man shouted, 'Father Abraham, have some pity! Send Lazarus over here to dip the tip of his finger in water and cool my tongue. I am in anguish in these flames.'
>
> "But Abraham said to him, 'Son, remember that during your lifetime you had everything you wanted, and Lazarus had nothing. So now he is here being comforted, and you are in anguish. And besides, there is a great chasm separating us. No one can

cross over to you from here, and no one can cross over to us from there.'

"Then the rich man said, 'Please, Father Abraham, at least send him to my father's home. For I have five brothers, and I want him to warn them so they don't end up in this place of torment.'

"But Abraham said, 'Moses and the prophets have warned them. Your brothers can read what they wrote.'

"The rich man replied, 'No, Father Abraham! But if someone is sent to them from the dead, then they will repent of their sins and turn to God.'

"But Abraham said, 'If they won't listen to Moses and the prophets, they won't be persuaded even if someone rises from the dead.'" (Luke 16:19-31)

There is much that can be drawn from this story about the nature of hell, but two elements stand out to me. First, the rich man was not enjoying his existence in hell. The highway to hell may be as fun as the band AC/DC have immortalized in their hit song, but according to Jesus once you get there no one is singing hell's praises. Hell is a place of conscious anguish meted out because of one's rejection of Jesus while on earth. Whether this anguish in hell is primarily physical or mental, we may not be able to say, but even in this life, both forms of anguish can be unbearable.

The second element of this story that stands out is that the rich man is forever separated from the heavenly goodness enjoyed by Lazarus. There is a chasm that cannot be crossed, and even the smallest measure of goodness is kept from relieving the rich man's anguish. C.S. Lewis aptly describes the banishment of hell with the title of his book *The Great Divorce*. In other words, hell, as Jesus speaks about it, is the result of the ultimate irreconcilable relationship, and it comes with a permanent restraining order.

So while hell may not be like the gruesome medieval paintings of the abyss, the Bible still provides a stark picture of its nature, one that includes conscious punishment and excludes even a small taste of the goodness of God. No wonder, then, that the rich man wanted to send a warning to his brothers to avoid hell.

At times, I have been asked to preside over or speak at a funeral for someone I did not know very well or for whom there was little indication of faith in Christ. On such occasions, I did not want to speak as though the deceased is in heaven today. That is not my call to make. So what I have said is that wherever that person is today, he would want his loved ones, as the rich man in Jesus' parable did, to know that this life is no game, that there is a judgment coming that puts us in heaven or hell.

Love and Hell

So far this chapter has largely been about describing what the Bible has to say about hell. You may have found it informative, but you've likely recognized that I haven't really addressed this chapter's question. If hell is as I have described it here, or even half of what I have described, it's reasonable to ask why a loving God would send anyone to hell. To some measure, I answered this question in the previous chapter where I discussed whether our goodness is sufficient to make us right with God. There, I made two big claims. The first was that none of us is all that good. We may be good relative to others, yet we all are guilty of not only dishonoring and disrespecting the Creator of the universe but also mistreating even our closest friends. Furthermore, I explained that our sin is never well contained. That is, it has an impact that goes far beyond the initial target. For instance, a simple lie does not just mislead someone about a particular point of fact; it can begin to erode trust in a way that can have far-reaching consequences that can affect parties even far removed.

Secondly, I made the case that love without justice would hardly count as love. If God simply ignored the hurt and pain we did to others and others did to us, it would be difficult to describe God as particularly loving. Imagine your loved one is defrauded out of his or her life's savings. The criminal has been properly identified and stands before the judge to be sentenced. If the judge pardoned the criminal out of love, we would cry foul. And we would cry foul because love without justice is shallow and even dangerous. So one way to answer the question of how a loving God could send anyone to hell is by saying that "true love cares enough to punish wrongdoing," and that hell is a place where punishment is properly executed for those who are unrepentant and do not seek the forgiveness found in Christ.

Bertrand Russell, one of the most outspoken atheists of the 20th century, wrote an essay entitled "Why I Am Not a Christian." In it, he said this about Jesus: "There is one very serious defect to my mind in

Christ's moral character, and that is that He believed in hell. I do not myself feel that any person who is really profoundly humane can believe in everlasting punishment."[7] But is Bertrand Russell correct? Personally, I don't think it would be humane if Jesus ignored the ways you and I have hurt others and the great ripple effect that undoubtedly has caused. Jesus loves us as the Bible says, but because his love is perfect, he does not wink at wrongdoing. He does not wink when others wrong us, and he does not wink when we wrong others.

Building a case that God can be loving and yet sentence someone to hell is not limited to understanding that we all have sinned and that love properly involves a judgment of that sin. There are other reasons that we can say that God is loving even if hell is a reality. Of course, these reasons call for some explanation.

God Gives Us Ample Warning

David Bernays and Charles Sawyer tried to save the residents of Yungay, Peru, from a massive avalanche. While exploring the area in 1962, the two American scientists discovered a massive, unstable slab of rock under a nearby glacier. Earthquakes were common to the area, and to warn the town, the two men published an article to tell the inhabitants of the looming disaster. Peruvian officials, however, did not take kindly to the warning and ordered the pair to retract their statement or be imprisoned. Instead, Bernays and Sawyer fled the country.

On May 31, 1970, the earthquake the scientists feared struck Peru. The quake destabilized the glacier on Mount Huascarán, and caused 10 million cubic meters of rock, ice, and snow to break away and slide down the slope at 120 miles per hour. Three minutes later the wave of debris had grown into a 3,000-foot-wide wall that instantly turned the 25,000-person town of Yungay into what remains a cemetery today.[8]

It's hard to know with certainty the motivation of Bernays and Sawyer when they made the initial report. They could have made the report out of a love for science or a desire for self-recognition. But a strong case could be made that they warned the people of Yungay because they cared. They did not want to see the inhabitants of the town killed, so they provided a warning of impending doom. The government and the inhabitants, however, refused to heed the warning. And it was their refusal—not the actions of Bernays and Sawyer—that was the reason for the destruction of the town and its inhabitants. The two scientists had shown love by providing the warning.

When we look at Jesus' words about hell, we consistently see that he speaks of hell as a warning. Even a casual reader of the Gospels will come to the conclusion that Jesus' intention in providing these warnings "was to stir a fear in us that would cause us to take hell seriously and avoid it at all costs."[9] That's what love does when danger is lurking; it warns people emphatically of what harm will come if action is not taken. What would not be loving would be for Jesus to know of hell and provide no warning at all.

God Provides a Way To Safety

One way we can know that God's love is not violated by the existence of hell is that Jesus provides a way to avoid it. I have watched a short film about Welles Crowther many times, and each time I cry. It is the story of a young man who worked on the 104th floor of the Trade Center's South Tower on September 11, 2001. As a teenager he volunteered regularly at a local fire station, and although he later pursued work in the financial sector, his heart still was with those at the station. When United Flight 175 struck the South Tower, he knew what he had to do. He located the only remaining stairwell and led people to safety, finally losing his life when he repeatedly went back to rescue more. One survivor recalls when Crowther arrived on her floor confidently saying, "I have found the stairs. Follow me."

It is loving to warn others of impending danger, but when one goes beyond that and provides a way out, even at the cost of their own life, that love is amplified. Crowther's father, when looking back on his son's sacrifice, said that what Welles did was "absolutely the most pure form of compassion and love." And I think few would disagree, because Welles at his own expense pointed others to safety.[10]

Jesus did no less. Throughout his ministry, he told people to repent of their ways and to put their trust in him for their salvation. He knew the danger of hell, and he knew the only way to avoid it is by following him. And then to prove such a warning wasn't about gathering a crowd for himself, Jesus offered his own life by taking on the judgment of our sin through an excruciating crucifixion. Jesus said hell was real and that people could be sent there, but it is difficult to sustain the idea that Jesus' position was unloving when he offered his own life so that we can avoid all that hell entails.

God's Heart Is for Us

The scene is played out over and over again in homes across the world. A child behaves poorly, and the parents must take corrective action. Perhaps the parents forbid the child to attend an event that she had looked forward to for weeks. Maybe the parents must take the drastic step of sending the child away to a center for teens whose ways have caused harm and destruction. But while the parents may be confident that their actions are the best for all involved, it does not mean that they take pleasure in meting out judgment. In fact, if the parents did express pleasure in doing so, we would be rather concerned, even if the parents had provided a warning beforehand or had provided a way for the child to avoid the consequences. In other words, when someone loves well, they do not take pleasure in seeing the ones they love experience painful consequences for their ways.

This is why it is so important to see that the loving God portrayed in the Bible not only shouts out a warning to us about hell and provides a way of escape at his own expense, but also has a heart that finds no pleasure in seeing any person sentenced to hell. Through the prophet Ezekiel, God said, "I take no pleasure in the death of wicked people. I only want them to turn from their wicked ways so they can live. Turn! Turn from your wickedness, O people of Israel! Why should you die" (Ezekiel 33:11). Jesus, just days before his crucifixion at the hands of those in Jerusalem, said, "O Jerusalem, Jerusalem, the city that kills the prophets and stones God's messengers! How often I have wanted to gather your children together as a hen protects her chicks beneath her wings, but you wouldn't let me" (Matthew 23:37). And Peter, when considering Jesus' patience in returning to judge the world, writes, "The Lord isn't really being slow about his promise, as some people think. No, he is being patient for your sake. He does not want anyone to be destroyed, but wants everyone to repent" (2 Peter 3:9).

From passages like these, the Bible reveals that God's heart is for us. He knows our failings. He knows our sin. He personally knows the ways in which we have offended him. And yet, he still has no desire to punish us. He is willing to let hell be the consequences of our sins, but he has no desire to see us spend eternity there. That is because he loves us.

Ensuring the Grandest Party

God is planning a big party, but throwing a big party for someone you love comes with a lot of decisions. You must decide when and where the event is to be, the food and beverage to be served, possible entertainment, and words that might be spoken or written or painted in the sky in celebration of the one for whom the party is given. But there is probably no greater decision when it comes to planning a grand party than the invitation list. If you plan a birthday party for your wife, you probably won't invite the guy to whom she was previously engaged and who publicly dumped her just days before their planned wedding. Similarly, if you are putting together a retirement celebration for a dear friend, it's not likely that you will invite the person he worked alongside who constantly undermined your friend's efforts. To grant such an invitation in either situation would at the very least create an uneasiness that would taint the celebration. If we are looking to create a great atmosphere for the one to be celebrated, as well as an environment that all who attend will enjoy, it is incumbent upon the host to invite those who will add to the celebration and leave off the invitation list those who will not.

In Matthew 22:1-14, Jesus described his return to judge the world like a wedding banquet, but he was clear to say that not everyone would be let in. Later in Revelation 5:1-14, we are told this "banquet" is all about celebrating the sacrificial death of Jesus that afforded people of any language or ethnic group or nation the opportunity to be made right with God. How good, however, would this party be if in addition to those who were excited to celebrate Jesus, the party included those who were unimpressed with Jesus, who sought to undermine Jesus all of their earthly life, who regularly mistreated others that loved Jesus, who actively taught people not to follow Jesus, or who repeatedly dismissed or ignored anything Jesus and his followers had to say? The obvious answer is that it wouldn't be a very good party at all. For it to be a truly great "banquet" certain people are going to be kept on the outside—an outside Jesus called hell.

For the goodness of heaven to be eternally preserved, it must be separated from those who have no interest in celebrating the good of the one who made heaven a possibility, namely Christ himself. Jesus, more than anything, wants the goodness he offers to triumph, and to triumph unhindered throughout all eternity. For that, we should be glad. But if we reject Jesus and believe ourselves in no need of his forgiveness and his life, we will be left outside of heaven. Not because God doesn't want us to enjoy heaven but because letting us in would ruin the party for everyone who readily accepts Jesus as Lord and Savior. Just as no one would consider it unloving to keep the man who previously dumped your wife from her birthday party, so too we should not call it unloving for God to keep those who reject the celebration of Jesus outside of heaven in a place called hell. Like it or not, love can't let everyone into the party.

God Respects Our Wishes

God, in his love, desires that all people be with him forever and enjoy his goodness, but he will not force us to do so. I have been blessed with a wonderful marriage. But others have not always been so fortunate. In some cases, a husband or wife has arduously sought to keep a marriage together, only to have a spouse walk out the door. In those instances, it would be possible, in the style of some Hollywood horror film, for the one wanting to avoid separation and divorce to steal away a soon-departing spouse and enslave him or her so as to avoid a dissolution of the marriage. But one wonders what that would accomplish. The one who wants the marriage to continue would have something far less than the joy and sweetness that my wife and I enjoy. And the one who wanted out of the marriage would hate to be enslaved and would simply grow in hatred toward the enslaving spouse. Like it or not, at times it is best to respect people's decision, even when we don't like the decision they have made.

As we have seen by the words of Jesus, God will honor the request of those who refuse to accept the Holy Spirit's assessment of their sin, Christ's free offer of forgiveness, and God's offer of an eternal relationship. In other words, hell is part of the dignity that God affords to those who reject him. Rather than require that people be forced into a relationship with him forever, God gives people the right to exclude him from their future. If a person wants to be separated from God for eternity, God will grant that desire. C.S. Lewis in speaking of this very topic writes: "There are only two kinds of people in the end: those who say to God, 'Thy will be done,' and those to whom God says, in the end, 'Thy will be done.'"[11] Maybe as you're reading this you recognize yourself as being in the latter camp. If so, know this: If you are willing to come to God on his terms, the love of God and the enjoyment of his goodness is yours forever. But if you do not want what God offers, he will respect your decision. God will let you reject the solution to our sin that Christ has provided and allow you to be forever estranged from God in hell, if that is your wish. This is not unloving of God. He is letting you live your future on your own terms.

More Questions About Hell

I hope I have answered the question of this chapter to some level of satisfaction. That is, I hope you have recognized, at least to some degree, that the biblical idea of God sending some people to hell is not inconsistent with the understanding that God is loving. And it is not inconsistent because:

- God has given us ample warning about hell.
- Jesus has provided us a way of escape from the hell.
- God takes no pleasure in keeping anyone out of heaven.
- God excludes people from heaven who wouldn't enjoy worshipping Jesus and would thus hate the party and ruin it for the rest.
- God respects our decision and does not force us into an eternity we do not want.

Even if you agree that love and hell are not necessarily at odds, I am under no illusion that the matter is all settled for you, and that you are now good with hell. Honestly, I am not sure that anyone should be all that comfortable with hell. It is an uncomfortable reality. It is meant to be. And in grappling with it, I suppose a few questions may have come to your mind.

Why would a loving God create us so that we could sin and thus be in danger of hell? A Christian believes God is the creator of all things. They believe that giraffes have long necks because God wanted them that way; that a redwood is "red" because that's the color God wanted for its bark; and that a dolphin playfully jumps out of the water because God designed it with that capacity. Could God have made you and me so that it was impossible for us to sin and thus be in danger of hell? I do not doubt he could have done so, but the question is just what kind of creature would we have been if we were not creatures with an ability to reject him? If a redwood were not red, would we still call it a redwood? Would giraffes still be giraffes without long necks? Maybe we would give them the same name, but I doubt they would capture our attention in the same way. God created humans with free will, so we may freely (not forcibly) reflect the image of God for which we were created. Without that free choice to follow God or not, we'd be more like robots incapable of love. Perhaps we wouldn't be able to sin, but would we be really human anymore?

But isn't eternal punishment disproportionate to finite sin? All of us have rightly received some sort of discipline for poor behavior, but at times the penalty for our waywardness may have seemed overboard. That's why if your parents grounded you for three weeks because you were one minute past curfew, the lesson you learned was probably not about respecting curfew but about the injustice of the heavy punishment enforced by your parents. Clearly, justice is not just about ensuring consequences for wrongdoing; it is also about ensuring that the consequences are handed out in proper measure. It is not unreasonable, then, to ask how eternal banishment to hell is the proper measurement of hell for a finite lifetime of sin. To this question, I give two answers.

First, it is not clear to me that the duration of the crime is always the best indication as to the proper duration of the penalty. In some cases, it might be. For example, your manager might require you to stay 15 minutes after your shift if you arrived 15 minutes late. In other instances, however, a penalty equal in duration to the crime itself is entirely unfitting. Jim Wallace, a career homicide detective, provides this example:

> If someone embezzles $5.00 a week from their employer's cash register they will have stolen $260.00 over the course of a year. If they're caught at the end of this time, they would still only be guilty of a misdemeanor in the State of California (based on the total amount of loss). Although the crime took a year to commit, the perpetrator wouldn't spend much (if any) time in jail. On the other hand, a murder can take place in the blink of an eye and the resulting punishment will be life in prison (or perhaps the death penalty).[12]

Of course, the point of this illustration is to say that even though our sins may be finite in duration, we should not think that the associated penalty can be only finite in nature.

Second, if it is not the duration of a crime but rather its gravity that is important, we must understand something about the nature of our sin to know whether the penalty is appropriate. As I have discussed, the gravity of a sin is often tied to the stature of the offended. This tells me that if God is of incalculable stature, then when we break his commands, our sin is worthy of incalculable punishment. Or, in other words, our finite sin is worthy of eternal punishment.[13]

But why eternal punishment and not reformation? People of many different religious persuasions do not find hell problematic as long as hell is viewed as a temporary means of reformation and not a place of eternal punishment. That is, they see hell as a place of purification or enlightenment that involves some hardship or pain that ultimately leads to restoration with God and entrance into paradise. I understand the appeal of such a viewpoint, particularly since in many instances we mete out discipline to others not because we want to punish them but because we hope that it teaches them a lesson and makes them better in the long run. The problem with this perspective, however, is that it makes a rather big assumption.

If we are inclined to think of hell as a place of temporary restoration and not eternal punishment, we are assuming that people, after spending time in hell, will eventually want to be restored. But what makes us so sure that will ever be the case? Undoubtedly, some people in your world have long displayed destructive behavior. As a result, they have endured substantial consequences. You may even shake your head wondering why they do not learn from their ways and change course. The simple answer is they are not willing, and no amount of re-education or punishment will make them "turn the corner." Scripture tells us that God is not above using hardship in this life as a means of turning our hearts toward him.[14] Nonetheless, many have suffered hardship and are angrier at God or more adamant that he does not exist than they were before the suffering ever occurred. Could not this be the same for those who are in hell? If so, reformation is not possible.

If God is loving, should he not be patient with people, hold back judgment, and lure them into goodness? This is the question posed and answered by Miroslav Volf, a prolific author and founder of Yale's Center for Faith & Culture. This is what he writes:

> Should not a loving God be patient and keep luring the perpetrator into goodness? This is exactly what God does: God suffers the evildoers through history as God has suffered them on the cross. But how patient should God be? The day of reckoning must come, not because God is too eager to pull the trigger but because every

day of patience in a world of violence means more violence and every postponement of vindication means letting insult accompany injury.[15]

Just after these remarks, Volf references Revelation 6:9-11. In this passage, those who had been martyred for their faith cry out to God, "How long before you judge the people who belong to this world and avenge our blood for what they have done to us?" God's response is one of patience, but not patience without a timeline. God said they were "to rest a little longer until the full number of their brothers and sisters—their fellow servants of Jesus who were to be martyred—had joined them." Such a response by God is unnerving. It is a response that emphasizes the fact that "God's patience is costly, not so much for God but for the innocent sufferers. Waiting for the evildoers to reform means letting suffering continue."[16] And so at some point, if God is loving, his patience must end and people must be judged for their sin.

What about my loved ones who have died? Are you saying that if they did not trust in Christ, they will go to hell? I do not know if your loved ones are going to hell. If a person rejects God, does not respond to the forgiveness afforded by the sacrificial death of Jesus, or chooses to trust in his or her own good works to be made right with God, Jesus tells us that he or she will be kept separate from God in eternity. But since I don't know where your loved ones stood with God, I do not know if they are in hell or not. What I do know is that there are many stories of people who in their final days, or hours, or moments cry out to Jesus for forgiveness. And for every cry that is heard by others, I have little doubt that there are countless unvoiced cries made in the final hours of life that God nonetheless hears.

When Jesus was crucified, he was not crucified alone. Next to him was a criminal who readily admitted to the worthiness of his own punishment. With his last gasps, he called out to Jesus and asked to be remembered in God's kingdom, not because he was worthy but because he knew only Jesus could grant him such a request. And Jesus responds, saying, "I assure you, today you will be with me in paradise" (Luke 23:43). If you asked the criminal's friends and family if he was in hell, they probably would have answered yes. But they would have been wrong, because they did not see what happened in the final moments of his life. This is why I would never definitively say that your loved ones are in hell, and you probably shouldn't either.

Two Final Struggles with Hell

My guess is that you have questions beyond what I have addressed here, but I hope you have seen that as difficult as the reality of hell may be to accept, it is not inconsistent with the love of God. If God is love, would not he care enough to seek justice for those who have been wronged? If God is love, wouldn't he be willing to take on the punishment we deserve? If God is love, would he force us to receive the pardon for our own errors that he offers? And if God is love, would he not cordon off those who refuse to rejoice in Christ, since heaven will be spent forever in Christ's presence? The answer to these questions seems to be yes. So rather than the reality of hell contradicting the love of God, perhaps we should view it as a product of it.

I wonder, however, if your struggle with hell isn't so much because it conflicts with God's love but because of a couple other issues. The first of these issues I touched on briefly a few pages back. It has to do with the comfort level you have with hell. Hell is a difficult notion for anyone to swallow because it is so very hard to *feel* good about it, even if it does not conflict with God's love. But maybe the reason we don't feel good about it is because God does not want us to feel good about it.[17] That is, maybe God doesn't want us to be at peace with any human rebellion (as tame as it may seem) that ultimately leads people to hell. When we see parents turn in a child to the authorities because of his or her grievous crime, we are grateful for their actions, but do we really feel good about the whole situation? Of course not, because things did not need to end up as they did. Yes, the penalty of prison is fitting, but if the child had not rebelled against the heart and ways of the parents, the prison sentence could have been avoided. That's why, in the case of hell, it is appropriate not to feel good about it and yet at the same time affirm that it is a fitting place for some.

A second concern you might have with the whole idea of hell is that some people, including Christians, seem so comfortable with it. At times, they even seem to take pleasure in others going to hell. Take, for example, the recent photo I saw of a man arrogantly carrying a sign saying that certain people are going to hell. Even if this is the case, should not the man mourn such a fact rather than seemingly rejoice in it? I know some rather unsavory characters, and I am sure you do too. But if we understand hell to be what Jesus described, our hearts should ache for those who may be headed there and not glorify their demise. Contrary to what some would suggest, hell is not about a triumphant doctrine; it is about people's destiny.[18]

I have not written this chapter to be harsh or judgmental. And Jesus did not speak about hell because he looked forward to seeing anyone go there. He spoke about it, and I speak about it, because if hell is real, it would be cruel to say nothing. Several years ago, Penn Jillette, of the magician act Penn & Teller, was given a Bible by a businessman whom he found to be very kind. He did not accept the offer to turn from his atheism to Christ, but he deeply respected the man's efforts, saying:

> I've always said that I don't respect people who don't proselytize. I don't respect that at all. If you believe that there's a heaven and a hell, and people could be going to hell or not getting eternal life, or whatever, and you think that it's not really worth telling them this because it would make it socially awkward . . . how much do you have to hate somebody to not proselytize? How much do you have to hate somebody to believe everlasting life is possible and not tell them that? I mean, if I believed, beyond the shadow of a doubt, that a truck was coming at you, and you didn't believe it, and that truck was bearing down on you, there is a certain point where I tackle you. And this is more important than that.[19]

Penn was right in saying that if hell is real, it presents a greater urgency than a truck bearing down on you. No one who says they believe in hell should be so comfortable with it that they say nothing about it. Yes, I have written this chapter because the topic of hell comes up frequently. But more importantly I have written it because if hell is real, something must be said about it. The stakes are simply too high to remain silent.

Key Points

- The concept of hell is not a scare tactic developed by Christians over the centuries. The Bible, particularly Jesus, speaks of it consistently. The picture of hell presented in the Bible is not pleasant and involves conscious punishment and eternal banishment from the goodness of God.

- Hell is not inconsistent with a loving God because:

  › God has given us ample warning about hell.

  › Jesus has provided us a way of escape from hell.

  › God takes no pleasure in keeping anyone out of heaven.

  › God excludes people from heaven who wouldn't enjoy worshipping Jesus and would thus hate the party and ruin it for the rest.

  › When assigning people in hell, God respects our decision and does not force us into an eternity we do not want.

- Some questions and answers about hell are:

  › *Why would a loving God create us so that we could sin and thus be in danger of hell?* Humans were created with free will. God could have made us as robots that did not sin, but would we really be human anymore?

  › *But isn't eternal punishment disproportionate to finite sin?* The duration of our sin is not a good indicator of the gravity of our sin. Furthermore, our sin is of greater gravity than we think because of the stature of the God we have offended.

  › *But why eternal punishment and not reformation?* Reformation is only possible for those who want to be reformed and discontinue their rebellion, but there is no indication that those in hell want to be reformed or have any desire to stop rebelling against God.

  › *If God is loving, should he not be patient with people, hold back judgment, and lure them into goodness?* God is patient, but his patience is costly to the victims of sin. Therefore, at some point, God must end the violence and judge people for their sins.

> › *What about my loved ones who have died? Are you saying that if they did not trust in Christ, they will go to hell?* Scripture is clear that faith in Christ is essential to enter into the kingdom of heaven, but since many have trusted in Christ with their last breath, it is not possible for us to know who is in heaven and who is in hell.

- Hell is not a comfortable reality. It is not supposed to be. But, like prisons, it is a proper destination for some. If hell is real, we should warn others of it. In fact, not to warn others of hell is not to love them as we should.

Additional Resources

Erasing Hell: What God Said About Eternity and The Things We Made Up, Francis Chan & Preston Sprinkle

Is Hell for Real or Does Everyone Go to Heaven? Christopher W. Morgan and Robert A. Peterson

"Hell," in *The Problem of Pain*, C.S. Lewis

"How Can Eternal Punishment Be Fair?" in *Why Does God Allow Evil? Compelling Questions for Life's Toughest Questions*, Clay Jones

14

Will God Judge People Who Have Never Heard of Jesus?

It was a holiday visit to relatives. I was probably five or six years old, and our family was at the home of my cousin who was a few years older than me. I can't recall what we were doing upstairs, but whatever it was, it gave me an occasion to give my cousin the middle finger. In a flash, he ran downstairs declaring to everyone that I was in big trouble because I had just given him "the bird." Honestly, I had no clue what he was talking about.

Moments later my father came up the stairs and pulled me into one of the bedrooms. And it was there I was enlightened. Little did I know that I could point three of my fingers or my thumb at someone, but if I lifted the middle one alone, I was making a statement, and an offensive one at that. Looking back on the incident, I'd have to say my father handled it all perfectly. I had acted in an offensive manner, but because I knew nothing about the rule of the middle finger, no punishment was forthcoming.

If you weren't sure what Christianity said about Jesus before you started reading this book, it is probably clearer now. Christianity claims that to end up on the good side of eternity, you must recognize your own waywardness and trust that Jesus Christ is the only means by which you can be made right with God. But if you are like many to whom I have spoken, it is natural to wonder what happens to those who have never heard of Jesus. And it's natural, because it seems terribly unfair for people to be judged by God for not trusting in Jesus if they have never heard of Jesus in the first place. It would be like my dad punishing me for "flipping the bird" when I had no idea what such a gesture meant.

No Knowledge? No Worries

I like that people want God to be fair. In fact, it's hard for me to think of God as good if fairness isn't an integral part of who he is. Perhaps that's why God seems to make a point of mentioning his fairness in the Bible. He declares, for example, that "I, the LORD, love justice" (Psalm 61:8) and makes it clear that "acquitting the guilty and condemning the innocent" are both "detestable to the LORD" (Proverbs 17:15). Best yet, God's justice is described as impartial, unaffected by one's earthly status or any attempt at bribery.[1] So, if you want God to be fair, I think your desire is good. It's right in line with what the Bible says is true of God.

If we say that God is fair, what then should we say about those who haven't heard of Jesus? For many, it is easy to jump to the conclusion that God would not condemn those who have never had a chance to hear of Jesus. Just as my father did not condemn me for the offense of the errant middle finger I knew nothing about, it seems right that God would also not condemn us for not trusting in Jesus, if we know nothing about Christ. There is some good logic to this conclusion, but sometimes even when an idea makes sense initially, it can be problematic in the end. And I think that is what happens if we say that God lets people off the hook who have never heard of Jesus.

Suppose I hear of Jesus and readily trust that he is the Savior I need given my frequently errant and immoral ways. Then, in the ensuing years my wife and I have four children. If it is true that those who do not hear of Christ are guaranteed a place in heaven, how should I raise my children to ensure that they end up on the good side of eternity? One approach would be to shield my children from learning anything about Christ. That way they would have no knowledge of Jesus, God would give them a free pass, and we would all be assured of enjoying heavenly bliss together. But doesn't something seem wrong with this arrangement? Doesn't it seem odd that Christians, if they really care about the eternal destiny of others, would have incentive to purposely hide the Jesus who they say is worthy of all honor and praise? Certainly, Jesus did not promote such a plan. He frequently talked about his desire for us to speak to others about him.

> Jesus came and told his disciples, "I have been given all authority in heaven and on earth. Therefore, go and make disciples of all the nations, baptizing them in the name of the Father and the

Son and the Holy Spirit. Teach these new disciples to obey all the commands I have given you. And be sure of this: I am with you always, even to the end of the age." (Matthew 28:18-20)

[Jesus replied,] "But you will receive power when the Holy Spirit comes upon you. And you will be my witnesses, telling people about me everywhere—in Jerusalem, throughout Judea, in Samaria, and to the ends of the earth." (Acts 1:8)

Jesus had no intention of our remaining silent about him to ensure that people get to heaven. So, while I understand the logic that says a fair God would not condemn those who have not heard of Jesus, I am not sure this conclusion works. At the very least, believing "there are no worries if there is no knowledge" puts Christians in the odd position of endangering the eternal destiny of others if they speak of Jesus.

No Knowledge? Too Bad

If it is problematic to believe that God will give a free pass to those who have not heard of Jesus, what about the alternative? What if God sends anyone who does not trust in Christ to hell regardless of whether or not he or she had a chance to hear of Jesus? This option doesn't sound too appealing either. It appears very unjust, especially if trust in Jesus is the *only* way to be made right with God, as I have suggested. Before we totally dismiss this possibility, however, we should recognize the logic to it.

Christians have long held that we are all sinners and worthy of God's judgment.[2] As such, whether someone has heard of Jesus or not, God would not be unfair in sending people to hell for their sin. Imagine if people became infected by a disease due to profound carelessness and ultimately died from it. Even if there existed an available cure they knew nothing about, you probably wouldn't think their death was unfair given their careless behavior. Similarly, even if some people do not hear of Christ—the cure for their sin—it could well be argued that God is still fair in judging them for their waywardness despite their ignorance of Jesus.[3]

So, we can find some logic to the idea that God could be fair and yet judge and sentence people to hell even if they have never had a chance to hear of Jesus. But I am not sure this line of reasoning completely absolves God of the charge of unfairness. Yes, God would be just in sending people to hell because of their sin, but it still doesn't seem right that God would tell some people where to find a "get out of jail free" card but hide that information from others. That's hardly my idea of fair, and I am guessing that's not your idea of fair as well.

More Knowledge Than We Think

If God gives some people an opportunity to hear about the forgiveness offered by Jesus that he does not give to others, then you could argue that God is unfair. But such a charge against God sticks only if it is true that God affords an opportunity to some that he denies to others. So far in this chapter we have assumed that some people have not heard enough from God to lead them to Jesus, and we have considered how God might judge them despite their lack of knowledge. But what if people have heard a lot more from God than is at first apparent? What if everyone, everywhere has been given ample opportunity to learn about 1) the existence and nature of God, 2) one's own personal shortcomings and waywardness, and 3) the need for God's forgiveness? And what if when people embrace such a learning opportunity, God is particularly good at getting news about Jesus to them? If this is all true, then our wondering whether God judges those who have never heard may not be the right question, for the simple reason that everyone has had the opportunity to hear. Of course, making the suggestion that people everywhere have been given an opportunity to learn of Jesus might seem a bit outlandish to you. Some people live in cultures that never speak of Jesus. And some people live in rather remote areas who have little, if any, contact with the outside world. How could they have an opportunity to hear about Jesus? Let me give you two answers from the Bible's point of view.

First, the Bible tells us that God has revealed himself to all people through creation. That is, the Bible says that by taking a look at the world, from the way a spider spins its web to the manner in which the stars move across the sky, we clearly should recognize that something big is behind it all. One passage in particular reads: "For ever since the world was created, people have seen the earth and sky. Through everything God made, they can clearly see his invisible qualities—his eternal power and divine nature. *So they have no excuse for not knowing God*" (Romans 1:20, emphasis added). Another states, "The heavens proclaim the glory of God. The skies display his craftsmanship. Day after day they continue to speak; night after night they make him known" (Psalm 19:1-2).

In other words, the Bible says that the very existence of nature in all of its complexity and beauty ought to give people everywhere a reason to believe in a great and mighty creator.

In an age when people are taught that the universe can be explained without the existence of God, the Bible's argument that we ought to know there is a powerful, creative God just by looking at nature may seem weak. But maybe it shouldn't. Imagine touring a factory for plastic chairs. Before you enter the building, you see hundreds of plastic chairs being loaded onto distribution trucks. Although the chairs are simple in design, it still never enters your mind that they came about because of a long series of unguided processes. You may not be aware of all the detailed and precise steps required to manufacture the chairs, but believing that the factory randomly received materials and randomly put them together in order to produce the chairs is so preposterous that the idea is not worth entertaining. Instead, without anyone having to teach you to do so, you assume that some smart people are behind it all. The Bible says we should have a similar response when we look at creation. What the universe has produced is far more intricate than a plastic chair and should have us concluding, without having to be taught by anyone, that a powerful creator is behind it all, just as I suggest in Chapter 2.

Many people suppose that belief in God is something that is learned, so it might surprise you to know that believing that God is responsible for our universe is not something that has to be taught but something that is naturally assumed. A number of studies have shown that children, regardless of the religious environment in which they are raised, inherently conclude that the world in which we live could not come about without the work of a divine agent. In other words, people are hard-wired to believe in God based simply on what they observe in the world, and it is only through intentional efforts that this belief is altered.[4] But why are such intentional efforts made and even encouraged today? According to the Bible, people suppress the truth about God's existence because they don't want there to be a God that tells them what to do.[5] Ignoring the existence of God means we can disregard the concern that our actions might be subject to a future judgment, thus freeing us up to do as we please. And doing what we please has always been a powerful incentive to ignore any voice of authority in our lives. Famous British writer and philosopher Aldous Huxley explained this dynamic well when he spoke of the motive behind dispensing with God and embracing a meaningless world:

> I had motives for not wanting the world to have a meaning; consequently assumed that it had none, and was able without any difficulty to find satisfying reasons for this assumption. . . .
>
> For myself, as, no doubt, for most of my contemporaries, the philosophy of meaninglessness was essentially an instrument of liberation. The liberation we desired was simultaneously liberation from a certain political and economic system and liberation from a certain system of morality. We objected to the morality because it interfered with our sexual freedom.[6]

Of course, ignoring the existence of a meaning-giving authority figure in our life doesn't actually make that authority figure go away. If God is a reality, then we will face his judgment whether we want him to be real or not, and our suppression of the knowledge of God's existence to suit our liberation will be our demise. In that case, we may be ignorant of God, but we are culpably ignorant because of our unwillingness to embrace what could easily be understood.

Second, the Bible does not just say that all people have been given evidence of God through creation; it also says everyone has been given a conscience that points not only to the manner in which God would have them behave but to the existence of a moral law giver. We often think that one's conscience is simply a passed-down set of cultural taboos, but I did not find this to be true of my children, who at the earliest age showed signs of discerning between right and wrong apart from any instruction of mine. And my kids are not the exception. An abundance of research on infants indicates that at a very young age, we all "have a moral sense that enables us to judge others and that guides our compassion and condemnation."[7] I suppose this is why the Apostle Paul explained that Gentiles, who at the time of his writing had not been exposed to the Jewish Scriptures, still showed evidence that they knew what God declares to be right and wrong. In fact, this is what Paul wrote:

> Even Gentiles, who do not have God's written law, show that they know his law when they instinctively obey it, even without having heard it. They demonstrate that God's law is written in their

hearts, for their own conscience and thoughts either accuse them
or tell them they are doing right. (Romans 2:14-15)

In suggesting that we all have a conscience, I am not saying that it perfectly reflects the standard of God at birth. I am also not saying that our
conscience cannot be seared over time and therefore lead us astray. It
most certainly can.[8] We can have guilt written all over our face when we
steal a piece of Cheerios from a sibling as an infant, but then later as an
adult justify stealing inventory from our employer. But just because our
conscience can be muted and twisted by our own selfish desires does not
mean our conscience lacks evidence of a "pre-wiring" that points to the
existence and expectations of God.

Recognition of an innate conscience helps support the idea that people have more knowledge of God and his ways than we often consider,
but this is not the only reason I bring up the matter of conscience. I also
bring it up because the existence of a conscience means that we all have
the means of recognizing the fact that we fall short of its standards. And
this is true whether our conscience at any given stage is pointing in one
direction or the other. Suppose, for example, that your conscience calls
for you to be honest in every situation. That's a high bar, and I am guessing that you'd find yourself falling short of living up to that standard on a
regular basis. Suppose, however, that your conscience tells you it is best
not to be honest when it keeps someone's feelings from being hurt. This
too is a high bar, as I am sure there are plenty of times you have spoken
truth and hurt someone's feelings because of it. In either case then, our
conscience lets us know of our inability to live up to the standard by
which we say we ought to live.

Let's take a step back now and review what the Bible tells us about
what people everywhere ought to know about God. First, it says that all
people who have graced planet Earth have been exposed to the handi-
work of God in creation. As such, they ought to be aware of God's power
and creativity, and even his right to rule over that which he has made.
Second, the Bible indicates that people have been given a conscience
that not only is designed to point them to the moral law giver and his
standard but also consistently shows them they have fallen short—even
when their conscience is not fully in sync with what God desires. What
is important to notice about the voice of creation or conscience is that
neither is dependent on living next to people who are Christians or on

hearing the message of Jesus. Both speak in a language that can be heard by people everywhere and in every period of history. In other words, while it is easy to assume that people are out there who know nothing of God, we have good reason to believe that assumption is incorrect.

What To Do with What We Know

Knowledge doesn't mean much if we don't do anything with it. This is true whether we are talking about sterilizing instruments to be used during surgery or about God and his ways. When it comes to the matter of sterilization, our knowledge should lead us to actively sterilize the instruments before surgery. If we don't do so, then all our knowledge about sterilization means nothing at all. Likewise, if we have knowledge about God and do nothing with it, our knowledge is of little value. But what should our knowledge of God and his ways lead us to do? It ought to lead us to seek out God's mercy.

As we have seen, the Bible tells us that creation points to the fact that God exists. He is the powerful maker of all and therefore our rightful judge. The Bible also tells us that our conscience regularly reminds us that we do not live up to the standard that we ought to keep. On the one hand, then, we are aware of a judge who has the right to rule, and on the other hand, we know we do not live up to our own moral standards, let alone God's. Such knowledge ought to have us worried. It ought to have us seeking out mercy.

Imagine traveling to New York City to enjoy a wonderful weekend of shows. Long ago you made reservations for your lodging, but when you arrive at your hotel, you are told it has been overbooked. Like it or not, there is no room for you in the inn. Despite your protests, the hotel management provides no alternatives because every hotel in the area is booked for the busy weekend. Of course, you are utterly distraught. At that point, a stranger who overhears your plight offers a solution. His brother owns a penthouse that is currently not in use, and the place is yours for the weekend if you would like it. Although the offer sounds too good to be true, you decide to give the penthouse a look. When you arrive, it is beyond your imagination. It has a gorgeous layout with views overlooking Central Park, and it is decorated beautifully. Clearly, the owner is well resourced and has impeccable taste. It is then that you ask if there are any conditions to your stay. The stranger answers by requesting only that you leave the penthouse in as good a shape as when you arrived. That, of course, seems more than reasonable, and you graciously express your gratitude for your wonderful weekend accommodations.

After enjoying an unforgettable day in the city and a fantastic evening musical, you arrive back at the penthouse ready for a perfectly appointed nightcap. Just then, however, you receive a call from someone at your office. The project you have been working on for a year has been lost. A glitch in the company's servers has completely erased 12 months of hard work. You are aghast, and in a moment of anger, you grab a decorative bowl on the table and throw it toward a painting on the wall, irreparably damaging both pieces of art.

What then should be your response? You are staying in a house that is not your own. It is the home of someone who clearly has the means to make life very difficult for you considering the way you have handled his belongings. You know that what you have done does not meet the conditions of your stay, and likely what you have damaged is beyond your means to repay. You could try to run from the scene, but you have a sense that sooner or later you will be found and made to pay for your angry outburst. So what do you do? Instead of running, you decide to fess up to your misbehavior and seek mercy from the owner of the penthouse.

This response is what God expects of you and me. He has created a beautiful world for us to live in that speaks loudly of his power and creativity to people everywhere. He has given us a standard by which we are to live in the world, and he has given us a conscience that, at least in part, lets us know that we have not met it. This is true whether we live on a remote island, in the Bible Belt of the United States, or in the deserts of the Middle East. That means that everyone everywhere ought to know that we have broken God's "pieces of art" and that we have damaged what is not our own. We could run from the scene, but we will be found. So what should we do? We ought to fess up to our mistake and seek mercy from God. And if we don't, can we really blame God for judging us?

God's Response to Our Interest

As we have seen, the Bible says that all people know *enough* and are therefore without excuse before God. And they are without excuse because God has provided evidence of himself and our condition before him based on what we can learn through creation and our conscience.

But you still might protest, saying, "Okay, I can go with what you say about everyone having enough information to know about God, but what about Jesus? You've said that people need to know about Jesus, and I don't see how looking at creation or listening to our conscience can lead us to knowing anything at all about Jesus." If this is your observation, it is a very astute one.

As mentioned previously, I have had the opportunity to teach many people how to play tennis over the years. Some people are very receptive to the coaching that I offer, and some, even though they want a lesson, quickly show they aren't too interested in learning much. When I encounter someone who is eager to learn, I find myself wanting to help that person even more. Knowing that my efforts will not be wasted, I gladly dispense as much instruction as he or she can absorb. My response, however, to those who don't have much appetite for learning is quite different. I tend to give out much less information. No need to dish out a great deal of understanding when it will be left on the plate. You've probably found yourself reacting in the same way with people you work alongside, or with family and friends.

This propensity to give more to those who are eager and less to those who are disinterested is not unlike what we see from God. This is what Jesus was getting at when he said, "To those who listen to my teaching, more understanding will be given. But for those who are not listening, even what little understanding they have will be taken away from them" (Mark 4:25). Throughout the Bible, we see statements like this: "Keep on asking, and you will receive what you ask for. Keep on seeking, and you will find. Keep on knocking, and the door will be opened to you" (Matthew 7:7). Or, "You will seek me and find me when you seek me with all your heart" (Jeremiah 29:13). The implication is that if we have an interest in God, he will respond. He will let himself be found.

Take, then, the idea that all have seen and heard enough about God and his ways through both creation and our conscience to seek God's mercy. What then should we expect from God if we are not willing to listen to what nature and our conscience are telling us? We probably ought to expect that God won't tell us a whole lot more about himself. It's not that he couldn't tell us more, but given our lack of receptivity, it may do little good. But, what if, on the other hand, we do respond to what we've heard from God and seek to know more about him and his mercy? In that case, it is not unreasonable to assume God will give us even more insight and understanding, including what we need to know about Jesus.

My wife grew up in a nonreligious home. Church was not a part of her upbringing, and Jesus and the Bible were completely foreign to her. Nonetheless, she could not get rid of the sense that a God must be out there. That's why she first prayed to him that the Houston Astros would win the 1980 playoffs. Okay, so that wasn't a particularly significant prayer, but it was still an indication she had at least a sliver of belief that something was out there that had the power to intervene. A few years later, after an enormously successful year in her collegiate tennis career, she found herself completely dissatisfied with her God-free life and seeking something more. It was in this very season that a new coach arrived who knew a great deal about Jesus. My wife will tell you that it was as if God put this coach in her path at just the time she was looking for God—at just the time when she was open to hearing about him. I share this story because it is an example of God's willingness to reveal more about himself when we begin to respond to what he has shown us through creation and our conscience. But there are far more dramatic stories than this.

In 1817 America's first foreign missionary, Adoniram Judson, arrived in Burma. His hope was to evangelize the Buddhist Burmese majority. He knew little of the minority *Karen* people who lived in their midst. As Judson settled into his work of translating the Bible into Burmese, he was completely unaware of the hymns that the Karen people were singing just outside his door:

O children and grandchildren! If we repent of our sins,
And cease to do evil—restraining our passions—
And pray to Y'wa, he will have mercy upon us again.
If Y'wa does not have mercy on us, there is no other one who can.
He who saves us is the only one—Y'wa.[9]

This was not a hymn taught to the Karen people by any outsiders. It is what they ardently believed on their own. They knew there was a God, they knew they were evil, and they knew they needed God's mercy. Furthermore, they were convinced that someone would come with a book to provide more details about the Y'wa to whom they prayed.

Not long after he arrived in Burma, Judson hired a Karen man, Ko Tha-Byu, to do a few odd jobs, but soon the man recognized what

Judson's work was all about. Judson was translating the book from Y'wa that the Karen people had long been awaiting. Accordingly, Tha-Byu spent every waking hour learning to read the new Burmese Bible as quickly as Judson could translate it. And as soon as Tha-Byu understood it, he embarked on countless trips to Karen villages. Nearly everywhere he went, people were amazed at what they heard, and soon there were tens of thousands of Karen who worshipped Christ. For centuries Burmese Buddhists had unsuccessfully tried to convert the Karen to Buddhism, but in a matter of years the Karen accepted the news of Christ's forgiveness in droves. Why is that? One way to explain it is to say that when the Karen honored Y'wa as the rightful judge, and when they recognized that their ways fell short of what he desired, God managed to get the message of Christ to them.[10]

The book of Acts is found in the New Testament and recounts the story of the nascent Christian church following the death and resurrection of Jesus. There we find a story of Philip, one of Jesus' twelve disciples, and are told that Philip was commanded by an angel to travel south from Jerusalem to Gaza. While on his way, Philip meets an important Ethiopian official who was in charge of all the treasury of Queen Candace of Ethiopia. The man had interest in God but was confused when reading the words of the prophet Isaiah concerning a coming messiah. When Philip meets the official, the Ethiopian asks him to explain what Isaiah the prophet wrote, and Philip tells him of Jesus, the promised messiah. It doesn't take long from that point for the Ethiopian to place his trust in Christ, and for Philip to go on his way. In other words, when the Ethiopian official had sought to know more of the God he worshipped, God saw that the official was able to learn of Christ from Philip.[11]

When speaking to others about Jesus, it is not unusual for me to be asked about those who grow up in Muslim cultures. People have heard enough to know that in many Muslim cultures open conversation about Jesus and Christianity is not welcome. If that's the case, people wonder how it would be possible for those who grow up in such an environment to ever learn about Christ. The evidence suggests, however, that getting the message of Jesus to people in this context has not proved too difficult for God. A large percentage of Muslim converts report that they experienced countless visceral dreams of Jesus that were then followed up by unexpected meetings with Christians or the gift of a Bible. That's why when Bibles are smuggled into places like Saudi Arabia or Somalia, they are gone in a day by those anxious to learn more about Jesus. So even in Muslim contexts, God seems to have little problem getting his message of Jesus to those who are interested.[12]

While we might question if people 100 years ago or more could have possibly heard about Jesus if they lived in remote or religiously insulated environments, it is much more difficult to question whether people today have a valid chance to learn about Jesus. I say this because of the access to information that technology now provides. Trans World Radio, for example, broadcasts Christian programs in more than 275 languages to 190 countries. Or consider Global Media Outreach (GMO). It has been answering people's questions about Jesus, the Bible, and Christianity through its online portals since 2004. When people ask spiritual questions through common search engines like Google and Bing, they are often pointed to websites hosted by GMO where they can get personal answers about Jesus and the Bible in their own language from trained volunteers. To date, over two billion people have received answers from GMO's volunteer staff. If you've done much traveling to remote or developing countries, you know that even in those locations cell phones are the norm. This means that people we may have assumed were out of reach when it comes to hearing of Jesus are not much more than a click away from learning of him if they show but a little interest in God.

I wonder if the reason we question whether people have really been given an opportunity to hear about Jesus is because we don't have a very big picture of God. If God, however, is the creator of the universe and all that is in it and if he desires that we live with him forever, it is not unreasonable to trust that God can get word about Jesus to someone who is seeking out God, regardless of where they are. Nonetheless, God's effectiveness in doing so still often comes as a surprise, even to Christians. Nineteenth-century Christian historian John Richardson Phillips speaks of such a surprise when he recounts the story of a 19th-century missionary to India.

> A caravan was crossing from one part of India to another, and in its company a missionary travelled. As it passed along, a poor Hindoo was so overcome by the heat and weariness, that he sank down, and was left to perish on the road. The missionary saw him, and kneeling by his side when the other travelers had passed on whispered into his ear, "Brother, what is your hope?" The dying

man raised himself a little, and with a great effort gasped out, "The blood of Jesus Christ His Son cleanseth from all sin," and immediately expired with the effort he had made. The missionary was greatly astonished at this reply, and from the calm peaceful expression of the man felt sure that he had died in Christ. "How or where," thought he, "could this man, to all appearance a heathen, have got his hope?" As he thought of it, he noticed a piece of paper grasped tightly in the dead man's hand. What was the missionary's surprise and delight, when he found that it was a single leaf of the Holy Book, containing the first chapter of the first epistle of St. John in which these words occur. On that single page the Hindoo had found the word of God.[13]

It is our tendency to assume that people who don't have the same religious training or cultural background as we do don't know the same things we know about God.[14] But that is not necessarily the case. No doubt, I would have been as surprised as that 19th-century missionary if I were placed in the same situation. The missionary probably thought that he was the one to bring Jesus to the people, and yet he finds that God was one step ahead of him. Too often we think that God is bound by our efforts, but that seems to make God rather small. While the Bible says he often delights to use us in sharing Christ with others, he is not dependent on us. God's heart is such that one way or the other, he will respond to the interest of any who are seeking him. As the Bible tells us: "For the Lord sees every heart and knows every plan and thought. If you seek him, you will find him. But if you forsake him, he will reject you forever" (1 Chronicles 28:9).

Knowledge and Responsibility

There are people who have never heard of Jesus, but that does not mean that God has been unfair. Sometimes we are responsible not just for what we know but also for what we should have known. If, for example, I order a chair that must be assembled but damage it during assembly because I choose not to read the instruction manual, I cannot ask for a refund because I didn't know better. Yes, I did not know how to assemble the chair properly, but I should have known because the instructions were provided. Likewise, while it may be true that some people have never heard of Jesus, that does not mean they did not have an opportunity for which they are responsible. They would be, as I stated earlier, culpably ignorant.

God has provided through creation evidence of his existence, power, and authority. He has also provided us a means to understand his standards and our inability to live up to it by giving us a conscience. With this information, we ought to seek the mercy of God. And when we seek his mercy, God is faithful to reveal himself and, in particular, reveal the person of Jesus. That means that if we do not know of Christ, we cannot cry foul, for the simple reason that we could have known about Christ had we simply shown some interest in what God has revealed to everyone.

Sometimes when people ask the question "Will God judge people who have never heard of Jesus?" they are hoping that the answer to this question will somehow absolve them from the responsibility to respond to what they know about Christ. But even if the question is unanswerable or its answer unsatisfactory, it is not really a question that applies to the asker. If you have made your way through the pages of this book, you are not counted among those who have not heard about Jesus. By now, you have heard of Jesus. You have heard that your good works are not enough to make you right before God. You have heard that your sin separates you from God. You have heard that Jesus died to pay the penalty for your sins and rose again so that you might enjoy life with God forever. You have heard that trusting in Christ is the only way to be made right with God. So even if it could be argued that others don't have all the same information you do, it does not change what you know. It does not change the knowledge for which you will be held accountable.

Afterthoughts

If repenting of your sin and trusting that Jesus' death and resurrection is what is necessary to put you in good standing with God, a couple of questions might arise: one has to do with those who lived before Jesus' time, and the other has to do with children or the mentally impaired.

What About People Who Lived Before Jesus' Time? The Bible indicates that God progressively revealed his plan to bring salvation to the world, and what was required of ancient peoples was that they trust in that which God had revealed up to the time they lived.[15] As I have covered, God has revealed himself through creation and human conscience. This has been true since the beginning of time. With the knowledge afforded by these two sources, people of all ages could readily recognize their need of God's mercy. At times, however, God went well beyond these two sources of revelation and made his presence even clearer. For example, when God freed the people of Israel from Egyptian captivity, he did so through a series of miraculous plagues that drastically impacted the land and people of Egypt. These plagues not only fanned the faith of the Israelites but also encouraged other people to follow the God of Israel.[16] So while people did not know of Christ, God did make himself known enough that people could readily seek his mercy and forgiveness.

In this book, I have spoken about the biblical claim that a person cannot be made right with God by doing good works. Further, I have shared the Bible's position that the only means by which we can have our sins forgiven and receive eternal life is by faith in the work of Christ. The necessity of faith over works, however, is not a post-Christ idea. It is what God required of all who would be accepted by God even before Christ came into the world. For example, the Bible tells us that Abraham, who lived about 2,000 years before Christ, "believed the Lord, and the Lord counted him as righteous because of his faith" (Genesis 15:6). So while Abraham would not have known the details about the coming Christ, he did know about God and his ways and placed faith in the mercy and provision of God. It could be said, then, that Abraham responded to the message of faith over works that God had established for all ages even before the coming of Christ.

As an expression of the need for God's mercy and forgiveness, God directed people before the time of Christ to offer regular sacrifices. These sacrifices, however, did not forgive the sin of the people.[17] They were simply reminders that a debt of sin needed to be paid. In effect, the sacrifices were only "interest payments" on the debt of sin that had accrued over a person's life. But they did nothing to affect the principal. The principal itself would be paid off only when the promised messiah came and suffered on behalf of humanity. Therefore, it was the death and resurrection of Jesus that ultimately sets people free of their debt of sin, whether they lived before, during, or after the time of Christ.

Imagine a family being in debt for decades. The best they can do is pay the minimum interest payments. The older members of the family die and leave the debt to their children. This carries on until a generous outsider comes and pays off all the debt incurred by past and present generations and even puts enough in the account to pay off all future expenses. This is what the Bible says Jesus did. He is the "outsider" who paid off the debt of all who in repentance sought mercy from God before the time of Christ, and he put enough in the account to pay off all future debt incurred by those who would seek the mercy and forgiveness of Jesus after his death.

What About Children or Those Who Are Mentally Impaired? Like many families, we lost a child before he or she was born. Others have lost a child in infancy or when the child was just a few years of age. And some have children who have significant cognitive challenges and their ability to understand the world around them is limited. What happens to these people? They can hardly be expected to trust in Christ.

The Bible does not explicitly address this question, but it does provide us with enough hints to suggest that God loves children and does not hold those accountable who lack the capacity to understand moral responsibility or the offer of salvation made possible through Jesus Christ. Jesus' interaction with children is particularly telling. When those around him sought to shoo children away, Jesus welcomed them, saying, "It is not my heavenly Father's will that even one of these little ones should perish (Matthew 18:14). And later, "Let the children come to me. Don't stop them! For the Kingdom of Heaven belongs to those who are like these children" (Matthew 19:14).

One helpful biblical example of a parent losing a child involves King David. Before the sick child died, David cried out to the Lord for the child's life, but once the child dies, David finds comfort in the fact that he will one day be reunited with his son, declaring, "I will go to him one day, but he cannot return to me" (2 Samuel 12:23). In other words, while David accepted that his son would not live with him on earth, he believed the child's death did nothing to prevent David from being with the child in the life to come.

Some wonder if there is an age when we become accountable to God. When the Israelites disobeyed God after the release from Egyptian captivity, God judged everyone who was 20 years or older.[18] This could point to an age of accountability, but it could just point to the fact that God was holding those under 20 *less* responsible for their actions than the older ones who were largely calling the shots. It is probably better to see God as holding people accountable who have sufficient awareness of their moral responsibility rather than judging them differently based on meeting a minimum age requirement. Consistently, we see Scripture say that all people will be judged on the basis of sins they willfully and consciously committed.[19] In other words, God's judgment is based on an informed rejection of what God has revealed through creation, conscience, or Christ.[20] Since it could be argued that infants or those who have severe mental impairment cannot make such informed decisions, it is reasonable to assume that they will not be held accountable before God for their lack of response to him and will enjoy an eternity with God. Similar to those who lived before the time of Christ, this gift of eternal life is still made possible by the life, death, and resurrection of Jesus.

When considering the fate of children or those who suffer from cognitive impairments, it is important to note that the Bible indicates that they will be given eternal life because they *could not* make a decision relative to Christ for which they will be judged. They will not go to heaven because their parents are Christians, and the parents of such heaven-bound children will not get to ride their children's coattails into God's presence.[21] If you are an adult, you are in the position where you *can* make a decision about Christ, and so it is incumbent upon you to seek Christ so that one day you can be reunited with any children who may have died before their ability to rightly respond to God.

Key Points

- If trusting in Jesus is the only way to be made right with God and live with him eternally, it is not unreasonable to ask about those who have never heard of Jesus. There are two common ways people approach this question, and both are problematic.

  › *People who do not hear about Jesus are given a "free pass."* The problem with this approach is that if people were given a "free pass" for not knowing Jesus, it would be better not to tell others of Jesus. This is inconsistent with Jesus' instructions to tell others about him.

  › *People who don't hear about Jesus are judged by God despite their lack of knowledge.* The problem with this approach is that it makes God out to be unfair. Our sin is worthy of judgment, so in that sense God could fairly judge us all, but it still seems unfair that some people would get to hear of the solution to their sin predicament and others would not.

- The two approaches explained above assume that people have not heard or do not have the possibility to hear about Jesus. Scripture indicates otherwise. It suggests that everyone has heard enough about God and his ways through creation and conscience. This knowledge should lead them to recognize that they fall short of God's standard and call out for mercy.

- Unfortunately, many people suppress the truth in order to remove any moral accountability to God, and thus no longer hear what they ought to hear. In doing so, they become culpably ignorant.

- Although not everyone has heard of Jesus, this does not mean that God is incapable of getting the message of Christ to all people who earnestly seek out God wherever they may be.

- Even if we are unsure as to how God will judge those we assume know nothing of Jesus, it does not change that we will be held accountable for the fact that we do know about Jesus.

- Those who lived before Jesus' time were responsible for what God had revealed up to that point. Again, through creation and conscience all people had enough knowledge to seek God's mercy and to look to him in faith knowing that their good works would never meet God's standard.

- The Bible indicates that children and those who are mentally impaired will not be judged for the lack of response to God because they do not have the capacity to willfully reject what God has revealed about himself, our sin, and the forgiveness offered by Jesus.

Additional Resources

Dreams and Visions: Is Jesus Awakening the Muslim World? Tom Doyle

Eternity in Their Hearts: Startling Evidence of Belief in the One True God in Hundreds of Cultures Throughout the World, Don Richardson

"Will God Judge Those Who Have Never Heard About Christ?" in *I'm Glad You Asked: How to Talk with Your Friends About Christian Faith and Their Questions*, Ken Boa and Larry Moody

15

If Christianity Is True, Where Do I Start?

Peter hadn't slept in days. At least, it's hard to imagine that he could have. Just a week ago, the man he had looked up to for years was greeted by the masses with stunning honor and respect. Many were calling him the Messiah, the promised one of God. Yet now, Jesus was dead. Crucified, naked, as a criminal. To make matters worse, the last words Jesus heard Peter speak were not ones of affection and support, but of repeated denial. How could Peter sleep?

The angst and confusion and disillusionment that Peter must have felt as he stirred in his bed is hard to imagine. Who was this man that he had followed for years? Who was this self-proclaimed Messiah who had given him so much hope? Was Jesus just a hoax? Was he just one more in a long line of disappointing religious hucksters? These are the questions that must have been racing through Peter's mind when suddenly a group of women burst into the home where he was staying. The women could hardly contain themselves. They spoke what seemed to be nonsense. They said Jesus was alive.

Alive? How could Jesus be alive? If there was one thing that the Romans did well, it was kill people. Peter may have been unsure of many things, but he was certain Jesus was dead. No one survives a crucifixion, and dead men don't break free from guarded tombs. So what was Peter to do with this report? Peter knew and trusted these women, but what they were claiming made no sense at all. There was only one thing to do—go and look for himself.

I don't know what made you pick up this book. No doubt, along the journey of life, you have heard your share of religious claims. At some point, you even may have thought there was something there for you, but then came the disappointment. Then came the disillusionment. Then came the unanswered questions. The last thing you want is to chase something that isn't real. And yet for some reason, you still picked up this book. Maybe it's a last-ditch effort to see if there is something more to Christianity. Maybe, like Peter, you had to go one last time and look for yourself.

I don't pretend to have addressed all the questions you might have about God, the Bible, or Christianity, or even to have answered the questions posed in these pages to your complete satisfaction. I do hope, however, that I have presented a case for following Jesus that gives you more evidence to consider than you've seen before. I don't know whether the evidence I have provided is enough for you, but this I do know: When it comes to Jesus, we cannot avoid making a choice.

Jesus said that he was God. Jesus said that we must trust in him, and that doing so is the *only* means by which we can enjoy eternal life with God. Either Jesus was right or he was wrong. Either we admit that we are lost and in need of being rescued by Jesus, or we believe such an admission is unnecessary. If what Jesus said, and what Christianity has declared, is true, there is no way to remain uncommitted. Philosopher Douglas Groothuis says this better than I can:

> Not to believe in Christianity, either as a committed unbeliever or as an agnostic, means to forfeit the *benefits* promised only to the believer (eternal life), should Christianity be true. Deciding not to choose has the same result as not believing in God. In this sense, "you are already committed."

Of course, you could say that you believe in Jesus, but only as you believe in a myth. His story and teachings inspire you to live a better life, but you need not pretend it all to be true. But I would suggest "the truth of the Christian narrative is precisely what makes the Christian life meaningful and worthwhile." Why bother with stories of Jesus and wishful thinking about eternity if it is not true? As Groothuis even more bluntly states:

> The only sufficient reason for wanting to blend one's own narrative with the narrative of the Bible is that what the Bible describes about creation, fall and redemption is true and worth believing and obeying. If it is not, then to live within this story line is literally to live a lie—and to advocate that others live this lie as well.

Ultimately, then, this book is not about persuading you to join my camp. Instead, my aim has been to provide you with facts and reasons and information for you to consider. Every person requires a different weight of evidence to be convinced of the truth; whether I have provided enough is your call to make. As I've suggested, it is a call no one can avoid making. You must answer the question Jesus asked: "Who do you say I am?" (Matthew 16:15).

This then brings us to the final question of this book: If Christianity is true, where do I start?

Look to Jesus

When I was growing up, there used to be a guy with a colorful afro wig who would show up at sporting events holding a sign that read, "John 3:16." Perhaps in those days a good number of people knew that he was referencing a Bible verse, but I still wondered if some folks thought he was attempting to convey a coded message to players on the field. If you're like those who didn't know the verse his sign referenced, it reads like this:

> For this is how God loved the world: He gave his one and only Son, so that everyone who believes in him will not perish but have eternal life. (John 3:16)

As you might guess, the "Son" in these words refers to Jesus. Jesus is the one who was sent because of God's love. Jesus is the one we are called to believe in if we are not to perish but have eternal life. Yet, as clear as these words might be, it's the words Jesus spoke before this famous verse I find to be even more instructive, even if they are a bit cryptic. Here is what Jesus said:

> And as Moses lifted up the bronze snake on a pole in the wilderness, so the Son of Man must be lifted up, so that everyone who believes in him will have eternal life. (John 3:14-15)

Of course, making sense of these words means you must know something of Moses and the snake, so let me explain. Moses was the leader of the Jewish people more than 1,400 years before Jesus came on the scene. He was the one who led the Israelites out of Egypt after 400 years of slavery. This was not without a lot of fanfare as God did quite a series of miracles to free his people from Egyptian bondage. Not long after escaping Egypt, however, the Israelites found themselves in the desert between Egypt and the promised land to which God was leading them. God saw to it that they had food and water while in the desert, but the menu was not up to the people's liking. So, the Israelites began to complain, and complain, and complain. God finally had enough. So, to teach the Israelites a lesson, God sent venomous snakes throughout their desert camp. Soon people were dying left and right.

Messing with God was clearly not working out well for the Israelites, and it wasn't long before they cried out to Moses to speak to God on their behalf. Moses did, and in response, God said, "Make a bronze replica of a poisonous snake and attach it to a pole. All who are bitten can look at it and live." Now, if I were Moses, I'd probably ask, "You want me to do what?!" But by this point in time, Moses had largely learned to just do what God told him. So, he fashioned together a bronze snake on a pole, placed it outside, and told the people that if they looked at it, they would be saved.

Now, suppose you are living in that time. The snakes start filling the landscape and you take your family and retreat into your tent. Eventually, however, the snakes make it in, and though you try your best to fend them off, they bite everyone in your family. The clock is ticking; like it or not, life will soon end for you and all you love. At just this point of desperation, a neighbor excitedly throws open the flap of your tent, crying, "Did you hear? Did you hear?" In response, you ask, "Hear what?" And your neighbor answers, "God told Moses to set up a bronze snake on a pole, and anyone who has been bitten can look at it and be saved."

Given this scenario, you could choose among a number of responses. If you are the independent type, you could say, "Thank you for the information, but I think we can handle this on our own." Or, if you are the analytical one, you may rebuff your neighbor, saying, "Look at a snake on a pole? How ridiculous! What good would that do?" Or maybe because you're the kind of person who doesn't like it when your options are limited, you reply, "Did you say there is only one pole I can look at? I am sorry, but that's too exclusive." Or perhaps if you're the noncommittal type, you could offer to make a donation to the cause but not bother with heading out to see the snake on the pole. The only problem is that if you choose any of these responses over getting out of your tent and looking at the bronze snake on a pole, you will die.

I am guessing at this point you now can see what Jesus was getting at when he brought up Moses and the bronze snake on the pole. Jesus knew that one day in the not-so-distant future, he would find himself fashioned to a crucifixion pole. And according to Jesus, if you do not want to perish because you have been bitten by the snake of sin, you have but one choice: to get out of your comfortable tent and look at him as the only means by which you can be saved. It may not make complete sense to you, and you may not like that Jesus is the only "bronze snake" on a pole that will make you well. You may even be the kind of person who would rather figure your own way out of your mess. Yet, if what Jesus says is true, and if what Christians have been declaring through the centuries is true, then the right place for you to start is by humbly acknowledging that your own sin has put you in a desperate state. And then, having done that, to look to Jesus as the only means by which you can be saved. As Peter declared soon after seeing the resurrected Jesus, "There is salvation in no one else! God has given no other name under heaven by which we must be saved" (Acts 4:12). Whether you do this is your call. But trusting in Jesus is the only way for you to start with God, if Christianity is true.

Part of the Family

In his book *The Case for Grace*, Lee Strobel shares the story of Stephanie Fast. She was an "illegitimate" child, born of a Korean woman and an American soldier. Soon she was abandoned on the streets and did whatever she had to do to survive. Eventually, she found herself in an orphanage, but who would ever want to adopt a sickly *toogee*—a nasty term reserved for half-breeds. In time, however, an American couple met Stephanie and felt compelled to adopt her into their family. At first, Stephanie could not comprehend what had happened; she figured they had bought her to be their servant. It finally sank in only after a friend emphatically explained, "You are their daughter."

If we turn to Christ and ask for his mercy, we might think that at best he'd make us his indebted servants going forward, but that's not what Scripture tells us happens. Instead, the Bible says that those who trust in Christ become children of God (John 1:12) as those adopted into his family (Galatians 3:26-4:7). This means that if you choose to look to Christ as the Israelites looked at the bronze snake, you will become a permanent member of God's family. And though at times you may struggle to be a very good son or daughter, nothing you can do will change your place in God's family. That's because there is nothing you can do to make God love you more as his child, and nothing you can do to make God love you less.

In the rest of this chapter, I will share with you a few things that Jesus would like you to do as a member of his family. But what I will share with you is not a long checklist to get you into heaven or keep you there. Even if you stumble in your efforts to live out what I share, you will not cease to be in God's family or fall away from his love. God's adoption of you is nothing but a gift when you trust in him, and his heart for you is that you enjoy an abundant, joy-filled life as a member of his family. In fact, Jesus said of those who trust in him, "My purpose is to give them a rich and satisfying life" (John 10:10). What you will find below, then, are not ways to earn God's grace (in that case it would no longer be grace) but rather a pathway to experience the deeply satisfying life Jesus offers.

Love Well

In Jesus' day, there was a definite line of authority. You didn't just start heading out on your own as a teacher without getting the seal of approval from the religious leaders. That's part of the reason Jesus met so much resistance. He didn't believe he needed any human stamp of approval to start preaching from town to town. It's not surprising, then, that the religious leaders would grill Jesus with questions at every turn. And what better way to get to the core of Jesus' teaching than to ask him which was the greatest of God's commandments. If Jesus was in error at this point, they easily could discredit his self-assigned authority. But Jesus did not stumble over the question. Without hesitation, he identified the greatest command: "Love the LORD your God with all your heart, all your soul, and all your mind" (Matthew 22:37). Then Jesus quickly added a related command that also had to do with love. It was not lengthy, but it was weighty and demanding. He said, "Love your neighbor as yourself" (Matthew 22:39).

Frequently, I am asked, "What is the purpose of life?" I can't think of a better way to sum it up than this: "Love God, love others, and encourage others to do the same." Of course, it can be helpful to define what it means to do each of these things, but sometimes I think people make the Christian life much too complicated. They figure it has to do with engaging in so many activities with a church, or reading the Bible so often, or helping so many poor people, or saying so many prayers. No doubt, those can all be valuable, but if in doing them, love gets squeezed out, Jesus says we've missed the boat. And it misses the boat because Christianity isn't about rules; it's about a relationship—a relationship that begins with God and spills out toward others. That's what the Apostle Paul was getting at when he wrote the words so often recited at weddings:

> If I could speak all the languages of earth and of angels, but didn't love others, I would only be a noisy gong or a clanging cymbal. If I had the gift of prophecy, and if I understood all of God's secret plans and possessed all knowledge, and if I had such faith that I could move mountains, but didn't love others, I would be nothing. If I gave everything I have to the poor and even sacrificed my body, I could boast about it; but if I didn't love others, I would have gained nothing. (1 Corinthians 13:1-3)

Imagine waking up tomorrow and beginning your day praying, "Lord, today I want to love you well, and I know loving you well means loving the people you have made. So, help me, Lord, to love the people in my world today—my family, my friends, the people I work with, the people I live by, the people I bump into along the way." And suppose, as best you can throughout the day, you do just that. According to Jesus, it's hard to go wrong living that way, and I'm guessing those around you won't mind it either. God simply made us to love—to love him and to love others.

Learn and Do

I've been married 33 years, and I'm pretty sure I love my wife better now than when we first got married. Some of that probably has to do with growing up a bit, but much of it has to do with learning better how my wife best knows my love. You might say, I have learned to better speak her love language. I now know, for example, that she prefers a new pair of running shoes over a vase full of flowers for her birthday, and I know that she'd rather go for a walk than go to a movie. I don't think it is just people like my wife, however, who have love languages. I think God does too.

On the evening before Jesus' arrest and crucifixion, Jesus had a great deal to say to his disciples. He knew his time with them was nearing its end, and he wanted to make sure they clearly understood a few things. At one point he told them rather bluntly, "If you love me, obey my commandments." If Jesus had said it just once, it would have been important enough to note, but a few moments later, he repeated himself, saying, "Those who accept my commandments and obey them are the ones who love me." I wonder what the disciples thought at that moment. Did they think, "Okay, Jesus, we've got that down. You've said it twice; we'll be sure to remember it going forward"? But if they did, they would have been surprised when a few seconds later, he nearly repeated himself again, saying, "All who love me will do what I say." And then if that was not enough, he made sure they understood his teaching from another angle, declaring, "Anyone who doesn't love me will not obey me." That's four times in a matter of minutes that Jesus essentially said the same thing (John 14:15, 21, 23, 24), which makes me think that if we are to make an educated guess at Jesus' love language, it has to do with obeying his commands.

So Jesus made his point clear, but here are the implications. If we are to love Jesus well, we have to know what his commands are. The first part calls us for us to keep on learning. I did not learn the way to love my wife overnight. I've had to study her. The same is true when it comes to Jesus. If you want to know what Jesus' commands are, you are going to need to learn them by reading what he had to say. And if you are like me, you are going to have to read them over and over through the years to keep them front and center. Take, for example, Jesus' teaching about loving your neighbor as yourself. Just after declaring the importance of this command, Jesus provided a vivid parable to let us know just what it looks like to love our neighbor, and not surprisingly, the story involves a lot more than just baking cookies for them at Christmastime. In fact, it is a parable that shows a traveling businessman reaching across the ethnic divide to help a dying man he did not know at great personal expense (Luke 10:30-37). Now, that's a much broader picture of loving your neighbor than I would have ever come up with on my own. That's why it is so important for me to keep on learning by reading the Bible nearly every day.

That brings up the second part of Jesus' love language. The first part has to do with knowing Jesus' commands, but the second part has to do with actually living them out. I am sad to say that there are far too many Christians today who have spent a great deal of time learning what Jesus has commanded us to do yet far too little time actually doing what he said. Jesus had a parable for folks like this:

> Anyone who listens to my teaching and follows it is wise, like a person who builds a house on solid rock. Though the rain comes in torrents and the floodwaters rise and the winds beat against that house, it won't collapse because it is built on bedrock. But anyone who hears my teaching and doesn't obey it is foolish, like a person who builds a house on sand. When the rains and floods come and the winds beat against that house, it will collapse with a mighty crash. (Matthew 7:24-27)

You probably noticed, but in this parable both the wise man and the foolish man have heard Jesus' teaching. That is, they had the same information about Jesus' commands. The difference between the two was that the wise man set out to do what Jesus said, while the foolish man continued to chart his own path. As you can see, it didn't turn out too well for the foolish man. And I don't think it will turn out too well for us if, like the foolish man, we leave Jesus' commands undone.

Let God into Every Room

When I was younger, a little book often made the rounds among Christians. It was a short story written by a Presbyterian minister, entitled *My Heart—Christ's Home*. It begins with a man who heard Christ knocking at the door of his proverbial home and freely invited him in. But not long after Christ came into the man's home, Jesus wanted to take a look around. First, there was the library—the place where the mind was filled with ideas and philosophies. After taking a look at the books on the shelves, Christ suggested changing out a number of books. Rather than the man reading books that encouraged perspectives and behaviors at odds with the heart of Christ, Jesus suggested the man begin to fill his mind with better things, particularly the Bible. As you can imagine, such a makeover of the library would not be easy. Some of the old books had once captured the man's imagination, and not in the best of ways.

The library, however, was just the beginning. Soon Christ wanted to visit the dining room, where soon he would address the man's "appetites and desires." Then it was on to the living room, or the place where Jesus would meet with the man every day. Next was the workroom, where Christ could see if the "tools" the man had been given were being used to their full potential. Christ even wanted to visit the rec room and had some things to say about the way the man entertained himself and his friends. Finally came the small, locked hall closet that held the secret things the man wanted no one to know about. In this hidden space was the stuff that had left a smell throughout the whole house.

Throughout the journey into each room of the man's house, Christ was gentle but nonetheless pointed. He simply was not satisfied with taking up residence in the man's life; Christ wanted to renovate each room. At first, the man was taken aback by Christ's plans for each room, but as he began to implement Christ's instructions, he saw the good in it. And instead of being restrictive or suffocating, the changes Christ sought brought about a newfound purpose, joy, and satisfaction.

Too often people see Jesus as an addition to their home—one more room among many that is visited on occasion (such as Easter and Christmas). But Jesus is never satisfied with that arrangement. His intent is to reshape the rooms in which we already live. In fact, even as the story of *My Heart—Christ's Home* concludes, Jesus wants us to sign over the deed—to say that our home is his home to do with what he deems best.

Of course, this kind of home makeover is a process, and at least in my experience, it seems that Christ keeps pointing out rooms and closets and drawers in my life that he'd like to improve. I suspect it will be the same for you as well. Sometimes the value of the changes Jesus encourages will be seen up front; at other times replacing something we have long loved with something new can be a scary proposition. But in the long run, I don't think you will be disappointed with the results. He is a better homeowner than we could ever be, and his ways can bring life, healing, strength, and hope, of unforeseen measure.

Don't Go It Alone

Each Friday morning, I meet with a group of men. We challenge each other with the things that we read. We talk about what is happening in the world and how we should respond. We let each other know what is happening in our families. We listen. We encourage. We pray. This morning was no different, except for the fact that one man among us was feeling the press. Yesterday, his brother died after a long battle with health issues, and today as we spoke his son was heading into surgery after breaking his jaw in several places due to a fall. To be honest, I did not expect him to join the group today. I figured that he would be too busy attending to family needs and concerns. And, yet, he was there right on time and was with us the whole hour. He did so because he needed us today. He needed us to listen. He needed us to pray. He needed our encouragement. Next week, it may be another of our group who is in his shoes. What a privilege at these times not to go it alone!

In one of the New Testament letters, readers are instructed to "think of ways to motivate one another to acts of love and good works" and more specifically not to forgo meeting together so that mutual encouragement can take place (Hebrews 10:24-25). This instruction is not because God is keeping attendance records but because he knows we are much more vulnerable on our own.

Sometimes people think I go to church because I am religious, but I've never attended church (as least as an adult) to check something off my religious to-do list. I have attended church because over the years I have recognized that I need to be reminded regularly of what is true and good and right, and at times I need to be there to do the same for others. Christ knows this, so he does not just call us to have friends but to be friends as well—friends who are there when the chips are down. To this point, I cannot agree more with the words of Rebecca McLaughlin:

> The further I go on in life, the more convinced I am that every Christian is a struggling Christian, dependent on help from brothers and sisters who know their needs and vulnerabilities. Lungs don't work without hearts, or legs without feet. We're simply not designed for solo flight.

Tell Others

If Christianity is true, if Jesus is the means by which we can enjoy life with God now and forevermore, and if rejection of Jesus has no good end, it is the kind of truth that ought to be shared with other people. Knowing that Jupiter is nearly 90,000 miles in diameter is probably a truth you could keep to yourself without impacting anyone's future, but not warning people of a tornado headed their way or telling people of the route to safety is a whole different matter. That is the kind of truth you should not keep to yourself.

Jews did not like Samaritans. Men did not respect women. And holy men certainly did not have conversations with a woman who had been married five times and was living with a sixth man. But Jesus rejected all these cultural standards and went out of his way to tell an adulterous Samaritan woman he was the Messiah. And what did she do? She ran back to her village to tell everyone about him (John 4:3-42). Soon, they came to check out Jesus for themselves, and in a matter of days Jesus had a whole host of new Samaritan followers.

In the days and months and years that preceded these events, no one in Samaria would have ever believed that the Messiah would take any interest in a woman like this. And certainly no one would have come close to imagining she would become the catalyst for a "Great Awakening" among the people of Samaria. Yet that is precisely what happened. The Samaritan woman could not keep the truth of Christ to herself. She had to share it with others. And if Christianity is true, we should do the same. We should point people toward Jesus so they too can learn that he is "the Savior of the world."

Remain Dependent

I wonder if in reading this chapter, you feel a bit overwhelmed. It is one thing to trust in Christ as the one who can heal the bite of sin, yet I have also shared with you Christ's desire for his children to love well, learn and do, let Christ into every room, not go it alone, and tell others about Jesus. All this may leave you feeling overwhelmed, but that has certainly not been my intent. A child does not learn to walk in a day, and the skills you possess today—whether as a student, parent, or professional—often took years, if not decades, to hone. And even then, you are still learning and growing. It is the same when it comes to walking with Christ. Am I better at loving Jesus and others today than in the past? I think so, but I am still learning. Are there times I forget to lean into others and try to fly solo? Of course, but those times are becoming less frequent. So do not feel overwhelmed; take one step at time: one step of learning more of Jesus' way and one step of putting what you have learned into action. You need not eat a lifetime's worth of meals in a day; you need to eat only the meal in front of you—the meal Jesus is calling you to eat today.

That said, there is one piece to following Jesus I have yet to share, and it's an all-important one. It's important because it has to do with finding the strength and power to take the next step Christ is calling you to take. I told you already that on the night before Jesus' crucifixion, he spoke about obedience, but that's not all he spoke about. He repeated something else of equal importance. He told his disciples over and over again that when he left the earth that he would leave with them his Holy Spirit (John 14:16-20, 26, John 16:7-15). Further, he said that this Spirit would give them the power to live out his instructions (Mark 13:11). In other words, not only did Jesus give his disciples instructions on how to drive the car, but also he filled the car with gas so they would not have to push it along. You might ask, "Okay, but how in the world does that work? How does the Holy Spirit give me what it takes to obey his commands?" Fortunately, it isn't all that tricky to explain.

In Paul's letter to the Colossians, he wrote these words: "And now, *just as* you accepted Christ Jesus as your Lord, you must continue to follow him" (Colossians 2:6, emphasis added). We've already seen how you can accept Christ Jesus as your Savior. You simply look to Christ in utter dependence. You recognize you have been bitten by the snake of sin, and you turn to Christ as the only means by which you can be saved. When Paul writes that you are to continue to follow him "*just as* you accepted Christ," he is saying that you are to follow him with the same sense of dependence every day. That is, as you wake, go to him saying, "Jesus, I need you today. Help me to love and follow you well."

When we maintain that sense of dependence, his Spirit goes to work. I've seen it over and over again for myself. There have been times I have not wanted to apologize to someone or confront a difficult situation. There have been other times when the work before me seemed daunting at best. Yet, when I have remembered to look to Christ in dependence rather than simply try to push the car of life on my own, I have found that the strength and the wisdom and the love the Spirit gives me is sufficient, and sometimes surprisingly so. I am confident the same will be true for you as you walk day by day with a sense of dependence on the one who has given you his Spirit.

Undoubtedly, there is much more I could tell you about getting started with Christ if Christianity is true, and much more I could tell you about being a member of God's family if you have trusted in Christ. But you don't have to learn that all from me. Besides, I'm still learning too. I am still asking questions and seeking answers. I am still trying to "see" when I find it hard to believe. I am still trying to make sense of it all. I hope you will too.

Key Points

- If Christianity is true, there is no way to remain uncommitted. You either take up Christ's offer of eternal life or you don't.

- The first step into Christianity is admitting that you have been bitten by "the snake of sin" and looking to Christ as the only one who can heal you.

- When we trust in Christ, we become God's children. As grateful children, we want to live in a way that pleases him, but even when we fail we will remain his children.

- As followers of Jesus, we are called to love God and love others.

- Like anything, walking with Christ is a learning process. It involves understanding Jesus' love language and then doing what he loves.

- Jesus gladly enters our life when we open the door, but he is not satisfied to stay in one room. He wants us to let him remodel every room of our life and be the Lord over all aspects of our life.

- The Christian life is not to be lived alone. Christians need the instruction, support, and encouragement of other believers.

- If Christianity is true, it is too good to keep to ourselves. Jesus came to seek and save the lost, and he invites us to be part of that same mission.

- Jesus doesn't expect us to live the Christian life by our own strength and wisdom; he gives those who trust in him the gift of the Holy Spirit. When we remain dependent on Jesus day to day, the Holy Spirit strengthens and guides us to accomplish all that God desires through our lives.

Additional Resources

NLT New Believer's Bible (There are plenty of Bibles you can choose, but you will find this one particularly easy to read with some side notes to help you understand what you are reading.)

Start Here: Beginning a Relationship with Jesus, David Dwight & Nicole Unice

The Purpose-Driven Life: What on Earth Am I Here For? Rick Warren

Postscript

In this book, I have attempted to answer fifteen questions. My guess is you have many more as well. In some cases, I may have answered the questions to your satisfaction. In other cases, I may have left you with more questions than when you began. Regardless, I hope you have discovered at least a few helpful answers to what I believe are very reasonable questions.

At the end of each chapter, I have presented some recommended readings. In many cases, the resources I suggest go into much more depth than I can offer here. So I encourage you to poke and prod and seek and knock. If you do, I am confident you will find that Christianity rests on more than wishful thinking or religious tradition. Better yet, the Bible says that God "rewards those who sincerely seek him" (Hebrews 11:6).

Finally, it is my privilege to work for Search, a national team of people dedicated to helping men and women like you find answers to their questions about God, Christianity, and the Bible. We don't do this through big seminars or splashy events. We do so in the context of friendly dialogue and lasting relationships. If there is a way we can help you in your own journey, I invite you to visit us at:

questioninggod.com

What a delight it would be to talk about questions like these face-to-face with a cup of coffee in hand.

Acknowledgments

I suppose some people could write a book like this with little help or encouragement along the way, but that is certainly not the case for me. I doubt I would have developed the interest to pursue a topic like this if I hadn't had parents who encouraged me to investigate God in the first place. Then, there is my wife, who has given up untold hours of my attention to the piles of books I have read, not just in preparation for this book but over several decades. My poor kids (Eric, Ian, Hudson, and Corrie) have had to endure me honing my answers to questions for years, and countless friends have kindly let me know my explanations were not as clear as I believed them to be. Many thanks to you all.

When Search decided it was time to create a new book for the kind of work we do, and then asked me to write it, I was honored. And scared! I knew putting my thoughts to paper would be a lofty task that would test me in many ways. I thank Tim Kilpatrick, Search's president, for trusting me with this project, and for the many Search staff who have reviewed various chapters over the last year. My good friend Rick Wittenbraker carried the biggest load, since he had to work his way through the very first draft of everything I wrote. After Rick's efforts, Blaine Larsen, Dave Krueger, Don Barkley, Josh Horton, and Mike Donahue took the time to read it all and give me invaluable feedback. I cannot thank them enough. That said, if what you read here is not to your liking, blame only me. No doubt, had it been their book, some or many parts would have been written differently.

Once the chapter drafts were done, then came the hard work of editing, with the final leg completed by the able Susan Alison. To put it mildly, this book reads a lot better because of Susan than if I had edited it on my own. Kyle Sacks and Bo Parker also put their creative touches on the final product with their publishing skills, without which the book you hold would probably look like a cheap novel.

Throughout the book, I have made a great effort to properly recognize those from whom I borrowed ideas, but having read so much over the years, I am quite sure that much of what I count as original is really a thought long ago garnered from someone much more studied and able than me. I am grateful to the likes of Josh McDowell, Norman Geisler, Tim Keller, Lee Strobel, Douglas Groothuis, J. P. Moreland, Garry DeWeese, and William Lane Craig—all of whose work has greatly impacted me over the years.

Finally, I want to thank the countless people who have financially supported the work I do. Mine is a quiet effort made up of an endless stream of conversations with real people who have real questions. To these supporters I owe a debt. May you receive dividends beyond anything I could ever pay.

About the Author

John Hopper has discussed questions about God and life with Muslim clerics in Uzbekistan, Buddhist monks in Canada, slum-dwellers in Guatemala, and tennis professionals at Wimbledon. Now, he serves as Houston Area Director for Search Ministries, a nationwide organization focused on creating opportunities for stimulating, sensitive, and respectful conversations for those wrestling with life's big questions. Prior to joining Search, John served for 16 years as a pastor at BridgePoint Bible Church in Houston.

John has always enjoyed learning and was in school far too long! He earned a B.A. in Economics at Trinity University, an M.Ed. at the University of Houston, an M.A. in Transformational Leadership at Bethel University, and a D.Min. at Biola University, where he focused on Christian apologetics and worldview studies.

John enjoys exercising, particularly on a tennis court, spending time with his wife at just about anything, and catching up with his four adult children and their great spouses.

Notes

Introduction

1. Matthew 3:13-17; John 1:29-34
2. Luke 3:19-20
3. Matthew 11:2-3
4. Matthew 11:4-5

Chapter 1

1. Steven Weinberg, *The First Three Minutes: A Modern View of the Origin of the Universe*, Rev. ed. (New York: Basic Books, 1993), chap. 8, Kindle.
2. Phillip Johnson & William Provine, "Darwinism: Science or Naturalistic Philosophy? Phillip Johnson vs William Provine," IDquest, debate, 41:10, https://www.youtube.com/watch?v=m7dG9U1vQ_U, emphasis added.
3. Arthur Schopenhauer, "On the Vanity of Existence," in *Exploring the Meaning of Life: An Anthology and Guide*, ed. Joshua W. Seachris (Chichester, UK: Wiley-Blackwell, 2013), 229.
4. Woody Allen, quoted in Frank Rich, "Woody Allen Wipes the Smile Off His Face," *Esquire*, May 1977, 76.
5. Richard Dawkins, *River Out of Eden: A Darwinian View of Life* (New York: Basic Books, 1995), 133.
6. By objective purpose, I mean it stands as the true state of affairs regardless of what I might feel about it in the moment. For example, some days a temperature of 70 degrees may seem cold to me, and other days it might feel hot, but the objective temperature is 70 degrees regardless of how I feel.
7. As quoted in William Lane Craig, *Reasonable Faith: Christian Truth and Apologetics*, 3rd ed. (Wheaton, IL: Crossway, 2008), 28.
8. Sam Harris, *Free Will* (New York: Free Will Press, 2012), 5.
9. Cris Evatt, *The Myth of Free Will* (Sausalito, CA: Café Essays, 2010), 25.
10. Adolf Hitler, *Mein Kampf*, trans. James Murphy, 238, https://greatwar.nl/books/meinkampf/meinkampf.pdf.

11.   Harriet A. Washington, *Medical Apartheid: The Dark History of Medical Experimentation on Black Americans from Colonial Times to the Present* (New York: Broadway Books, 2006), chap. 1, Kindle.

12.   Martin Luther King, Jr. "Letter from Birmingham Jail," April 16, 1963, page 7, http://okra.stanford.edu/transcription/document_images/ undecided/630416-019.pdf.

13.   Paul M. Churchland, "Eliminative Materialism and the Propositional Attitudes," *The Journal of Philosophy* 78, no. 2. (February 1981), 67.

14.   Churchland, "Eliminative Materialism," 88.

15.   An adaptation of similar words found in Taylor Marshall, "How Do Atheists Define Love?" Strange Notions, https://strangenotions.com/atheists-love/.

16.   Jean-Paul Sartre, *Being & Nothingness: An Essay in Phenomenological Ontology*, trans. Hazel E. Barnes (New York: Washington Square Press, 1956), 478, https://archive.org/stream/in.ernet.dli.2015.69160/2015.69160. Jean-paul-Sartre-Being-And-Nothingness_djvu.txt.

17.   Francis Crick, *The Astonishing Hypothesis: The Scientific Search for the Soul* (New York: Charles Scribner's Sons, 1994), 262.

18.   Steven Pinker, *How the Mind Works* (New York: W. W. Norton, 1997), 305.

19.   Charles Darwin, *The Autobiography of Charles Darwin: 1809-1882*, ed. Nora Barlow (London: Collins, 1958), 93, http://darwin-online.org.uk/content/ frameset?itemID=F1497&viewtype=text&pageseq=93.

20.   Charles Darwin to William Graham, July 3, 1881, Darwin Correspondence Project, "Letter no. 13230," accessed February 15, 2021, https://www. darwinproject.ac.uk/letter/DCP-LETT-13230.xml.

21.   For a very similar argument, see C.S. Lewis, *The Case for Christianity* (New York: Macmillan, 1943), 32.

22.   "Alan Lightman Shares His Worldview," Veritas Forum, September 16, 2011, video, 0:01, https://www.youtube.com/ watch?v=6Ny30CgaRmU&list=PLpVxnnpiCUnNv9roPQWGbV6Hc_ t9C7Zuh&index=6&t=0s.

23.   Francis Crick, *What Mad Pursuit: A Personal View of Scientific Discovery* (New York: Basic Books, 1988), 10.

24.   Crick, *The Astonishing Hypothesis*, 3.

25.   Blaise Pascal, *Pascal's Pensées* (New York: E. P. Dutton, 1958), 67, https:// www.gutenberg.org/files/18269/18269-h/18269-h.htm. For more on Pascal's Wager, see Peter Kreeft, "The Argument from Pascal's Wager," https://www. peterkreeft.com/topics/pascals-wager.htm.

Chapter 2

1.   I learned to use the circle illustration from Ken Boa and Larry Moody, *I'm Glad You Asked: How to Talk with Your Friends About Christian Faith and Their Questions*, Rev. ed. (Ellicott City, MD: Search Ministries, 2013), 19.

2.   Stephen Hawking, "The Beginning of Time," 1996, https://www.hawking. org.uk/in-words/lectures/the-beginning-of-time.

3. Alexander Vilenkin, *Many Worlds in One* (New York: Hill and Wang, 2006), 176.

4. This kind of thinking gave rise to the words of Francis Collins, current Director of the National Institute for Health and former lead of the Human Genome Project: "We have this very solid conclusion that the universe had an origin, the Big Bang. Fifteen billion years ago, the universe began with an unimaginably bright flash of energy from an infinitesimally small point. That implies that before that, there was nothing. I can't imagine how nature, in this case the universe, could have created itself. And the very fact that the universe had a beginning implies that someone was able to begin it. And it seems to me that had to be outside of nature. And that sounds like God." Steve Paulson, "The Believer," Salon, August 7, 2006, https://www.salon.com/2006/08/07/collins_6/.

5. The Bible describes God as standing outside of time (Jude 24-25), not confined by space (Jeremiah 23:24), immaterial (John 4:24), and a powerful agent of change (Psalm 115:3).

6. Robin Collins, "The Teleological Argument: An Exploration of the Fine-Tuning of the Universe," in *The Blackwell Companion to Natural Theology*, eds. William Lane Craig & J. P. Moreland (Chichester, UK: Wiley-Blackwell, 2012), 215.

7. For more about finely-tuned constants see Martin Rees, *Just Six Numbers: The Deep Forces that Shape the Universe* (1999; repr., New York: Basic Books, 2000); Geraint F. Lewis and Luke A. Barnes, *A Fortunate Universe: Life in a Finely Tuned Cosmos* (Cambridge: Cambridge University Press, 2016); Jay W. Richards, "List of Fine-Tuning Parameters," Discovery Institute Center for Science and Culture, accessed July 19, 2020, https://www.discovery.org/m/securepdfs/2018/12/List-of-Fine-Tuning-Parameters-Jay-Richards.pdf.

8. Edward L. Wright, "Flatness-Oddness Problem" in Cosmological Tutorial, accessed July 13, 2020, http://www.astro.ucla.edu/~wright/cosmo_03.htm#FO; Stephen M. Barr, *Modern Physics & Ancient Faith* (Notre Dame, IN: University of Notre Dame Press, 2003), 129-130.

9. Stephen Hawking & Leonard Mlodinow, *The Grand Design* (New York: Bantam, 2012), chap. 7, Kindle; emphasis added.

10. Paul Davies quote taken from *Horizon*, 1987, episode 18, "The Anthropic Principle," BBC, https://archive.org/details/BBCHorizonCollection512Episodes/BBC+Horizon+-+s1987e18+-+The+Anthropic+Principle.avi, 14:54; emphasis added.

11. John Polkinghorne, *Science and Theology: An Introduction* (Minneapolis, MN: Fortress Press, 1998), 75; emphasis added.

12. Fred Hoyle, "The Universe: Past and Present Reflections," *Engineering and Science* 45, no. 2 (November 1981), 12.

13. G. H. Hardy, *A Mathematician's Apology* (1940; repr., Edmonton, AB: University of Alberta Mathematical Sciences Society, 2005), 20, https://www.math.ualberta.ca/mss/misc/A%20Mathematician%27s%20Apology.pdf.

14. Eugene P. Wigner, "The Unreasonable Effectiveness of Mathematics in the Natural Sciences," in *Communications in Pure and Applied Mathematics* 13, no. 1 (February 1960), 1-14.

15. John Lennox, *God's Undertaker: Has Science Buried God?* (Oxford, UK: Lion, 2009), chap. 4, Kindle.

16. Friedrich Nietzsche, *The Twilight of the Idols and The Anti-Christ*, ed. and trans. Anthony M. Ludovici (n.p.: Evergreen Classics, 2019), "The 'Improvers' of Mankind," sec. 1, Kindle.

17. Richard Dawkins, *River Out of Eden: A Darwinian View of Life* (New York: Basic Books, 1995), 133.

18. One prominent view as to how objective morals can exist without God is *moral platonism*. It is the idea that moral values such as goodness, justice, or mercy just exist as brute facts of the universe. Not only should we wonder why we have a duty to live up to them, but also we should wonder how moral values could have come into being as abstract entities. See William Lane Craig, *On Guard: Defending Your Faith with Reason and Precision* (Colorado Springs, CO: David C Cook: 2010), 136-138.

19. Timothy Keller, *Making Sense of God: An Invitation to the Skeptic* (New York: Viking, 2016), 42.

20. I especially like how C.S. Lewis spoke to this point: "Whenever you find a man who says he does not believe in real Right and Wrong, you will find the same man going back on this a moment later. He may break his promise to you, but if you try breaking one to him he will be complaining 'It's not fair' before you can say Jack Robinson." C.S. Lewis, *Mere Christianity*, Rev. ed (New York: Macmillan, 1960), 19.

Chapter 3

1. Calvary Tucson & Hot Topics with Robert Furrow, "Prof. J. Warner Wallace—Cold Case Christianity," October 25, 2020, video, 2:48, https://youtu.be/7xqVpiZ85Zo.

2. Nagel lays the foundation for his case in Thomas Nagel, *The Last Word* (New York: Oxford University Press, 1997), but he more directly addresses his objections to neo-Darwinian evolution in Thomas Nagel, *Mind & Cosmos: Why the Materialist Neo-Darwinian Conception of Nature Is Almost Certainly False* (New York: Oxford University Press, 2012).

3. Nagel, *The Last Word*, 130.

4. To be fair, Thomas Nagel also admitted that it is irrational to not believe in God simply because one hopes there is not a God. See Nagel, *The Last Word*, 131.

5. Douglas Groothuis, *Christian Apologetics: A Comprehensive Case for Biblical Faith* (Downers Grove, IL: IVP Academic, 2011), 141.

6. Alan Deutschman, "Change or Die," Fast Company, May 1, 2005, https://www.fastcompany.com/52717/change-or-die.

Chapter 4

1. Frequently, people use Galileo to illustrate an inherent conflict between faith and science, since he and the Pope found themselves at odds over Galileo's suggestion that the Earth revolved around the sun and not the other way around. But Galileo's scientific pursuits were not in conflict with faith in God, only with a certain biblical interpretation. In response to a friend who challenged his theories, Galileo wrote of his unswerving belief in Scripture. See Darrel R. Falk, *Coming to Peace with Science* (Downers Grove, IL: InterVarsity Press, 2004), 28.

2. Baruch Aba Shalev, *100 Years of Nobel Prizes* (New Delhi, India: Atlantic Publishers, 2003), 57-61.

3. Elaine Howard Ecklund is the Herbert S. Autrey Chair in Social Sciences, Professor of Sociology, and director of the Religion and Public Life Program at Rice University, Houston, TX.

4. Elaine Howard Ecklund, *Science vs. Religion: What Scientists Really Think* (Oxford, UK: Oxford University Press, 2010), chap. 2, Kindle.

5. Ecklund, *Science vs. Religion*, chap. 1, Kindle.

6. Ecklund, *Science vs. Religion*, chap. 2, Kindle.

7. Quoted in Natasha Crain, *Talking with Your Kids about God* (Grand Rapids, MI: Baker Books, 2017), 111-112.

8. John C. Lennox, *Can Science Explain Everything?* (Epsom, UK: The Good Book Company, 2019), 32-33.

9. Melissa Cain Travis, *Science and the Mind of the Maker: What the Conversation Between Faith and Science Reveals About God* (Eugene, OR: Harvest House, 2018), 24.

10. Joseph Liu, "The 'Evidence for Belief': An Interview with Francis Collins," Pew Research Center, April 17, 2008, https://www.pewforum.org/2008/04/17/the-evidence-for-belief-an-interview-with-francis-collins/.

11. J. P. Moreland, *Scientism and Secularism: Learning to Respond to a Dangerous Ideology* (Wheaton, IL: Crossway, 2018), chap. 1, Kindle.

12. Ian Hutchinson, Professor of Nuclear Science and Engineering at the Massachusetts Institute of Technology, speaks to this point: "Many of life's most important matters simply do not possess reproducibility. History, for example, cannot be understood by appeal to reproducibility. Its most significant events are often unique, never to be repeated. There is no way to experiment on history, and no way to repeat the observations. Some parts of historical study benefit from scientific techniques, but the main mission of history cannot be addressed through reproducibility; its methods are not those of science. Yet history possesses real knowledge." Quoted in Mike Gene "More Thoughts on Scientism," The Design Matrix, March 6, 2011, https://designmatrix.wordpress.com/2011/03/06/more-thoughts-on-scientism/.

13. The boiling pot example is borrowed from Lennox, *Can Science Explain Everything?* 36.

14. Robert Oppenheimer, *Some Reflections on Science and Culture* (Chapel Hill: The University of North Carolina, 1960), 20-21.

15. Richard C. Lewontin, "Billions and Billions of Demons," review of *The Demon-Haunted World: Science as a Candle in the Dark*, by Carl Sagan, The New York Review of Books, July 9, 1997, https://www.nybooks.com/articles/1997/01/09/billions-and-billions-of-demons/?lp_txn_id=1026791.

16. To read of these men's contribution to the development of the scientific method, see Hanne Andersen & Brian Hepburn, "Scientific Method," *The Stanford Encyclopedia of Philosophy*, November 13, 2015, ed. Edward N. Zalta, https://plato.stanford.edu/archives/sum2016/entries/scientific-method/.

17. Nancy R. Pearcey & Charles B. Thaxton, *The Soul of Science: Christian Faith and Natural Philosophy* (Wheaton, IL: Crossway Books, 1994), 17.

18. Vishal Mangalwadi, *The Book That Made Your World: How the Bible Created the Soul of Western Civilization* (Nashville, TN: Thomas Nelson, 2011), 220.

19. Mangalwadi, *The Book That Made Your World*, 221.

20. Alfred North Whitehead, *Science and the Modern World: Lowell Lectures, 1925* (Cambridge: Cambridge University Press, 1929), 15-16.

21. See Pearcey & Thaxton, *The Soul of Science*, 17-42, and Stephen C. Meyer, *Return of the God Hypothesis: Three Scientific Discoveries that Reveal the Mind Behind the Universe* (New York: HarperCollins, 2021), 13-29, for a discussion of why many recognize the Christian worldview as setting the stage for the scientific revolution.

22. Because Islam is monotheistic and believes in a God separate from creation, it would also seem to have been an appropriate framework on which to birth modern science. But historically Islam has struggled with the idea that God would create natural laws. To the Muslim this would limit God, since Allah does as he pleases, and what he pleases is variable. Furthermore, early Muslim thinkers fully embraced Greek thought even to the point of believing that the world was "a huge, conscious living organism, having both intellect and soul." See Rodney Stark, *For the Glory of God: How Monotheism Led to Reformations, Science, Witch-Hunts, and the End of Slavery* (Princeton, NJ: Princeton University Press, 2003), 154-156.

23. The four worldview elements mentioned here are part of a larger treatment of the topic in Pearcey & Thaxton, *The Soul of Science*, 22-37.

24. Hans Halverson, "Why Methodological Naturalism?" in *The Blackwell Companion to Naturalism*, ed. Kelly James Clark (Hoboken, NJ: Wiley-Blackwell, 2016), 140.

25. Some say that Christian thought impedes science because the Christian is more concerned about the life to come than the present life. But this is rarely the case. The Christian believes the present life has great purpose *because of* the life to come. God gave the command to rule over the fish of the sea, the birds in the air, and the living creatures that move on the ground, as well as to care for every form of vegetation (Genesis 1:28-30). This, of course, requires an understanding of how biological life flourishes

as well as the larger environment in which Earth exists. If God takes note of how we obey this command, then there is value in attending to it well for the life to come. God also commands us to love those around us and to help the poor and the sick. Science plays a role in fulfilling this command (such as in the discovery of vaccines and the development of sustainable farming practices), meaning the Christian has further impetus to excel in the world of science. In addition, God wants the Christian to recognize how praiseworthy the Creator is. This in part comes from studying the beauty, intricacy, and magnificence of creation at both the microscopic and telescopic level. In fact, the Bible says that creation provides a witness to the world of God's "eternal power and divine nature" (Romans 1:20). By studying science, Christians are then able to appeal to "public" evidence that can draw people to God. All in all, then, there is great motivation for the Christian to engage in scientific pursuit and understanding.

26. Thomas Y. Lo, Paul K. Chien, Eric H. Anderson, Robert A. Alston & Robert P. Waltzer, *Evolution and Intelligent Design in a Nutshell* (Seattle, WA: Discovery Institute Press, 2020), 96-98.
27. Halverson, "Why Methodological Naturalism?" 140.
28. To better understand how Christians differ in interpreting the Genesis narrative regarding creation, see David G. Hagopian, ed., *The Genesis Debate: Three Views on the Days of Creation* (Mission Viejo, CA: Crux Press, 2001).

Chapter 5

1. Sigmund Freud, *The Future of an Illusion*, ed. and trans. by James Strachey (New York: W. W. Norton, 1961), 30.
2. Thank you to Sarah Stone, Young Adult Outreach Director, Memorial Drive Presbyterian Church, Houston, TX, for sharing her story with me.
3. Holly Ordway, *Not God's Type: A Rational Academic Finds a Radical Faith*, (Chicago, IL: Moody Publishers, 2010), 16.
4. Ordway, *Not God's Type*, 24.
5. Ordway, *Not God's Type*, 25.
6. Ordway, *Not God's Type*, 26.
7. Ordway, *Not God's Type*, 15-16.
8. Ordway, *Not God's Type*, 16.
9. Paul C. Vitz, *Faith of the Fatherless: The Psychology of Atheism* (Dallas, TX: Spence Publishing, 1999), 4.
10. Vitz, *Faith of the Fatherless*, 16.
11. Douglas Groothuis, *Christian Apologetics: A Comprehensive Case for Biblical Faith* (Downers Grove, IL: InterVarsity Press, 2011), 16.
12. Lee Strobel, *The Case for Grace: A Journalist Explores the Evidence of Transformed Lives* (Grand Rapids, MI: Zondervan, 2015), 15-19.
13. Lee Strobel, "The Search for Grace: My father and My Father," FaithGateway, June 15, 2019, https://www.faithgateway.com/search-for-

grace-my-father/#.X75_TM1KhPY.

14. Lee Strobel, *The Case for Christ: A Journalist's Personal Investigation of the Evidence for Jesus* (Grand Rapids, MI: Zondervan, 1998), Introduction, Kindle.
15. Strobel, *The Case for Christ*, Introduction, Kindle.
16. Lee Strobel, "Nothing Is More Important Than Your Response to Jesus," Crosswalk, September 13, 2016, https://www.crosswalk.com/faith/spiritual-life/nothing-is-more-important-than-your-response-to-jesus.html.
17. Ordway, *Not God's Type*, 18.
18. Ken Boa and Larry Moody, *I'm Glad You Asked: How to Talk with Your Friends About Christian Faith and Their Questions*, Rev. ed. (Ellicott City, MD: Search Ministries, 2013), 66.
19. C.S. Lewis, *Mere Christianity*, Rev. ed. (New York: Macmillan, 1952), 120.
20. Clifford Williams, *Existential Reasons for Belief in God: A Defense of Desires and Emotions for Faith* (Downers Grove, IL: InterVarsity Press, 2011), chap. 3, Kindle.
21. Williams, *Existential Reasons*, chap. 2, Kindle.
22. Williams, *Existential Reasons*, chap. 2, Kindle.
23. Williams, *Existential Reasons*, chap. 2, Kindle.
24. Williams, *Existential Reasons*, chap. 2, Kindle.
25. Williams, *Existential Reasons*, chap. 2, Kindle.

Chapter 6

1. "Authorities: Retired Pa. Pastor Killed Both Wives," *USA Today*, September 29, 2012, https://www.usatoday.com/story/news/nation/2012/09/29/adultery-murder-pastor-wives/1602405/.
2. "Chicago Pastor Steals $1 Million from Church Funds to Buy a New Bentley," Black Enterprise, January 31, 2020, https://www.blackenterprise.com/chicago-pastor-steals-1-million-from-church-funds-to-buy-a-new-bentley/.
3. Leonardo Blair, "Hillsong Says Church Took Action after Claims of 'Inappropriate' Sex between NYC Staff and Volunteers," www.christianpost.com, accessed February 8, 2021, https://www.christianpost.com/news/hillsong-says-it-took-action-after-claims-of-inappropriate-sex.html.
4. See, for example, Matthew 5:23-24; Luke 3:1-14, 19:1-10; Acts 3:19, 17:30; 1 John 1:8-10.
5. Matthew 23:1-33
6. Matthew 23:33
7. For more on the Greg Kelley story see Eric Huffman, narrator, "What If He Didn't Do It?" *Maybe God*, season 4, December 9, 2020, Maybe God Podcast, https://maybegodpod.com/what-if-he-didnt-do-it/.
8. Robert Lewis Wilken, "Christianity Face to Face with Islam," First Things January 2009, https://www.firstthings.com/article/2009/01/christianity-face-to-face-with-islam.

9. Thomas F. Madden, author of four books on the Crusades, explains Muslim expansionism into Christianized countries in this way: "Christians in the 11th century were not paranoid fanatics. Muslims really were gunning for them. While Muslims can be peaceful, Islam was born in war and grew the same way. From the time of Mohammed, the means of Muslim expansion was always the sword." See Thomas F. Madden, "The Real History of the Crusades," Crisis Magazine, April 1, 2002, https://www.crisismagazine.com/2002/the-real-history-of-the-crusades-2.

10. Wilken, "Christianity Face to Face with Islam."

11. Madden, "The Real History of the Crusades."

12. Rodney Stark, *The Triumph of Christianity: How the Jesus Movement Became the World's Largest Religion* (New York: Harper Collins, 2011), 217.

13. Dan Arnold & Alicia Turner, "Why Are We Surprised When Buddhists Are Violent?" The New York Times, March 5, 2018, https://www.nytimes.com/2018/03/05/opinion/buddhists-violence-tolerance.html.

14. See, for example, Eliza Griswold, "The Violent Toll of Hindu Nationalism in India," The New Yorker, March 5, 2019, https://www.newyorker.com/news/on-religion/the-violent-toll-of-hindu-nationalism-in-india; "Hindu Nationalism, The Growing Trend in India," NPR, April 22, 2019, https://www.npr.org/2019/04/22/715875298/hindu-nationalism-the-growing-trend-in-india; William Dalrymple, "India: The War Over History," The New York Review, April 7, 2005, https://www.nybooks.com/articles/2005/04/07/india-the-war-over-history/.

15. See a full treatise on deaths related to 20th-century genocides in R. J. Rummel, *Death by Government: Genocide and Mass Murder Since 1900* (1994; repr., New York: Routledge, 2017).

16. "The killing machine that is Marxism," WND, December 15, 2004, https://www.wnd.com/2004/12/28036/.

17. Stark, *The Triumph of Christianity*, 335.

18. Stark, *The Triumph of Christianity*, 335-336.

19. Stark, *The Triumph of Christianity*, 337-338.

20. Stark, *The Triumph of Christianity*, 338.

21. Stark, *The Triumph of Christianity*, 339.

22. Stark, *The Triumph of Christianity*, 339.

23. Stark, *The Triumph of Christianity*, 350.

24. Robert D. Woodberry, "The Missionary Roots of Liberal Democracy," *American Political Science Review* 106, no. 2 (May 2012), 244-274.

25. This summary statement is taken from Andrea Palpant Dilley, who provides a highly accessible article on Woodberry's work at Andrea Palpant Dilley, "The Surprising Discovery About Those Colonialist, Proselytizing Missionaries," Christianity Today, January 24, 2014, https://www.christianitytoday.com/ct/2014/january-february/world-missionaries-made.html.

26. Dilley, "The Surprising Discovery."

27. Dilley, "The Surprising Discovery."

28. Dilley, "The Surprising Discovery."

29. Stewart Gill, "Conquerors or Saviours?: The Aboriginal and the United Aborigines Mission," *Kategoria* 7 (Spring 1997), 10.

30. "7 Surprising Trends in Global Christianity in 2019," Lifeway Research, June 11, 2019, https://lifewayresearch.com/2019/06/11/7-surprising-trends-in-global-christianity-in-2019/.

31. Joey Marshall, "The World's Most Committed Christians Live in Africa, Latin America – and the U.S.," Pew Research Center, August 22, 2018, https://www.pewresearch.org/fact-tank/2018/08/22/the-worlds-most-committed-christians-live-in-africa-latin-america-and-the-u-s/.

32. Russell, *Exposing Myths about Christianity*, 124.

33. Don Richardson, "Do Missionaries Destroy Cultures?" *Perspectives on the World Christian Movement: A Reader*, eds. Ralph Winter & Steven C. Hawthorne (Pasadena, CA: William Carey Library, 1981), 483.

34. See Philip J. Sampson, *Six Modern Myths about Christianity and Western Civilization* (Downers Grove, IL: InterVarsity Press, 2000), 92-112; and Richardson, "Do Missionaries Destroy Cultures," 482-493.

35. *Trinummus* 2.338–39 as quoted in Schmidt, *How Christianity Changed the World* (2004; repr., Grand Rapids, MI: Zondervan, 2004), chap. 5, Kindle.

36. Schmidt, *How Christianity Changed the World*, chap. 5, Kindle. Also, see 2 Corinthians 8:1-9:15.

37. William Edward Hartpole Lecky, *History of European Morals: From Augustine to Charlemagne*, Vol. 2 (London: Longmans, Green and Co., 1920), 79.

38. Karl Zinsmeister, "Less God, Less Giving? Religion and Generosity Feed Each Other in Fascinating Ways," The Philanthropy Roundtable, Winter 2019, https://www.philanthropyroundtable.org/philanthropy-magazine/less-god-less-giving.

39. *Works of Dionysius*, Epistle xii, 5, https://www.ccel.org/ccel/schaff/anf06.iv.iii.ii.xii.html.

40. George Grant, *Third Time Around: A History of the Pro-Life Movement from the First Century to the Present* (Brentwood, TN: Wolgemuth and Hyatt, 1991), 27.

41. Schmidt, *How Christianity Changed the World*, chap. 5, Kindle.

42. Schmidt, *How Christianity Changed the World*, chap. 5, Kindle.

43. Schmidt, *How Christianity Changed the World*, chap. 7, Kindle.

44. Schmidt, *How Christianity Changed the World*, chap. 7, Kindle.

45. Nancy R. Pearcey and Charles B. Thaxton, *The Soul of Science: Christian Faith and Natural Philosophy* (Wheaton, IL: Crossway, 1994), 22.

46. D. James Kennedy & Jerry Newcombe, *What If Jesus Had Never Been Born?* Rev. ed. (Nashville, TN: Thomas Nelson, 2001), chap. 4, Kindle.

47. Donald Jay Grout, *A History of Western Music*, 3rd ed. (New York: W. W. Norton, 1980), 2.

48. Pliny the Younger reported to Emperor Trajan early in the second century that Christians "sing responsively a hymn to Christ as to a god" (Pliny, *Letters*, 10.96).

49. Kennedy & Newcombe, *What If Jesus Had Never Been Born?*, chap. 12, Kindle.
50. Schmidt, *How Christianity Changed the World*, chap. 13, Kindle.
51. Tom Holland, *Dominion: How the Christian Revolution Remade the World* (New York: Basic Books, 2019), 17.
52. Tyler J. VanderWeele & John Siniff, "Religion May Be a Miracle Drug," USA Today, October 28, 2016, https://www.usatoday.com/story/opinion/2016/10/28/religion-church-attendance-mortality-column/92676964/.
53. Tyler VanderWeele, "Religion and Health: A Synthesis," in *Spirituality and Religion within the Culture of Medicine: From Evidence to Practice*, ed. Michael J. Balboni & John R. Peteet (New York: Oxford University Press, 2017), 357-401.
54. VanderWeele, "Religion and Health," 366.
55. Ying Chen & Tyler J. VanderWeele, "Religious Upbringing Linked to Better Health and Well-Being During Early Adulthood," Harvard T. H. Chan School of Public Health, September 13, 2018, https://www.hsph.harvard.edu/news/press-releases/religious-upbringing-adult-health/.
56. VanderWeele, "Religious Communities and Human Flourishing," 477-478.
57. Tyler J. VanderWeele, "Religious Communities and Human Flourishing," *Current Directions in Psychological Science* 26, no. 5 (October 2017), 476.
58. Jonathan Haidt, *The Happiness Hypothesis: Finding Modern Truth in Ancient Wisdom* (New York: Basic Books, 2006), chap. 5, Kindle.

Chapter 7

1. See F. F. Bruce, *The New Testament Documents: Are They Reliable?* 6th ed. (Downers Grove, IL: InterVarsity Press, 1981), 14-15. For a full treatment of textual criticism, particularly as it relates to the New Testament, see Bruce M. Metzger and Bart D. Ehrman, *The Test of the New Testament: Its Transmission, Corruption, and Restoration*, 4th ed. (New York: Oxford University Press, 2005).
2. Individual books of the New Testament were written on scrolls. Scrolls were not of sufficient size to include the entire New Testament. Larger written formats capable of including the entire New Testament (known as *codices*) were not used widely until the fourth century. Thus, it is not surprising that the oldest, complete New Testament is not dated prior to this time period.
3. Information in this chart is largely taken from Josh McDowell & Sean McDowell, *Evidence That Demands a Verdict: Life-Changing Truth for a Skeptical World* (Nashville, TN: Thomas Nelson, 2017), 56.
4. McDowell & McDowell, *Evidence That Demands a Verdict*, 54.
5. McDowell & McDowell, *Evidence That Demands a Verdict*, 54.
6. Information in this chart is largely taken from Joseph M. Holden & Norman Geisler, *The Popular Handbook of Archaeology and the Bible* (Eugene, OR: Harvest House, 2017), 33-53.

7. Holden & Geisler, *The Popular Handbook of Archaeology and the Bible*, 44-46.

8. Walter C. Kaiser Jr., *The Old Testament Documents: Are They Reliable & Relevant?* (Downers Grove, IL: InterVarsity Press, 2001), 164.

9. Mark D. Roberts, *Can We Trust the Gospels? Investigating the Reliability of Matthew, Mark, Luke, and John* (Wheaton, IL: Crossway Books, 2007), 33.

10. Bart D. Erhman, *Misquoting Jesus: The Story Behind Who Changed the Bible and Why* (San Francisco: HarperSanFranciso, 2005), chap. 3, Kindle.

11. This illustration is adapted from a similar illustration found in Roberts, *Can We Trust the Gospels?* 33-34.

12. Roberts, *Can We Trust the Gospels?* 34.

13. Bruce M. Metzger, *The Text of the New Testament: Its Transmission, Corruption, and Restoration*, 3rd ed. (New York: Oxford University Press, 1992), 15-19.

14. F. F. Bruce, *The New Testament Documents*, 10.

15. For more on the "gospels" that are not part of the Bible, see Josh McDowell and Sean McDowell, "Gnostic Gospels and Other Biblical Texts," in *Evidence That Demands a Verdict*, 124-139.

16. "Gospel of Thomas," trans. Thomas O. Lambdin, accessed June 5, 2020, https://www.marquette.edu/maqom/Gospel%20of%20Thomas%20 Lambdin.pdf.

17. See 1 Corinthians 15:14-17 where Paul, the great leader of the early church, wrote: "And if Christ has not been raised, then all our preaching is useless, and your faith is useless."

18. See Holden & Geisler, *The Popular Handbook of Archaeology and the Bible*, 222-224. Holden and Geisler also note that Egyptologists often date the *Ipuwer Papyrus* a few hundred years before the time of the Exodus, but that nothing in the text itself necessitates an earlier date.

19. Holden & Geisler, *The Popular Handbook of Archaeology and the Bible*, 229.

20. Holden & Geisler, *The Popular Handbook of Archaeology and the Bible*, 250.

21. Holden & Geisler, *The Popular Handbook of Archaeology and the Bible*, 267.

22. Richard A. Burridge, *What Are the Gospels? A Comparison with Graeco-Roman Biography*, 2nd ed. (Dearborn, MI: Eerdmans, 2004), 254-255. To say that the Gospels were similar to biographies of the day is not to say that they are similar in shape to modern biographies. For a full discussion on the historical nature of the Gospels in their context, see Craig S. Keener, *The Historical Jesus of the Gospels* (Grand Rapids, MI: Eerdmans, 2009), 71-125.

23. To further investigate the evidence supporting the claims of the four biblical Gospels, see J. Warner Wallace, *Cold Case Christianity: A Homicide Detective Investigates the Claims of the Gospels* (Colorado Springs, CO: David C. Cook, 2013); Peter J. Williams, *Can We Trust the Gospels?* (Wheaton: IL: Crossway, 2018), Mark D. Roberts, *Can We Trust the Gospels?*

24. Shlomo Pines, *An Arabic Version of the Testimonium Flavianum and Its*

Implications (Jerusalem: Israel Academy of Sciences and Humanities, 1971), 16, http://khazarzar.skeptik.net/books/pines01.pdf. The quote is a translation of a tenth-century Arabic text that does not include the overtly Christian references found in other Greek versions of Josephus' accounts. As such, this translation by Pines, an Israeli scholar of Jewish and Islamic philosophy, is considered to best represent the original words of Josephus.

25. Williams, *Can We Trust the Gospels?* 24-26.

26. Williams, *Can We Trust the Gospels?* 26.

27. Williams, *Can We Trust the Gospels?* 25.

28. W. M. Ramsay, *St. Paul the Traveler and the Roman Citizen* (Grand Rapids, MI: Christian Classics Ethereal Library, 2000), 15, http://www.ntslibrary. com/PDF%20Books/WM%20Ramsay%20Paul%20the%20Traveler%20 &%20Roman%20Citizen.pdf.

29. Frederic C. Putnam, *Ten Key Finds in Bible Archaeology: Behistun to Ebla, The Digs That Made a Difference*, (n.p., Evangelical Ministries, 1981), unnumbered.

30. See Ryan Nelson, "How Did the Apostles Die? What We Actually Know," OverviewBible, December 17, 2019, https://overviewbible.com/how-did-the-apostles-die/.

31. A review of evidence strongly supports the martyrdom of four of the initial 14 church leaders (the 12 disciples, plus Paul of Tarsus and James, the brother of Jesus), and moderately supports the martyrdom of two others. See Josh McDowell and Sean McDowell, "The Martyrdom of the Apostles," in *Evidence That Demands a Verdict*, 360-367.

32. See, for example, Exodus 8:1; Joshua 20:1; 2 Samuel 7:4; 1 Kings 17:2; Isaiah 43:1-28.

33. Armand M. Nicholi, Jr., *The Question of God: C.S. Lewis and Sigmund Freud Debate God, Love, Sex, and the Meaning of Life* (2002; repr., New York: Free Press, 2003), 123-124.

Chapter 8

1. Lee Strobel, *The Case for Miracles: A Journalist Investigates Evidence for the Supernatural* (Grand Rapids, MI: Zondervan, 2018), 101-105. For further information about the case of Barbara Cummiskey, see Thomas Marshall, "Praying for a Miracle," in Scott J. Kolbaba, ed. *Physicians' Untold Stories* (Self-Published, CreateSpace, 2016), chap. 2, Kindle.

2. See Craig S. Keener, *Miracles: The Credibility of the New Testament Accounts* (Grand Rapids, MI: Baker Academic, 2011), for discussion of miracle accounts around the world.

3. Ken Boa & Larry Moody, *I'm Glad You Asked: How to Talk with Your Friends About Their Objections to Christian Faith*, Rev. ed. (Ellicott City, MD: Search Ministries, 2013), 44.

4. Bradley Donn Snyder, "Celebrating the 38th anniversary of Barbara's Dramatic Miraculous Healing!" June 7, 2019, https://bit.ly/3yeU3nK

5. This is an adaption of an illustration used in C.S. Lewis, *Miracles: How God Intervenes in Nature and Human Affairs* (1947; repr., New York: Macmillan Publishing Co., 1978), 58.

6. Candy Gunther Brown, Stephen C. Mory, Rebecca Williams & Michael J. McClymond, "Study of the Therapeutic Effects of Proximal Intercessory Prayer (STEPP) on Auditory and Visual Impairments in Rural Mozambique," *Southern Medical Journal* 103, no. 9 (September 2010), 864-869.

7. Clarissa Romez, Kenn Freedman, David Zaritzky & Joshua W. Brown, "Case Report of Instantaneous Resolution of Juvenile Macular Degeneration Blindness after Proximal Intercessory Prayer," *Explore* 17 (2021), 79-83.

8. My interest in miracles seems to be the same as the apostle John's. At the end of his gospel, John writes that Jesus performed many miracles, and that the miracles John chose to include in his gospel were written to give credence to what Jesus said about being the Messiah, the Son of God, in whom we find life (John 20:30-31).

9. Craig S. Keener, *Christobiography: Memory, History, and the Reliability of the Gospels* (Grand Rapids, MI: Wm. B. Eerdmans, 2019), 12.3, Kindle.

10. Keener, *Christobiography*, 12.3, Kindle.

11. William D. Edwards, Wesley J. Gabel & Floyd E. Hosmer, "On the Physical Death of Jesus Christ," *JAMA* 255, no. 11 (March 21, 1986): 1463.

12. Some argue that Jesus was not buried formally by Joseph or anyone else, since those who were crucified were placed in mass graves and not given a dignified burial. This may have been the case for some, but archaeological evidence in the form of skeletal bones pierced by crucifixion have been found in tombs. One of these artifacts was discovered in 1968 just outside of Jerusalem and is dated to 20AD. The other was discovered in 2019 in a grave outside of Venice, Italy. See Kristina Killgrove, "Heel Bone from Italy Is Only Second Example of Crucifixion Ever Found," Forbes, December 23, 2019, https://www.forbes.com/sites/kristinakillgrove/2019/12/23/heel-bone-from-italy-is-only-second-example-of-crucifixion-ever-found/#7926c84f129a.

13. Collins is quoted in Lee Strobel, *The Case for Christ: A Journalist's Personal Investigation of the Evidence for Jesus* (Grand Rapids, MI: Zondervan, 1998), chap. 13, Kindle.

14. It is not completely clear based on the biblical text whether the guard was made up of temple guards approved by Pontius Pilate or Roman soldiers supplied by Pilate (see Matthew 27:65-66). In either case, the guard would have been a formidable deterrent to theft. Furthermore, the tomb was officially sealed by Pilate, which meant any attempt at theft would likely carry a death sentence.

15. The four Gospels are credited to Matthew, Mark, Luke, and John. Matthew and John were two of Jesus' twelve disciples. Mark was in close relationship with Peter, and the unanimous account of early church leaders (Papias,

Irenaeus, Justin Martyr, Clement of Alexandria, Eusebius, and Tertullian) is that Mark was basically a scribe for Peter's account of Jesus' life and ministry. Luke was a traveling companion of Paul and had access to the testimony of eyewitnesses, including some of the disciples, when he wrote the Gospel of Luke.

16. Flavius Josephus, among others, strongly discounted the value of a woman's word: "Let not the testimony of women be admitted, on account of the levity and boldness of their sex." *Antiquities* IV. 8.15.

17. Marjorie Hyer, "Colson Preaches That Watergate Proves the Bible," The Washington Post, September 28, 1983, https://www.washingtonpost.com/archive/local/1983/09/28/colson-preaches-that-watergate-proves-the-bible/e4978ba1-795b-44ed-b9e8-2cfe90e6e2d2/.

18. Most stories of a rising god involve mythological figures, but even in the case of the story of Apollonius, who may well have been a historical figure, his life after death is not experienced in a human body. For more about the contrast between pagan myths and the biblical resurrection account, see N.T. Wright, *The Resurrection of the Son of God* (Minneapolis, MN: Fortress Press, 2003), 74-75. To see how unique the entire biblical story is relative to ancient myth, see John N. Oswalt, *The Bible Among the Myths: Unique Revelation or Just Ancient Literature?* (Grand Rapids, MI: Zondervan, 2009).

19. Wright, *The Resurrection of the Son of God*, 33.

20. Wright, *The Resurrection of the Son of God*, 77.

21. Wright, *The Resurrection of the Son of God*, 77.

22. J. Ed Komoszewski., M. James Sawyer, and Daniel B. Wallace, *Reinventing Jesus: How Contemporary Skeptics Miss the Real Jesus and Mislead Popular Culture* (Grand Rapids, MI: Kregel Publications, 2006), 231-234. To understand other ways the biblical account of Jesus' birth, death, and resurrection are not analogous to pagan myths, see Mary Jo Sharp, "Is the Story of Jesus Borrowed from Pagan Myths?" in *In Defense of the Bible: A Comprehensive Apologetic for the Authority of Scripture*, ed. Steven B. Cowan & Terry L. Wilder (Nashville, TN: B&H Publishing Group, 2013), 183-200.

23. The Gospels report that James, along with his brothers, was an unbeliever during Jesus' ministry (Mark 3:21, 31, 6:3-4; John 7:5). The resurrected Jesus appeared to James (1 Corinthians 15:7) according to Paul, and after the resurrection, James became a leader in the Jerusalem church (Acts 15:13-21; Galatians 1:19).

24. 1 Corinthians 15:3-5. To read about the dating of this creed, see Gary R. Habermas & Michael R. Licona, *The Case for the Resurrection of Jesus* (Grand Rapids: MI: Kregel, 2004), 260-261.

25. See Habermas & Licona, *The Case for the Resurrection of Jesus*, 48-77.

26. This example is taken from J. Warner Wallace, *Cold Case Christianity: A Homicide Detective Investigates the Claims of the Gospels* (Colorado Springs, CO: David C Cook, 2013), 35-38.

27. Gary R. Habermas and Michael R. Licona, *The Case for the Resurrection of*

Jesus (Grand Rapids, MI: Kregel Publications, 2004), chap. 8, Kindle.

28. Habermas is quoted in Strobel, *The Case for Christ*, chap. 13, Kindle.

Chapter 9

1. J. I. Packer, "Is Systematic Theology a Mirage? An Introductory Discussion," in *Doing Theology in Today's World: Essays in Honor of Kenneth S. Kantzer*, ed. John D. Woodbridge and Thomas Edward McComiskey (Grand Rapids, Mich.: Zondervan, 1991), 21.

2. Barry Cooper, *Can I Really Trust the Bible? And Other Questions About Scripture, Truth and How God Speaks* (Epsom, UK: The Good Book Company, 2014), 35-36.

3. Philip K. Wilson, "Popular Support for Eugenics," Britannica, accessed May 8, 2021, https://www.britannica.com/science/eugenics-genetics/Popular-support-for-eugenics.

4. Mortimer J. Adler, *How to Think About the Great Ideas: From the Great Books of Western Civilization* (Peru, IL: Carus Publishing Co., 2000), chap. 46, Kindle.

5. C.S. Lewis, *Mere Christianity*, Rev. ed (New York: Macmillan, 1960), 36.

6. Lewis, *Mere Christianity*, 36.

7. The destruction of Israel by Assyria is found in 2 Kings 17:1-23. The biblical record is corroborated by the ancient *Taylor Prism* and the near identical *Prism of Sennacherib* as discussed in Chapter 7.

8. Martin Luther King, Jr., "Nonviolence and Racial Injustice," *Christian Century* 74 (February 6, 1957): 165-167. Article may be found online at https://kinginstitute.stanford.edu/king-papers/documents/nonviolence-and-racial-justice.

9. Dacher Keltner, *The Power Paradox: How We Gain and Lose Influence* (New York: Penguin Book, 2016), chap. 10, Kindle.

10. Keltner, chap. 4, Kindle.

11. Sarah Sin, *Beyond Colorblind: Redeeming Our Ethnic Identities* (Downers Grove: InterVarsity Press, 2017), 67, 70.

12. For review of research on forgiveness and health, see Tyler VanderWeele, "Religion and Health: A Synthesis," in *Spirituality and Religion within the Culture of Medicine: From Evidence to Practice*, ed. Michael J. Balboni & John R. Peteet (New York: Oxford University Press, 2017), 371-373.

13. Melanie Curtin, "This 75-Year Harvard Study Found the 1 Secret to Leading a Fulfilling Life," Inc., February 27, 2017, https://www.inc.com/melanie-curtin/want-a-life-of-fulfillment-a-75-year-harvard-study-says-to-prioritize-this-one-t.html.

14. The book of Ecclesiastes speaks well to the inability of even grand success, achievement, and wealth to bring about deep satisfaction in life.

15. Timothy Keller, *Making Sense of God: An Invitation to the Skeptic* (New York: Viking, 2016), 103. For more on the idea that we are not free from constraints, see the entire chapter from which this quote is taken. It is titled "Why Can't I Be Free to Live As I See Fit, as Long as I don't Harm Anyone?"

Chapter 10

1. Micha Boyett, "Andrea Palpant Dilley: Doubt, Flat Tires and the Goodness of God," Patheos, April 12, 2012, https://www.patheos.com/blogs/michaboyett/2012/04/andrea-palpant-dilley-doubt-flat-tires-and-the-goodness-of-god/.
2. C.S. Lewis, *Mere Christianity*, Rev. ed. (New York: Macmillan, 1952), 45.
3. Ken Boa & Larry Moody, *I'm Glad You Asked, How to Talk to Your Friends about the Christian Faith* (Ellicott City, MD: Search Ministries, 2014), 119.
4. My purchase of the doll was prompted by an illustration of the Mr. Wonderful Doll in J. P. Moreland & Tim Muehlhoff, *The God Conversation: Using Stories and Illustrations to Explain Your Faith* (Downers Grove, IL: InterVarsity Press, 2007), 23-25.
5. David Benatar, *Better Never to Have Been: The Harm of Coming into Existence* (New York: Oxford University Press, 2006). For a brief summary of Benatar's views see Joshua Rothman, "The Case for Not Being Born," The New Yorker, November 27, 2017, https://www.newyorker.com/culture/persons-of-interest/the-case-for-not-being-born.
6. This illustration plays off the words of the famous colonial American theologian Jonathan Edwards, who wrote: "So that sin against God, being a violation of infinite obligations, must be a crime infinitely heinous, and so deserving of infinite punishment. Nothing is more agreeable to the common sense of mankind, than that sins committed against any one, must be proportionably heinous to the dignity of the being offended and abused." Jonathan Edwards, "The Justice of God in the Damnation of Sinners," Christian Classics Ethereal Library, accessed September 5, 2020, https://www.ccel.org/ccel/edwards/sermons.justice.html.
7. C.S. Lewis, *The Problem of Pain* (New York: HarperCollins, 1996), 91.
8. D. A. Carson, *"How Long, O Lord?" Reflections on Suffering & Evil*, 2nd ed. (Grand Rapids, MI: Baker Academic), chap. 10, Kindle; emphasis added.

Chapter 11

1. I first learned of the examples of Jim Marshall and the Carriage-by-the-Lake nursing home in Ken Boa & Larry Moody, *I'm Glad You Asked: How to Talk with Your Christian Friends about Christian Faith and Their Questions*, Rev. ed. (Ellicott City, MD: Search Ministries, 2013), 140.
2. This quote is consistently attributed to Jim Rohn; however, I could not locate the origin of this quote.
3. Acts 9:2, 19:9, 19:23, 24:14, 24:22.
4. Mark 14:61-64. Even prior to Jesus' trial, his claim to be God was also met with disdain and persecution. See Luke 5:20-21; John 5:17-18, 8:57-59, 10:30-33.
5. C.S. Lewis, *Mere Christianity,* Rev. ed. (New York: Macmillan, 1952), 55-56.
6. Sura 5:72; Saheeh International, *The Qurʾān: Arabic Text with Corresponding*

English Meanings (Jeddah, Saudi Arabia: Abul-Qasim Pub. House, 1997).

7. Pantheism is the belief that God is everything and everything is God. Monism is the idea that everything is One. The two systems of belief often overlap.

8. See, for example, "Inside Delhi: Beaten, Lynched and Burnt Alive," The Guardian, March 1, 2020, https://www.theguardian.com/world/2020/mar/01/india-delhi-after-hindu-mob-riot-religious-hatred-nationalists; Adrija Bose, "Chhattisgarh: Mob Chanting 'Jai Sri Ram' Vandalises Church, 5 Injured," *The Huffington Post* (Indian ed.), March 6, 2016, https://www.huffingtonpost.in/2016/03/06/chhattisgarh-church_n_9393258.html?utm_hp_ref=in-chhattisgarh.

9. I mentioned a similar line of reasoning in Chapter 3 when discussing the law of non-contradiction.

10. Thallus, Tacitus, Mara Bar-Serapion, Phlegon, and Josephus were not supportive of Christianity yet spoke of Jesus' crucifixion within 100 years of his death.

11. See, for example, Mark 5:21-43, 12:13-17; John 7:1-10, 7:14:24, 11:32-36.

12. See, for example, Matthew 12:1-14; Luke 7:11-17, 36-50; John 11:38-44. That the miracles were meant to authenticate Jesus' claims, also see John 10:2-24-25, 20:30-31; Acts 2:22.

13. Matthew 8:1-4

14. Luke 19:1-10

15. John 4:1-38

16. Mark 2:15-16; Luke 7:34, 7:36-63, 15:1-2

17. Sura 40:55

18. See, for example, Matthew 16:1, 19:3, 22:15-18, 22:34-36; Mark 12:13-15; Luke 11:53-54.

19. Mark 14:55-64; Luke 22:66-23:25

20. The conversation with the Cambridge professor is found in Duncan Campbell, *Revival in the Hebrides* (n.p.: Kraus House, 2015), chap. 5, Kindle. For details on Sundar Singh's life, see Friedrich Heiler, *The Gospel of Sadhu Sundar Singh*, abridged trans., Olive Wyon (London: George Allen & Unwin Ltd., 1927), https://livres-mystiques.com/partieTEXTES/SundarSing/gospel.pdf.

Chapter 12

1. Howard Chai, "The Entire List of Actions and Their Scores On 'The Good Place'" Medium, September 21, 2016, https://medium.com/@howard24/a-look-at-the-moral-point-system-of-the-good-place-7858215fd9dc.

2. Exodus 20:1-17; Deuteronomy 5:1-22

3. See, for example, Deuteronomy 7:9; Psalm 86:15, 136:1-26; Isaiah 54:10; Romans 8:37-39; 1 John 4:7-8, 16.

4. Bryan Chapell, *What Is the Gospel?* (Wheaton, IL: Crossway, 2011), 10.
5. See, for example, Proverbs 14:12; Isaiah 59:2; John 3:18, 36; Romans 1:18, 3:23, 5:12, 6:23; James 1:15; Revelation 21:8.

Chapter 13

1. For example, *Sheol* is used in reference to the righteous in Psalm 16:10, 30:3; Isaiah 38:10; and to the wicked in Numbers 16:33; Job 24:19; Psalm 9:17.
2. See Isaiah 2:12, 13:6, 9; Ezekiel 13:5, 30:3; Joel 1:15, 2:1-2, 11, 31, 3:14; Amos 5:18-20; Obadiah 15; Zephaniah 1:7-9, 14-18; Malachi. 4:5.
3. See Romans 2:5; 2 Thessalonians 1:5-10; Hebrews 6:1-2, 10:27-31; James 5:1-5; 2 Peter 2; Jude 12-16; Revelation 14:9-11, 20:10-15, 21:8, 22:14-15.
4. There are those who make a case that the Bible does not speak of hell as I have outlined, but instead paint hell as a temporary place of purification or rehabilitation, or as a place of due suffering according to one's sin before complete annihilation. In my opinion, those who take this route do so by embracing passages that are more ambiguous and ignoring passages like those I have presented above. Francis Chan and Preston Sprinkle do a good job of addressing those who believe a lesser view of hell is biblically sound in an easy-to-read book: Francis Chan & Preston Sprinkle, *Erasing Hell: What God Said About Eternity and The Things We Made Up* (Colorado Springs, CO: David C. Cook, 2011). See also, Christopher W. Morgan & Robert A. Peterson, ed., *Is Hell for Real or Does Everyone Go to Heaven?* (Grand Rapids, MI: Zondervan, 2011).
5. In writing this, I do not mean to completely disparage the medieval depictions of hell. They still can have their intended effect of awakening people to the judgment to come. One recent example of a medieval painting changing the course of an atheist is that of Peter Hitchens. You can read his account in Peter Hitchens, *The Rage Against God: How Atheism Led Me to Faith* (Grand Rapids, MI: Zondervan, 2010), chap. 7, Kindle.
6. See Matthew 8:12; 13:42, 13:49-50, 22:13, 24:51, 25:10, 25:30; Mark 9:48; Luke 12:45-47, 16:24; Revelation 14:17-20, 20:15, 21:8.
7. Bertrand Russell, "Why I Am Not a Christian," The Bertrand Russell Society, 1927, https://users.drew.edu/~jlenz/whynot.html.
8. Alan La Rue, "Yungay 1970-2009: Remembering the Tragedy of the Earthquake," *Peruvian Times,* May 31, 2009, https://www.peruviantimes.com/31/yungay-1970-2009-remembering-the-tragedy-of-the-earthquake/3073/.
9. Chan & Sprinkle, *Erasing Hell*, 86, Kindle.
10. Information about Welles Crowther came from the ESPN documentary *The Man in the Red Bandana*, written by Tom Rinaldi, https://www.espn.com/video/clip/_/id/11505494.
11. C.S. Lewis, *The Great Divorce* (New York, NY: Macmillan, 1946), 72.
12. J. Warner Wallace, "Why Would God Punish Finite, Temporal Crimes

in an Eternal Hell?" *Cold-Case Christianity,* September 6, 2017, https://coldcasechristianity.com/writings/why-would-god-punish-finite-temporal-crimes-in-an-eternal-hell/.

13. In saying that all sin makes us worthy of separation from God in hell is not to say that God weighs all sins the same. For example, according to Jesus, the punishment received in hell will be different depending on how much Christ has been revealed to us. The implication is that if God has revealed his son to us in extraordinary ways, and yet we still reject him, the punishment will be greater if we have been exposed to some lesser degree of the life of Christ. See Matthew 11:20-24; Luke 12:47-48.

14. See, for example, Psalm 119:67; 2 Corinthians 1:8-9, 4:17; Hebrews 12:7-11.

15. Miroslav Volf, *Exclusion and Embrace: A Theological Exploration of Identity, Otherness, and Reconciliation,* Rev. and upd. (Nashville, TN: Abingdon Press, 2019), chap. 7, Kindle.

16. *Volf, Exclusion and Embrace,* chap. 7, Kindle.

17. Jones, *Why Does God Allow Evil?* 106.

18. Chan & Sprinkle, *Erasing Hell,* chap. 3, Kindle.

19. Jillette Penn, "A Gift of a Bible," YouTube video, 3:00, July 8, 2010, https://www.youtube.com/watch?v=6md638smQd8.

Chapter 14

1. Deuteronomy 10:17; Job 34:18-19; Acts 10:34-35; Romans 2:11; Ephesians 6:9; Colossians 3:25

2. Romans 3:9-18, 23

3. Some might argue that people in every time and place cannot be expected to know what God's standard is, so it is not right to categorize their sin as careless activity. As I outline later in the chapter, the Bible is rather clear that while people may not innately know all of God's standards, they know enough, and have been careless with what they know.

4. Casey Luskin, "More Studies Show Children Are Wired for Religious Belief: A Brief Literature Review," *Evolution News & Science Today,* August 7, 2014, https://evolutionnews.org/2014/08/more_studies_sh/.

5. See Romans 1:18-25. An example of suppressing possible knowledge about God because of a desire that there not be a god can be seen in the words of Thomas Nagel that were presented at the end of Chapter 3: "It isn't just that I don't believe in God and, naturally, hope that I'm right in my belief. It's that I hope there is no God! I don't want there to be a God; I don't want the universe to be like that." Thomas Nagel, *The Last Word* (New York: Oxford University Press, 1997), 130.

6. Aldous Huxley, *Ends and Means: An Inquiry into the Nature of Ideals and into the Methods Employed in Their Realization* (1937; repr., London: Chatto & Windus, 1941), 270, 273.

7. Paul Bloom (Yale University professor) outlines this research in Paul

Bloom, *Just Babies: The Origins of Good and Evil* (New York: Crown Publishers, 2013), 8-9. Bloom is an atheist and does not suggest in his book that the moral intuition of children points to God; nonetheless, his research and that of others supports the biblical notion that God has provided all people with a conscience.

8. 1 Timothy 4:2 speaks of the capacity of our conscience to become "dead" or "seared" such that we don't see right and wrong properly. Famed philosopher Alvin Plantinga describes well how the "natural knowledge of God," or *sensus divinitatis*, that should come through our conscience is weakened by sin: "This natural knowledge of God has in many or most cases been compromised, weakened, reduced, smothered, overlaid, or impeded by sin and its consequences. Due to sin, the knowledge of God provided by our *sensus divinitatis*, prior to faith and regeneration, is both narrow in scope and partially suppressed. The faculty itself may be *diseased* and thus partly or wholly disabled." See Alvin Plantinga, *Knowledge and Christian Belief* (Grand Rapids, MI: Wm. B. Eerdmans, 2015), 37.

9. Don Richardson, *Eternity in Their Hearts: Startling Evidence of Belief in the One True God in Hundreds of Cultures Throughout the World* (Ventura, CA: Regal Books, 1981), 82.

10. Richardson, *Eternity in Their Hearts*, 92-98.

11. Acts 8:26-40

12. See Tom Doyle, *Dreams and Visions: Is Jesus Awakening the Muslim World?* (Nashville, TN: Thomas Nelson, 2012), and Tom Doyle, *Killing Christians: Living the Faith Where It's Not Safe to Believe* (Nashville, TN: Thomas Nelson, 2015).

13. John Richardson Phillips, *Remarkable Proofs and Providence of a Divine Revelation*, 2nd ed. (London: S.W. Partridge & Co, 1876), 226-227.

14. Ken Boa and Larry Moody, *I'm Glad You Asked: How to Talk with Your Friends About Christian Faith and Their Questions*, Rev. ed. (Ellicott City, MD: Search Ministries, 2013), 158.

15. Hebrews 1:1-2 speaks of God's progressive revelation.

16. The story of the plagues is found in Exodus 7:14-12:30. We are told that after witnessing the plagues many non-Israelites joined the Israelites and followed them out of Egypt (Exodus 12:37-38).

17. Hebrews 10:1-10

18. Numbers 14:26-35

19. Romans 2:6-8; 1 Corinthians 6:9-10; 2 Corinthians 2:5-10; Revelation 20:11-12

20. Sam Storms, "Do All Infants Go to Heaven?" The Gospel Coalition, August 20, 2015, https://www.thegospelcoalition.org/article/do-all-infants-go-to-heaven/.

21. Ezekiel 18:20; John 1:12-13

Chapter 15

1. Douglas Groothuis, *Christian Apologetics: A Comprehensive Case for Biblical Faith* (Downers Grove, IL: InterVarsity Press, 2011), 159.
2. Groothuis, *Christian Apologetics,* 76.
3. Groothuis, *Christian Apologetics,* 76.
4. Lee Strobel, *The Case for Grace: A Journalist Explores the Evidence of Transformed Lives* (Grand Rapids, MI: Zondervan, 2015), 21-43.
5. The secure position in the family of God of all who trust in Christ is expressed in verses such as John 4:14; 5:24, 6:37-40, 10:28-29, 14:1-3; Romans 8:1, 8:15-16, 8:38-39; Ephesians 1:13-14; Colossians 1:12-14; 1 Peter 1:3-4; 1 John 5:13.
6. Philip Yancey, *What's So Amazing About Grace?* (Grand Rapids, MI: Zondervan, 1997), 70.
7. Robert Boyd Munger, *My Heart—Christ's Home,* Revised (Downers Grove, IL: InterVarsity Press, 1986). An older version of this booklet can be accessed at https://www.usna.edu/Navigators/_files/documents/MHCH.pdf.
8. Rebecca McLaughlin, *Confronting Christianity: 12 Hard Questions for the World's Largest Religion* (Wheaton, IL: Crossway, 2019), 167-168.

The text face is Minion Pro, designed by Robert Slimbach. It was issued by Adobe Systems in 1989.

The heading face is Akzidenz-Grotesk Next, designed by Bernd Möllenstädt and Dieter Hofrichter. It was issued by Berthold Type Foundry in 2006.